12.3
11.7

12.3
11.7

2

1.2

SWIMMING AND DIVING

The V-Five Physical Education Series

ORIGINALLY PREPARED for physical conditioning of naval aviators, the V-Five Physical Education Series includes manuals on basketball, boxing, conditioning exercises, football, gymnastics and tumbling, hand-to-hand combat, intramural programs, soccer, and track and field.

Maintenance of high standards of physical fitness in the nation's young men is considered a prerequisite to national preparedness. Accordingly, this series is continually revised to keep it compatible with civilian educational interests.

This series is published by the United States Naval Institute, a non-profit organization founded in 1873 for the advancement of professional, literary, and scientific knowledge in the Navy.

SWIMMING AND DIVING

THIRD EDITION
PREPARED BY

JOHN H. HIGGINS, *Coach of Swimming*
United States Naval Academy
Annapolis, Maryland

ALFRED R. BARR, *Coach of Swimming*
Southern Methodist University
Dallas, Texas

BEN F. GRADY, *Coach of Swimming*
University of Pennsylvania
Philadelphia, Pennsylvania

FOR

THE V-FIVE ASSOCIATION OF AMERICA

UNITED STATES NAVAL INSTITUTE
Annapolis, Maryland

SWIMMING AND DIVING
(Formerly *Swimming*)

Printed in the United States of America
BY GEORGE BANTA COMPANY, INC., MENASHA, WISCONSIN

Preface to the Third Edition

DURING WORLD WAR II, the United States Navy trained thousand of young aviation cadets to be combat pilots. At the same time, these men received rigorous phyiscal training aimed at the development of quick reaction, coordination, accurate timing and cool judgement. Because most naval air action took place over the sea, it was of first importance that aviators who crashed or were shot down be able to swim and to survive in the sea while awaiting rescue. Accordingly, while it taught men to fly, the Navy also taught them to swim.

The Navy's World War II physical training program was conducted by some two thousand of the nation's leading physical educators and coaches, commissioned in the Navy as Reserve Officers. Many of these officers contributed to the preparation of this and other physical training manuals which were designed to standardize teaching methods. Since World War II, this manual has found wide usage in programs outside the field of naval aviation training, and has been revised, when necessary, by the V-Five Association, a peace-time organization built around coaches who served in the Navy's World War II training program. These revisions are aimed at keeping the manual current, with added descriptions of new techniques and methods, and to adapt the experience and lessons learned for instruction in proper gradations at high school and college level.

It is no longer possible to name all those who have contributed to making this manual the success it has become, but the V-Five Association joins with me in sincere appreciation of their efforts.

T. J. HAMILTON
Rear Admiral, USNavy (Retired)
Executive Director
Athletic Association of Western Universities

Introduction to Third Edition

THE BASIC MATERIAL in this manual is considered as sound today as it was when the first edition was issued in 1943. However, changes and additions have been made to update the book. Some portions of the second edition which pertained purely to the teaching of swimming and administration of swimming programs on naval stations have been eliminated or rewritten so as to make the book generally applicable to all swimming programs, whether military, educational, or associated with a community. New features or sections in this edition include descriptions of the Butterfly and Breaststroke, instructions for the Mouth-to-Mouth method of artificial resuscitation, and an appendix on Olympic Swimming and Diving, with present Olympic records.

The Revision Committee
JOHN H. HIGGINS
ALFRED R. BARR
BEN F. GRADY

Table of Contents

SWIMMING AND DIVING

CHAPTER I

History of Swimming

Swimming, like warfare, has played an important role in every century. Beginning with the primitive carvings on cave walls and continuing through the pages of history, literature, art, and education, there is evidence that the knowledge of swimming is vital for survival.

Whether it be the consideration of peacetime trade, colonization, sea battles, sea raids, or the transportation of armies by water, the historical accounts of the Phoenicians, Carthaginians, Vikings, Caesar's conquest of Britain, and the Spanish Armada are full of references to swimming.

By viewing the present in the light of the past, it is possible to have greater judgment and appreciation of aquatics today.

The popularity of swimming during the Sung Dynasty, the Egyptian wall reliefs, the paintings on Grecian vases, the 29-acre Caracalla baths of Rome, the accomplishments of Barbarossa and Otto II, all bear witness to the background of swimming, but it is upon the military aspects that emphasis is placed, and history provides abundant reference.

First Depiction of Swimming

This is to be found in the wall carvings of Wadi Sori in the Libyan desert. Created in 9000 B.C., it is described as the only known picture of swimmers in pre-historic art.

First Teacher of Swimming

It was written during the Middle Kingdom in Egypt, 2160-1780 B.C., that the children of a nobleman and the children of the king took swimming lessons together.

Swimming was a part of the required curriculum for young Greek and Roman boys, and the educational organization characteristic of these peoples lends strong probability that planned instruction was given.

First Military Use of Swimming

Egyptian wall reliefs picture the story of the rout of the Hittites by Rameses II (1292-1225 B.C.) across the Orontes River in northern Syria. One Hittite, in flight to the safety of the far shore, is shown in what might be either a position of completion of breast stroke or one of death. Another, who shows an excellent position for elementary back stroke, might also be dead. Still another is shown in what may be either the glide position in the side stroke or excellent execution of the trudgen or crawl strokes, with breathing position, body position, kick, and arm reach and timing. Only the arms of another overhand or crawl swimmer appear on the relief and two other warriors are to be seen being drawn from the water by their comrades on shore.

Two Assyrian reliefs picture soldiers in the act of swimming. One appears at first glance to be executing a breast stroke arm pull, but the fact that the right palm is turned downward and the left is turned forward and upward strongly implies that the picture is intended to represent the use of trudgen or crawl strokes. Doubt is further banished by the portrayal of an attendant in prone, face down position, head held high, right arm extended forward with palm down, left arm drawn backward with the palm up, the legs in flutter position but with toes pointed downward.

According to the historian, Cornelius Tacitus, the island of Mona was taken, in the absence of boats, by soldiers who were good swimmers.

Appreciation of the importance of swimming was perpetuated by the fact that superior aquatic ability was possessed by such military greats as Charlemagne, Barbarossa, Carl the Great, Otto II and Olaf Trygvesson.

First Use of Life Saving

In the relief depicting the battle of Kadesh, primitive methods of resuscitation are represented. King Aleppo's soldiers have grasped him by the ankles and are supporting him, head downward, to hasten his recovery. His Majesty appears to have shipped an uncomfortable amount of Orontes River water. The outstretched hands of men on shore, extended to swimmers in the water, illustrate earliest rescue method.

Although Shakespeare cannot be taken as a factual reference, it may be noted that the words of Caesar, "Help me Cassius, 'ere I sink!", prompted the latter Roman to perform a water rescue.

First Use of Artificial Support

The Assyrian Nineveh reliefs provide earliest example of the use of inflated skins to provide support in the water. Forerunners of the modern lifejacket and life raft, the use of them appears to have been finely developed. The Assyrian warrior lay chest down upon the skin, which was equipped with an opening permitting oral inflation, and was about two and one half feet in length. The float was grasped with the left arm and the right arm was employed in a downward-backward pull similar to the stroke common to the use of paddleboards of today. A leg kick with slight knee bend, in flutter or scissors fashion but with toes pointed toward bottom, supplemented the arm action.

Alexander the Great (356-323 B.C.), although unable to swim, was not to be denied when a deep river separated his army from a city named Nyda in Asia. By holding his shield under his left arm and supporting himself upon it, he led an unsuccessful assault against the coveted prize.

In later years, the Franconians once crossed the Rhine on their shields.

First Military Transportation Over Water

In 490 B.C., after disaster had struck against one expeditionary force, the Persians sent 100,000 foot soldiers and 10,000 cavalry on 660 ships across the Aegean to punish the Greek city-states. Again in 480 B.C., a large fleet carried an army against Greece; an army which was to win for Xerxes at Artemisium and to lose the battle of Salamis.

The Romans successfully crossed the English Channel to conquer Britain but the Spanish Armada failed of realization of the same objective. One half of the 132 vessels carrying 21,621 soldiers and 8066 sailors were lost in battle with the English and because of gales of unprecedented violence.

During World War I, more than 2,000,000 American soldiers were transported to Europe. Losses were negligible because bombings were virtually unknown and submarines concentrated against merchant shipping. In World War II, however, the addition of the airplane and the increased number and efficiency of undersea craft made transportation of men far more hazardous.

First Instruction in Swimming

In Persia, every boy became the property of the state at the age of six and he was thenceforth thoroughly trained to become a defender of the Persian borders. Training was extremely rigorous and included forced marches during which the youthful warrior was required to cross streams with weapons held above the water.

In Sparta, similar training began at the age of seven, and swimming held a prominent place in the daily program of activities. The Romans considered aquatic ability an essential possession and practice in swimming in full armor and without armor comprised one of the phases of training to be undergone at Camp Martius. Later, a daring Batavian won public acclaim, bestowed by Emperor Hadrian, for swimming the Danube in complete armor.

During the middle ages, the training for knighthood was a well-defined course of education, requiring active participation in vigorous activities. Swimming was one of the skills in which participation prepared the page and squire to assume the role of knight.

First Swimming Competition

With competition in the use of weapons prevalent in the training of youth from China to the Atlantic, it is probable that competition in swimming was not uncommon to the Egyptians, Assyrians, and Persians. It is written, however, that swimming was one of the activities in which contests were held at the Grecian Hermine Games.

Vittorino Da Feltre, humanistic educator of the early 15th Century, conducted a school in Italy called the "Pleasant House" and the broad physical training, designed to prepare young men to meet the demands of rigorous warfare, included competitions in swimming.

First Commando Raids

Here, again, history undoubtedly can present earlier instances, but the best known examples of the employment of such tactics are presented by the Vikings. Daring the seas in their small craft, they swooped down upon the coast of France to sack and flee. An outstanding Viking was Olaf Trygvesson, King of Norway and a proficient swimmer.

And so we find that in swimming there is little new under the sun. We have only been tearing out the pages of history and rewriting them to meet the demands of our own times. The strokes that are taught today are but refinements of those known to the Egyptians of ancient history. However, every new development in warfare may present a new problem in swimming, and it is an ever responsible task to make certain that swimming makes every change that will insure adjustment to those new developments.

Swimming in World War II

For millions of men in World War II, knowing how to swim was almost as important as knowing how to use a gun. All sailors, of course, should know how to swim, because there is always the chance that their ship may be torpedoed, bombed, or burned, and their escape and rescue depends on swimming away and staying afloat until help comes. But in World War II it was equally necessary that soldiers and flyers know how to swim, because they all crossed the ocean on their way to war, either in troop transports or in aircraft, and if a ship sank or a plane crashed, the men had to swim to survive.

Swimming was especially important for aviators. Almost all Air Force bombers and fighters flew across water to and from their targets, everywhere in the world. Navy pilots flew from dozens of aircraft carriers. If a plane was shot down or ran out of fuel over the water, the crew had to swim. The Navy established an intensive swimming training program for all enlisted recruits, and for its flyers it set up a Naval Aviation Training Program which trained thousands of pilots to be expert swimmers. The Navy still teaches all aviation cadets how to swim, and much of this book is based on the Naval Aviation Training Program.

During World War II thousands of men were saved by the simple ability to keep afloat in the water—and many others died because they could not swim. When the Navy troop transport *President Coolidge* sank in the Southwest Pacific with 5,000 American troops aboard, only two lives were lost. But when the British transport *Llandaf Castle* sank in the Indian Ocean with 1,000 South African troops aboard, only 40 men were saved. A Navy pilot, shot down in the Battle of Midway, floated most of one day with the plane's seat cushion over his head to hide from the enemy, and was rescued the following day. When the U.S.S. *Indianapolis* was torpedoed in July, 1945, hundreds of men, huddled in life rafts and clinging to their sides, survived in the water for some hundred hours before rescue came.

Swimming Means Survival

Swimming is a required part of all military training, but it may mean the difference between life and death for anyone. Every day in the United States, lives are needlessly lost when fishermen wade in over their depth, passengers tumble out of pleasure boats, children fall into flooded excavations, or flood waters catch people in their homes or cars. You may swim for recreation, or for sport. You may also have to swim to live. When you need to know how to swim, it is too late to learn. Learn to swim the right way, now.

CHAPTER II

Preliminary Teaching Procedures

Every workman hopes for the best of tools but it is certain that at some time he will have to perform an important task by improvised methods and makeshift implements. No matter what the problems, no matter how poor the tools, the task must be done. Navy coaches have faced these situations:

For example, one base has an outdoor pool with the water unheated. At another station, 15,000 enlisted men must be instructed. The nearest facilities to one particular base are 18 miles distant. One administrator must make provision for the instruction of WAVES, another must arrange that the men are transported from outlying bases to a pool at the main base. Perhaps no instructor for swimming has been provided, perhaps large groups are scheduled for very small pools, perhaps no provision is made in the station schedule for "subsquad" swimming instruction.

The answers to specific problems must be sought out by each officer in charge of swimming. Some of the solutions to general problems found in the following pages apply to Naval and civilian schools alike.

PLATE 1. *Effective Teaching Depends on Discipline*

7

Some Common Problems in Navy Training

1. There is no Naval officer to teach swimming. This was the major problem as the Flight Preparatory Schools were becoming established. In every case, capable civilian instructors were obtained and these men did extremely well.

2. Insufficient officer personnel is available to teach swimming. Some stations have organized training classes for officers. Some bases use Chief Petty Officers. Several Flight Preparatory Schools used cadet instructors.

3. The pool is too small for the numbers assigned for instruction. Officers in charge of swimming have solved this problem by organizing all procedures in detail, so as to obtain fullest utilization of the limited facilities, such as:

   Motion pictures and lectures are used to instruct before work in the water. Divide the class into two or three groups. One group is in the water at one time, and that group works without any rest or waste of time.

   Drills are used that will give activity to numbers.

   Formations are used that will crowd the greatest number into a small place. Military procedures are emphasized.

   Land drills are practiced to perfection before entry into the water.

4. There is no pool available. The solution rests in making a survey of the surrounding area. Attempt is made to obtain Y.M.C.A., private and school pools. The loan of such pools has been obtained. Distances of from two to thirteen miles have been traveled.

5. The swimming pool sanitation is unsatisfactory. Full cooperation can be obtained from the Medical Department whose word is final.

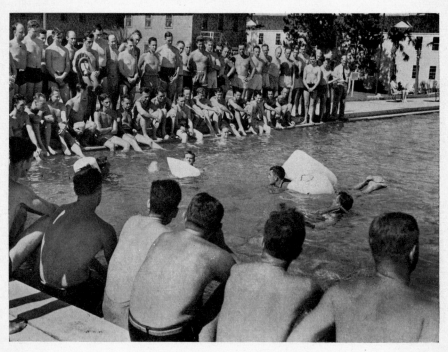

PLATE 2. *Attention of Class Important*

6. Civilian groups must also use the pool. This problem may arise out of the fact that an outside pool must be used, or is due to the fact that complete details of the Navy contract with an institution have not been consummated. In the first case, there is no general solution. In the second instance, the Commanding Officer will obtain the best conditions that he can.

7. The distance to be traveled is too great. An adjustment can possibly be made whereby fewer classes are held, but those will be of longer duration.

8. The weather is cold. An outdoor pool must be used. Best procedure is to so organize the schedule and period so that frequent periods of short duration are held, and each practice is uninterrupted by instructions once the swimmers are in the water.

9. No time is provided for "subsquad" swimming practice. Periods may be scheduled during sports program, during the athletic instruction periods, in the evenings, on Saturdays and Sundays, during study periods, and by station order issued by the Commanding Officer.

10. The pool is a "snare drum." The acoustics are poor, making teaching difficult. Complete instructions out of the water precede instruction in the water. The men may stand at ease but may not walk. Deck drills are held in an area removed from the pool. Water practice instructions are given by briefest possible command, by hand signals or by whistles.

11. The pool is oddly shaped or has insufficient deck space. In this case land drills are given elsewhere.

The Teaching Load

How many hours, and how many periods, shall an instructor of swimming teach each day? How many men shall be assigned to each class?

PLATE 3. *Partner Support for Glide*

PLATE 4. *Partner Support for Frog Kick*

The solution does not lie in the answer, "As many as he can stand." The important consideration is concern for the student. The instruction must be complete, the instructor must be alert. It is recognized that this can come to be only if some rest and relaxation is possible. An instructor should teach or coach for no more than three periods out of four, and the number of students he is responsible to instruct in each period should number between 20 and 30.

Training Swimming Personnel

When there are instructors assigned to any school, station or center, whose specialty is some sport other than swimming, it may be necessary to prepare them for work in the Swimming Department. It will be found that under pressure a surprising amount of knowledge can be acquired, certainly enough to begin teaching and to enable younger coaches to grow along with the sport.

A few methods have been tried and found successful. Pre-Flight Schools have adopted a plan which designates certain officers as supernumeraries who undergo a training period in every sport. Clinics for coaches have been held and many of these men are now teaching swimming.

The "Subsquad"

The most important single duty of an instructor is to teach swimming to those who cannot swim. Time and space tend to rule the aquatic program. If these two factors are present in abundance, they are the highway to accomplishment. If they are available only in a limited measure, that insufficiency becomes the shackles which bind the teaching personnel. Consequently, whatever space and time there is that can be used must be expended carefully and completely.

This fundamental truth may necessitate a search for odd moments not in demand or use by other aspects of training. This quest will most certainly direct attention to Saturdays and Sundays and to the evenings, if those hours are free of other obligations.

These salvaged moments must be devoted to those of poorest ability. Additional practice periods for "subsquad" men will, in all probability, be necessary if those men are to be clear of all swimming deficiencies before the set date of transfer or graduation. Men who fail to remove themselves from the deficiency group should not be permitted to graduate until they have demonstrated abilities equal to the minimum requirements. A "subsquad" will therefore include all men who fall short of the minimum standard for that base.

It will require the exercise of diplomacy and tact to put over the idea that attendance at "subsquad" is a privilege and not a requirement, yet to do so is extremely important. If the cadet is to receive the greatest possible benefit, he should regard these extra sessions with appreciation and not with resentment. In fact, it is a doubtful policy where the practice periods deprive the "subsquad" men of all shore liberty, unless there is definite evidence of lack of determination to master the required skills.

Scheduling further presents problems of selection, time and numbers. In general, those battalions with the earliest graduation date should be given preference. Each session may be divided into periods of any length, varying from 30 to 90 minutes. The periods may be devoted to instruction, practice or testing, or to all three. The number of cadets to attend any one period should be kept small, thus preventing confusion; due attention must be given to the limitations of time and space. Men lacking the same strokes or the same skills should be scheduled for the same period.

Swimming Pool Watch

The creation of a swimming pool watch will help reduce the supervisory duties of instructors. Only men who possess a background of life saving or life guard experience may qualify for this watch. Each will be required to pass the tests up to and including the "AA." Greater safety is assured because of the known abilities of these men. In addition, the members of this watch are not only qualified to serve as guards but also to assist and instruct "subsquad" swimmers. A sample organization for an evening period is given below.

Organization

To stand watch in the evenings, Monday through Friday.

The hours of the watch are to be from 1930 to 2110.

Either two or three men are to be on duty each night, depending upon the number of qualified men available. One of these is to be designated as senior member of the watch.

Men are to be qualified to serve on this watch by an acceptable showing in the tests administered by the head of the swimming department.

The list of qualified men must be approved by the Head of the Athletic department and by the Swimming Coach.

The approved lists will be submitted to the Senior Watch Officer, who will make the watch assignments.

General Instructions

All men on watches are responsible for the safety and lives of all men in the pool area.

This will be concretely true on the swimming pool watch with respect to the men immediately under your supervision. *You will be severely held to account for any accident which is the result of your carelessness or your inattention to duty.*

The watch will not study, read or write letters while on duty. It will be especially important that you be constantly alert to note any swimmer in need of assistance.

You must insist upon immediate obedience to all of your orders. The name of any man who fails to give such obedience must be reported. Any advanced swimmers who may come to the pool to assist "subsquad" shipmates are also subject to your orders. *You are in charge.*

The Swimming Pool Watch Bill must be read by you prior to opening the pool.

Report to the Security Watch Officer any condition which might make the opening of the pool to swimmers inadvisable.

Report the discovery of any faulty equipment to the Security Watch Officer and forbid any swimmer to use such equipment.

You will be required to perform the following specific duties.

1. Open and secure the pool on time.
2. Make an examination of the pool bottom at the beginning and end of each watch.
3. Require every man to abide by the pool regulations.
4. Permit no unauthorized person to swim.
5. Obtain the name of every person present and record it on the attendance sheet.
6. Stow all equipment properly when the pool is secured.
7. Make the proper entries in the swimming pool log:
   a. Time of opening of pool.
   b. The names of those on duty.
   c. Any particular occurrence.
   d. Time of securing the pool.
8. Keep control over all swimmers. Forbid dangerous stunts.
9. Do not leave the pool unguarded for any reason.
10. Instruct beginning swimmers that they must limit themselves to the shallow area unless they inform one member of the watch that they wish to go into the deep area.
11. Log the details of every accident, no matter how trivial it may seem.
12. If the lights are doused, immediately line up all of those present and examine the pool bottom with your flashlight. Do not leave the pool to ascertain the cause.

Sample Time Schedule (for Naval station.)

     1910   Muster with the Officer of the Day.
            Log out the keys to the swimming pool and towel room.
            Log out the Swimming Pool Watch Bill.
            Log out the Swimming Pool log.
     1915   Report to the swimming pool. Put on swimming gear.
            Log in on the pool log.
            Read the Swimming Pool Watch Bill.
            Examine the pool bottom.
            Have all necessary equipment at hand.
     1930   Open the pool.
            The junior member of the watch will take the name of every cadet entering upon the pool deck. He will require every cadet to take a

cleansing shower. He will permit only "subsquad" men to enter, with one exception; Advanced swimmers may be admitted to assist "subsquad" shipmates.

2110   Secure all swimmers from the pool.
       Examine the bottom of the pool.
       Stow all equipment. Return the attendance sheet and clipboard to the towel room.
       Douse the lights. Secure the pool.
2112   Secure all men from the showers. They must be in barracks by tattoo.
2120   Return keys to the Watch Officer.
       Log in keys, Watch Bill, and pool log.
       See that you are logged off the watch.
       Return to barracks.

The Silent Instructor

One very effective visual aid is the "Silent Instructor." In reality it is a bulletin board display, but the similarity extends only as far as does the similarity between king and commoner. Careful arrangement gives the display an attractive appearance. Complete instructions accompany every picture series to provide a dual approach to the learner. Selected photographs presented in series portray the skills taught in the instruction periods. A centrally placed card gives information relative to abandon ship and open water skills, and serves as a constant reminder that these skills may have a very practical future application.

The arrangement of the board should be frequently changed. Each display should be left up only long enough to have served its immediate purpose, and then should be put away to be brought out again for repetition at a later date.

The Introductory Talk

It will only sometimes be possible to meet with an incoming group prior to the first day of instruction. If such a meeting can be scheduled, the officer in charge of swimming must take advantage of this opportunity to welcome the new arrivals, to impress upon them the importance of swimming, to make the point emphatic that every man on the swimming staff will be eager to help them and does not want to see any one of them bilge out, to invite them to discuss any problem with a member of the staff, and to briefly explain to them the swimming requirements and the date they will be tested.

There will always be a first meeting of the class and it is on this occasion that the officer in charge of swimming must so introduce these men to aquatics that they are impressed with the importance of this instruction, are informed of the rules and procedures they must follow, understand what will be expected of them, and are imbued with a desire to cooperate to the fullest possible extent. Each officer must give this presentation in his own way. He must decide what he believes should be said, and he must say it in the way that he is convinced will best reach his listeners.

Rules and Regulations Related to Sanitation, Hygiene and Safety

Efficient administration of the swimming pool demands that certain rules and regulations governing the conduct of those using the facilities, be drawn up, posted

PLATE 5. *"Silent Instructor" Bulletin Board*

and enforced. It is only too true that the state of purity of the water depends greatly upon the extent to which the swimmers abide by these necessary regulations.

If swimmers and teaching personnel are lax in their attention to these rules, it is possible for infection to result. If proper methods of sterilization of the water are employed and if proper precautions are taken in conduct, the possibility of ill effect is extremely remote.

Such regulations also help to insure against accident. Unrestrained swimming may easily become boisterous or daring. The rules which govern swimming conduct need not detract from the amount of enjoyment which may be derived from participation any more than do regulations at a busy intersection restrict driving pleasures.

In a Navy program, a platoon or other unit will be informed of these regulations on the occasion of the first meeting. From that moment, non-adherence to any one of those rules is unpardonable. Much fuller cooperation will be obtained, however, if the necessity for it is explained, and obedience to the rules is made a matter of obligation rather than requirement.

The regulations which can be listed are varied and many. Placards and announcements must, however, be kept brief and this will necessitate that only those be chosen which careful analysis indicates have most practical application. The following list of swimming pool rules and regulations is therefore intended to serve as a source rather than as a model:

These rules must be enforced in order that the safety and health of all swimmers be protected.

No swimmer will maliciously break any one of these rules. It may, however, be necessary to remind some person who has for the moment become careless.

Sanitation

1. A cleansing soap shower must be taken by every swimmer, and the soap suds rinsed off, before he puts on trunks or suit.
2. Any swimmer with a communicable disease, nasal or ear discharges, boils, open sores, or who is wearing bandages is forbidden to enter the pool.
3. No person wearing street or athletic shoes may walk on the deck.
4. No swimmer will be permited to spit, spout water or blow his nose in the pool.

Safety

5. All swimmers are forbidden to run, wrestle or push others when on the deck, on the springboard, or in the shower or locker rooms.
6. No swimmer may enter the pool when no instructor, attendant, guard or C.P.O. is present, or when the pool has been secured.
7. All swimmers must keep clear of the jumping area.

Instruction

8. Towels and trunks must be placed in proper receptacles
9. All equipment must be carefully used. Permission to check out any item of equipment must be obtained from the instructor.
10. Every swimmer must keep himself informed of tests and instruction being given, in order that he may avoid interference.

Additional

In the instructions given to the class from time to time, mention may be made of rules to cover the following:

Athletic supporters and other outside articles.	Report cuts and abrasions
Shower after going to head.	Attitude, actions and speech.
Use of footbath	Throwing polo balls at jumpers.
Food and beverages	Number on diving board at one time.
Smoking	Bottles, glasses, cans.
Dogs or other pets	Leaving kickboard adrift
	Report broken equipment.

At some time during the instruction, swimmers should be advised of the following:

11. Don't blow nose forcibly. It forces water into sinus.
12. Don't swallow while head is submerged.
13. Take cool, not cold, shower before dressing.
14. A good form of ear plug is lambs' wool.
15. Don't talk to the guard unnecessarily.
16. Never dive or jump without looking.
17. Read and know the posted and announced rules.

Taking A Muster

There are a number of methods possible for the taking of a muster. Selection of the method to be used will depend upon the nature of the general organizational plan, the manner in which swimmers are routed to the swimming pool, station or school policies and regulations, the amount of time which may be devoted to it, the number to be mustered, and similar considerations.

If a military procedure is to be followed, it may be taken by the instructor or by swimming officer in charge, who calls off each name and awaits the reply, "Here, sir!" The second plan calls for attendance to be taken by mustering petty officers and squad leaders. Both methods will still apply if the entire group is broken down into smaller sections for the specific assignments.

The following plan for muster procedure is the plan selected for use. The officer in charge of the swimming department must so modify and improve upon it that the resulting revision will be best suited to the needs of his particular situation.

Procedure for Military Muster

1. At the appropriate minute, the senior swimming officer will:
   a. Blow a whistle, *or*
   b. Give the command, "Fall in for muster."
   Cadets should not enter the water before mustering. The swimming staff assigned to this period should be on the pool deck ten minutes prior to the command to fall in, or the senior swimming officer for the period may be the only one to delay his arrival until the appropriate minute for the muster.
2. The senior swimming officer stands on the deck at one end of the pool. He may be flanked by other officers assigned to the period.
3. Upon the command, "Fall in for muster," each cadet platoon commander will form his platoon at close intervals, on the deck.
4. The platoon of the senior battalion will fall in on the right side, the junior platoon on the left side, and any third unit will form at the opposite end of the pool. The mustering P.O. will report to the senior swimming officer to receive the muster lists.
5. When the platoon is formed, the mustering petty officer will take the muster, receiving reports from the squad leaders.
6. The muster will be taken by:
   a. Noting the absentees on prepared muster slates, or
   b. Noting the absentees on prepared clipboard lists, or
   c. Writing out the names of absentees on absentee forms attached to the clipboards.

    d. Each cadet is checked as:
      1. Present and participating.
      2. Present, observing only.
      3. Absent.

7. When the muster has been taken and all mustering petty officers have returned to their positions in front of their platoons, the senior swimming officer will call for, "Mustering Petty Officers—Report."

8. Each platoon mustering petty officer will report, "The platoon has been mustered, sir."
The platoon of the senior battalion will report first, followed by the platoon of the junior battalion.

9. The command will then be given by the senior swimming officer present, to "Fall out and report to assigned swimming group."

10. On the occasion of the first meeting, and in the event that it is desired to give announcement or instruction to the entire group, the cadet platoon commanders may be instructed to give their men, "Parade rest."

11. Copies of this procedure will be made available to all cadet platoon officers, who will, in turn, instruct the men of the platoon prior to reporting to the first swimming period.

Excuses

Since all cadets will not be able to participate in swimming on every instructional day, some definite procedure must be used to determine the validity of requests to be excused. The common practice is to excuse a cadet only upon request of a medical officer.

Classification for Instruction

No instructor should hold to a rigid pattern. There are two major methods most prevalent. The first method provides that the cadets attending any one period be classified as basic or advanced, or as beginners and qualified. By the second method, three groups are created and are termed non-swimmer, beginner and qualified, or beginner-intermediate-advanced.

The abilities of the swimmers will not remain the same. Cadets who might fall into three equal groups on the first day of instruction may, during the second week, best be classified into two groups. Men who progress rapidly should be permitted to advance to another and superior classification.

Organization for Teaching

There will always be some differences of opinion with respect to the choice of method to be employed in instructing others to swim. Most instructors have the same preference. Demonstration and explanation of the skill is first given, followed by land or deck drills, and then the swimmers practice the techniques in the water.

Assuming that the cadets have been classified according to ability, the manner in which even smaller groups will be created will differ in accordance with specific problems. The men who have not yet passed the "D" test may be considered as one group and be given water drills as a unit. The intermediate and advanced groups may each be divided, one half of each group to be on deck for land drills and the other half working in the water. Or a rotation system may be used with three or four groups, with but one of the three or four on the deck for drill at any one time.

Still another plan for division provides that the intermediate group be broken down into four deficiency squads, one for each of the basic strokes. Finally, those not able to pass the minimum test may be assigned to the shallow area, and all others segregated into as many groups as there are additional instructors. Each of these groups is simultaneously practicing the same skill or skills.

Specific Organization Procedures for Drills

Regardless of the size of the pool, the instructor should plan to conduct all practice according to drill pattern. A triple purpose is thereby served. Control of the group is enhanced, greater benefit is obtained from instruction and practice, and the greatest use is made of available space.

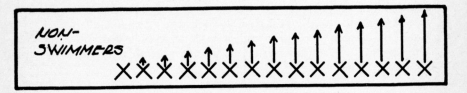

Single Echelon. Cross Pool or Lengthwise.—The swimmers may or may not be required to count off. In either case they will peel off in order from one end of the line.

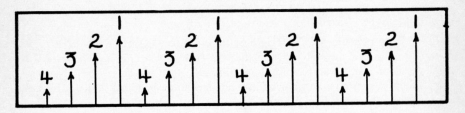

Multiple Echelon. Cross Pool.—The cadets (when in single line against the bulkhead, at close intervals), are directed to count off by fours.

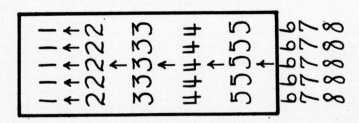

Wave Plan. Cross Pool or Lengthwise.—If five men may swim at one time and there are 40 men to swim, they would be directed to count off by eights, to give eight waves with five men in each wave.

Circle Swimming. Cross Pool or Lengthwise.—This is used primarily for distance swimming or testing. The entire group is sub-divided into smaller groups, the number of groups to be equal to one-half the number of lanes available. If the length of the two lanes will not accommodate all of the men in a sub-group when spaced at from 10-20 foot intervals, the sub-group must be sub-divided. In this pattern each man swims down one assigned lane and returns in an adjacent one and continues in this circle pattern for a designated number of times.

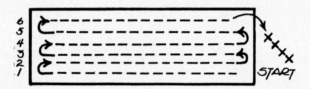

Weaving Pattern. Cross Pool or Lengthwise.—This is used for testing and for short distance swimming or interrupted distance swimming. The men push off in alphabetical or numerical order, at 10 or 20 foot intervals, swim down the first lane, return in the second lane, down the third lane, return in the fourth. When a man has completed the swim, he again lines up at the start.

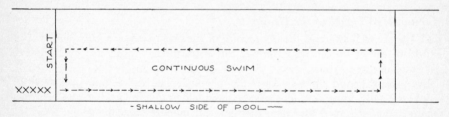

Subsquad Drill—A fairly large squad can be kept busy in this manner. All men in the lane adjacent to the bulkhead are swimming the same stroke with correction and encouragement by the instructor. They return in the other lane to the starting end by swimming any stroke taught to date which should be their best and easiest stroke. Less correction is needed and they will relax more, ready for the return instruction length.

Dividing the Pool into Sections.—With the class subdivided into classification groups, the use of lines will permit the sectioning of areas for each practice unit. The number of areas to be sectioned will depend upon the number of groups. The same procedure can be used to segregate sports program teams for practice and for cross-pool meets.

Pattern for Practice of Release from Strangle Holds.—The group is divided into two equal sections. Those cadets effecting the release are in the water facing the bulkhead and grasping the gutter. On command, the cadets jump into the water

and apply the hold. The position against the gutter is held until the hold has been applied. (Plate 102, p. 168)

For Shallow Water Drills, Standing—This pattern can be formed by having the squads execute a half facing and it is especially useful for armstroke and breathing drills.

Double Rank Pattern for Life Saving Drill Practice.—This enables the instructor to stand at either end of the two ranks to give instructions and directions, and permits him to walk behind either of the two ranks to check performance techniques.

Circle Pattern for Life Saving Drill Practice.—On deck or in shallow water. This makes it possible for the instructor to take a position in the center of the group. From this point he may both give instruction and direct the drill. Single circle for instruction and demonstration. Double circle for practice.

Maintaining Control of the Group

Cadets are well aware of the importance of the possession of aquatic ability. Poor control of the group can result only if the instructor has failed to give thought to class organization.

Every class period must be carefully planned. The cadet must feel that this lesson is vitally important. Every step should logically follow the one before it, there should be limited confusion despite great numbers, and the lesson should be arranged so that every cadet will be doing something every minute.

The adoption of military commands and movements will enhance this feeling. The cadets should be required not only to assemble in military manner for muster and dismissal but also to move from deck to water or station to station in formation.

Finally, effort must be made to present the demonstrations, drills and explanations in a manner which will be both interesting and challenging to the learners. The instructor must have the conviction that the material he is presenting is worthwhile. He must also talk to and not down to his listeners. He should be neither too dramatic nor too matter-of-fact. The cadets should know that he is cognizant of their aspirations and aware of their problems.

However, no matter what the teaching personality of the instructor may be or by what method he chooses to conduct the training procedures, he must never lose sight of the fact that, during the period of instruction, he is the officer in command of those cadets under his supervision.

PLATE 6. *Know Everyone's Name*

Military Commands.—All of the common military commands are familiar to Navy personnel. A swimming instructor will not have occasion to use all of them in order that he may conduct his class in a military manner but he must know all commands sufficiently well to permit him to select and use the commands which best fit any given need or situation.

Supplemental Commands.—Each swimming department may find it necessary to devise certain descriptive commands. They may be necessary because no standard military command can bring about the desired action. For example:

Peel off!
Take off!
Fix gear!
Into water, close to bulkhead, jump!

Standardizing Commands and Procedures.—It is essential that all persons who give swimming instruction on the same station shall use the same commands in approximately the same manner. The commands which are to be employed should be typed or mimeographed and a copy placed in the hands of every person who has anything to do with the direction or instruction of swimmers. Obviously these commands should be consistent with the common military usage of the station. Below is a sample form used at one station:

HANDLING SWIMMING AND WATER TRAINING DETAIL

1. Give all directions, instruction and commands in a military manner, in a clear voice, using few and simple words.
2. Have detail fall in along deck with toes hooked over the edge.
3. Have detail seated when not actually in the water, also while giving instructions or demonstrating.

4. For giving instructions and for demonstrating, have detail "close toward center." To have them open out, "Give way both ends to regular interval, or one arm's length."

5. When ready for men to enter water "stand by on apron around pool," then "shove off" or dive into pool. As soon as men have finished assignments in pool, they resume sitting position on edge of pool deck.

6. Check off assignments as completed (will result in effort and more serious work on the part of the men). Give a grade for fairly good performance, for below par, and for poor performance.

7. Insist on proper performance of each assignment. Point out general faults and give simple corrections.

8. Give individual instructions, or corrections, when necessary, quickly and in a simple manner. Don't keep a detail waiting while one man is training.

9. To secure detail, have men line up in dress-right, along edge of deck.

10. While a detail is working, secure the pool and pool deck.

Picture Words and Descriptive Phrases

The value inherent in the use of picture words must not be underestimated. These picture words can be used to best advantage when they are such as to describe an action or fault. "Think of your legs as a pair of green willow sticks, whipping up and down" helps to describe the crawl kick to the beginner. For example:

1. Crawl stroke kicking	"Make a splash"
2. Sidestroke kick	"Kick for the sidelines"
3. Drill singly from rank formation	"Peel off"
4. Stand up in shallow water	"Drop your landing gear"
5. Balancing the body	"Keep an even keel"
6. Starting a swim	"Take off"
7. Passing a test	"Receiving an Up-Check"
8. Failing a test	"Receiving a Down-Check"
9. Correct performance	"Hitting the target"
10. Drills	"Maneuvers"

Suggestions

Every instructor has need of some check list by which he may take personal inventory and by so doing improve the quality of his teaching. The following list is the kind of one that will be forever incomplete, for ever teacher of swimming has discovered something which might be added.

The inexperienced teacher will profit most by these suggestions and he will be wise to review them frequently. Every instructor should feel challenged to begin a supplemental list of hints which have come to him in his own experience. As that supplementary list grows, and assuming that he will put those ideas into practice, he will have measurable proof that his teaching is constantly improving.

1. Know completely the information and materials to be presented.
2. Before every class, have the procedures definitely planned and the equipment ready.

3. Arrange the class for explanations and demonstrations so that every member can see and hear.
4. Use clear diction. Speak with conviction, brevity and clarity. Avoid lengthy explanations. Make each talk short, concise. Avoid shouting.
5. Put your own personality into your teaching.
6. Use visual aids; motion pictures, posters, photographs, demonstration.
7. Begin each class by outlining what is to be done that day.
8. Know the names of everyone in the class.
9. Keep your teaching alive by the use of current examples and terms.
10. Never criticise a colleague or assistant in public.
11. Be critical of your own teaching. Get the opinion of others.
12. Avoid getting the men out of the pool too often for explanations or drills. Confusion results from re-adjustment to the water.
13. Know the drill patterns well. Insist that the swimmers learn and follow them from the beginning.

CHAPTER III

Teaching the Beginner

The common problem, what stroke shall be taught first, cannot be completely answered because of the many influencing factors. It may be the age, needs, past experience and interests of the learners, or it may be the limited knowledge of the instructor, which determine the primary stroke. In the past most popular choices as the lead-off strokes were the dog-paddle and crawl.

The Navy program, however, specifies that after the five-minute or horizontal float with kick has been mastered, the first stroke to be taught is the elementary back stroke. This selection is made on the basis of advantages of simpler breathing, similarity of position to that of the horizontal float supplemented by kick and scull, and because the kick is similar to the breast stroke, treading water and life saving carries. Its possible utility exceeds that of the crawl stroke. Proficiency is next acquired, in order, in the breast, side and overarm strokes.

TEACHING DEVICES

Visual aids such as photographs, moving pictures and demonstrations, can be overstressed but the possible advantages of their use certainly should not be ignored. The beginner learns by doing, and only a limited amount of seeing will be beneficial. Nevertheless, the beginner is in this manner given an understanding of what it is that he must do to achieve success.

Demonstration is the visual aid of greatest value, preferably accompanied by verbal explanation, comment and analysis. Actual demonstration is of greater benefit than is the motion picture, but the contribution of the latter is well worthwhile.

Photographs and still pictures do not, of course, show action unless they are of the "magic eye" serial type. Such reproduction of movement in series helps the beginner set the mechanics of the skill in his mind. Black and white stick figure drawings make a similar contribution. For example see cartoon below:

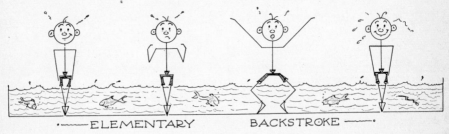

— ELEMENTARY   BACKSTROKE —

It should be noted that pictures, as well as demonstrations, call for verbal explanations. It is quite possible to look at a picture and see nothing, if the mind is not challenged to analyze it; or it is possible to look at a drawing and mentally strip it of all that it has to offer. Verbal explanation and analysis will aid this process.

The use of supporting devices in teaching brings out loud and perhaps rash statements from both the opponents and advocates. In the main the opponents state that the learning process must be repeated when the beginner is shorn of his support and so time is lost through the use of them. The advocates argue that the learner, having less fear of sinking, will concentrate on the exact movements and so will learn less haphazardly and emerge with better form. Also larger numbers can be kept moving which is good pedagogy. Regardless of different views, aids are not indispensable for it can be done either way. Past experience with the use of aids, numbers in the group, depth of the water and the age of the group may be factors that will determine whether the aids will or will not be used.

Benches and Tables

These may be considered artificial aids. They are of value in land drills and the use of them is intended to aid learning by permitting the novice to practice the stroke movements while he is in a position closely approximating the position he will assume in the water.

Diving Pits and Tumbling Belts

These devices also are for use in land drills, but the use of them applies only to advanced divers and not to beginners. They permit the diver to concentrate upon the movements involved in the performance of certain parts of a difficult dive and to perfect it before he attempts it from the board.

Poles

Rather than use the pole to hold one beginner in deep water while he attempts to swim it should be used as a device to assist beginners to the bulkhead for further instruction. In addition it can be used as an aid to secure the attention of those whose ears or eyes, or both, are submerged. At this point verbal instruction or signaling with hands may be given.

Belts

These have been used both in the teaching of beginners and in the coaching of advanced swimmers. This belt is sturdily supported so that when the swimmer snaps it around his waist he is in position to practice movements without sinking. Advanced swimmers use this device to build up a stronger arm pull.

Swim Cans

Swim cans may be made inexpensively by soldering two number ten fruit juice cans together and painting them. Two loops can be soldered on to hold an inexpensive web belt. It can be strapped around the waist or legs and placed on the front or back, depending on the stroke. The can should not have an over all length of more than 15 inches so that it does not impede movements.

Kickboards

These are used by beginner and expert alike. In both cases, this device provides a means whereby the techniques can be practiced to the isolation of all other movements. They should be buoyant and light and have inset hand grips on the sides. If a commercial product is not used, they may be constructed of balsa, fir, pine, or spruce. The edges should be beveled. The wood should be thoroughly treated with linseed oil and then shellacked or coated with acid resisting paint in color. Dimensions should not exceed 1½″ thick by 18″ wide by 30″ long.

Balls

Balls or similar floats are sometimes used by competitive swimmers to support the legs while drilling on arm stroke. The ball is enclosed in mesh netting and strapped to the ankles. A ball may also be held in the hands to serve the same purpose for which a kickboard is employed.

PLATE 7. *Swim Cans Can be Effective Aids*

Partner Support

When a beginner first takes to the water in the practice of the horizontal float or elementary back stroke, assistance may be given by a partner who places one hand under the back, the other hand grasping the chin of the novice while he repeats movements practiced in land drills.

BEGINNERS' SKILLS

A discouraging number, between 15 and 20 per cent, of young men of military age cannot swim. Not many, but a few of these non-swimmers, have in the past had a frightening water experience and that conditioned fear has kept them from further pursuit of the acquisition of aquatic ability. Although these young men report for swimming instruction with doubt and trepidation, this fact does not justify any less insistence that every command be obeyed or that every skill be practiced without hesitation, but it does advise that the instructor express himself as possessing full understanding of the extent to which this fear dominates the learner. Time will be saved, and the beginner will be helped, if but a minute or two is taken for an expression of the following points:

1. Skills necessary for swimming are easy to acquire.
2. Once these skills are obtained you have CONFIDENCE.
3. You have no reason to lack confidence if it is remembered that in a few minutes of practice in warm water—
   a. You can hold your breath for thirty seconds.
   b. You can swim 20 feet with arms alone.
4. You must listen carefully to instructions, and if directions are not clear, ask questions.
5. You must have confidence not only in yourself but in your instructor.

The Five-Minute Test

No swimming test is as important as the one requiring the novice to support himself on the water's surface for five minutes; no other one is so vital to the survival of the pilot when he suddenly ceases to be flier and becomes swimmer. If a man can stay afloat for five minutes, he has a fighting chance. Once the beginner has this mastery over time in his favor, more advanced achievement rapidly follows.

The requirements of this test may be satisfied in a variety of ways, such as: Treading, the float with or without the use of hands, as in sculling and finning, the dog paddle, or any stroke or combination of strokes. Regardless of method, the prime requisite for the beginner is confidence.

After these and additional preliminary skills have been practiced and the five-minute float techniques have been tried in shallow water, the following recapitulation may be given before the beginner advances into the deep water area:

1. Hold breath 30 seconds underwater.
2. Paddle to the surface.
3. Level out to horizontal position on chest.
4. Swim at least 20 feet with arms.

Note again that this line of reasoning will be used only for beginners with past history experience of near drowning and is not to be accepted as a general method.

Customary procedure in the teaching of beginners has been to restrict instruction to the shallow area until such time as the novice acquires sufficient proficiency to make certain that he can venture into the deep water with utter safety. Moreover, the beginner is not hurried in his learning; he is baited with stunts and games, and even coaxed to undertake a simple step at which he hesitates.

Much of this sugar-coating springs from peacetime concern lest the pupil fail to reappear for the subsequent lesson if the first is not to his liking. Part of this gentle teaching is due to an honest appreciation of the problem of the beginner who may have undergone a terrifying water experience.

One of the greatest truths, however, that has come out of wartime swimming instruction has been that the beginner may be taught to swim in a fraction of the customary time if the instruction proceeds on the basis of, "This must be done— and quickly." Instruction and encouragement of a hesitant novice in the perform- ance of a turtle float can consume as much time as would be required to run the entire gamut of preliminary skills in a "Do it *now*" manner.

Mental Attitude.—One unfortunate outcome of teaching in the past has been the development of an attitude of, "If you don't make it this time, there will al- ways be another chance to try." This is evidenced time and time again when cadets are given the five-minute test and with the first onset of fatigue or the first mouth- ful of water, quit and reach for the gutter. And then the worst happens; they draw themselves from the pool with a burst of energy that bears certain testimony that they had abundant energy to carry them through the trial.

This mental attitude must not be permitted to exist. A determined aviator will force himself to withstand even severe punishment and extreme fatigue in order to pass this test. Men fail the five-minute test because they do not try to pass it; because they throw their hands in the air as the first water washes across the face; because they grasp for any support that presents itself; because they begin the test with the conviction that they will not finish it; or because they doubt themselves.

A cadet should be instructed in a few simple skills which are necessary for a five-minute test. He may fail subsequent attempts, but he must not have failed having made reasonably great demands upon mind and muscle. Hence, men are not encouraged to come to the bulkhead because a gulp of water has been taken. When moving toward the bulkhead he is told, "No, stay with it," and the rescue pole is withheld until it is obvious that the cadet will not come out of his difficulties himself. If a breath of air is lost and he cannot rise high enough in the water to obtain another, he is told to sink to bottom, shove up to the surface and take a breath as he emerges.

Skills to be Acquired Before the Five-Minute Float

Ducking.—First with support, then without. Take a breath, grasp the gutter or other support with one or both hands, and squat to a depth in the water sufficient to submerge the entire head. The nose may be held with one hand. Repeat without holding on to the gutter.

Breath Holding.—First above the surface, then below. Take ten deep, rapid breaths, the final inhalation to fill only three-quarters of the lung volume. Hold the breath while the passage of thirty seconds is counted off. Repeat, holding the breath while the head is submerged.

Opening Eyes.—This skill calls for a mind set to perform it before it is attempted. Make up your mind that you *will* do it. Your eyes will feel the presence of water but that is all. Although vision will not be as clear as it is above the surface, try to count your fingers or look at the feet of the person next to you. Take a breath, submerge and open your eyes.

Exhaling.—You will do most, if not all, of your breathing through the mouth. That breathing should be done easily and without strain. You will find it helpful at the beginning, however, if you will breathe under pressure by performing a Bronx cheer or razzberry. Forcing your breath out in this manner will give you confidence. First above water, and then below, take a breath and force the air out. Grasp the gutter on the first trial. Repeat while submerged. Now try doing it slowly five times in succession, on your own time. Next, stand in shallow water away from the gutter and bob up and down, exhaling each time you submerge.

Relaxing.—The sooner you can acquire the feeling of what it is like to be relaxed in the water, the more quickly will you master every phase of swimming skill. Droop, let your arms hang limply from the shoulders. Let your knees buckle. Loosen every muscle. Slump into the water.

PLATE 8. *Tuck Float*

Tuck Float.—Carefully follow these directions. You will probably find that you will float, that you can't sink. That will mean that it is silly to fight to stay *up:* you need only to learn how to move *across* the water. Now, *slowly,* take a deep breath, submerge and go into a tuck position with legs doubled up, knees drawn to chest, forehead on knees and arms clasped around the legs. If your feet leave bottom, you will float with your back at the surface; if your feet stay on bottom, it means that you are a sinker rather than a floater, but the planing action of your momentum as you swim through the water later will be the margin of difference sufficient to keep you at the surface.

Prone Shove-off, Glide and Stand.—Be sure that you understand the method of regaining standing position before you practice the shove-off and glide. Three simple things must be done at the same time: Go into a tuck position; bring the arms and hands sharply down to the knees; and raise the head. Now for the skills in

PLATE 9. *Partner Support for Glide*

order. Stand with your back to the gutter, facing cross pool, or stand in chest deep water facing the shallow end bulkhead. Bend the knees and bend the body forward to bring the body in forward leaning position with only the head above water. Extend the arms forward across the surface; lean gently forward off balance; place the face down in the water; push off gently from the bottom or bulkhead; raise your feet behind you to the surface. You are now in the glide position, body coasting across the surface. Later, you will find this an important part of the breast stroke. When the body glide is spent, execute the three movements to regain standing position and straighten the legs to stand.

Back Shove-off, Glide and Stand.—Take a standing position facing the side bulkhead, or facing deep water and with back toward the shallow end bulkhead, bend the knees and sink down in the water to neck depth; hold the hands at the sides and take a breath and lay the head back into the water with face up, lean backward and gently shove off with the feet. Glide in this position, relaxed, as far as the momentum will carry you. To regain standing position, do these three things: Tuck the legs, bend forward at the hips and neck and draw the elbows backward; straighten the arms downward and scoop upward with the palms; straighten the legs and stand. The head must not be raised during the glide; the entire body must be in the straight position you would assume in lying on the deck with chin tucked slightly toward the chest.

PLATE 10. *Front Glide*

Reaching the Surface.—Two methods may be employed, but neither may be considered successful unless performed easily and without panic. The first is the dog paddle arm action in which the hands alternately draw up from the waist past the chest to approximately head height and then, with flexed wrist, pull down to the waist again.

The second method is to employ the arm action of the breast or elementary back strokes. The breast stroke arm action will bring the beginner to the surface in a vertical or forward leaning position and will permit him to continue stroking to the bulkhead. The advisability of teaching the breast stroke arm action at this early period of instruction is to be questioned. There is greater probability that proficiency in the elementary backstroke arm action will have been acquired. This action will, when the beginner arches his back, permit him to come to the surface at an angle and plane into a back float position.

Leveling with Tuck and Extension.—The beginner goes into a tuck float, straightens the arms forward and the feet backward to bring him into prone float or glide position and begins arm stroke or performs the turn from front to back.

To the Rear.—To change to a back down position from a face down position and reverse direction at the same time, the body is tucked and the feet swung underneath in pendulum fashion as the arm circles backward in an arc. Simultaneously the elbows draw backward, the arms are extended downward and backward and then are drawn in the original direction of progress. As the back of the head lies back in the water, the hips and knees are straightened to extend the feet and a float or form of backstroke is begun.

Elementary Diving. Distance Dive with Glide.—These skills are discussed in Chapter VIII.

The Horizontal Float

The term horizontal float implies that body position and buoyancy will suffice to maintain a person at the water's surface. Despite the fact that such a float is easier in salt water than in fresh, a large percentage of persons lack sufficient body buoyancy to perform it with ease. Consequently, it is found to be much more efficient to supplement the pure float with leg and arm action. These actions keep the body in a consistently higher position and contribute to confidence.

Body Position.—The body is in a reclining, horizontal position, hips at the surface and the head back to leave only the face above the water.

Arm and Hand Action.—The arms, shoulders and wrists are loose, relaxed. The hands move in a figure eight path beside the hips, sculling, or slowly move up and down in a paddling action. (See Sculling)

Leg Action—The leg action is used mainly to keep the legs near the surface so the body will not assume a vertical position and sink. The action of the legs is quite similar to riding a bicycle. The calf of one leg presses down on the water until the angle of the knee is at 45 degrees. At this time the other leg is being raised by lifting the knee to the surface. Too deep a press with the calf will cause the body to assume a vertical position. Too much upbeat will cause forward motion of the body and an unnecessary expenditure of energy.

Breathing.—Buoyancy will be improved by holding the breath, performing quick exhalation and inhalation every fifteen or twenty seconds. This, however, is fatiguing. A normal respiration rhythm will be found to be most effective, but it is essential that the breathing be shallow with the lungs one-half to three-quarters full of air at all times. Breathe in through the mouth; exhale through either the mouth or nose.

Eight Common Faults

1. The body is in a sitting position instead of lying on the water. The hips are too low. Body is in pike or tuck position. Knees are too close to chest.
2. The head is held too far back. The nostrils are inclined downward and water runs down the nose.
3. The head is held too far forward or is raised forward in strained position. Neck muscles are tensed. The ears are not submerged.
4. The arms are brought out of water. The head will sink if the hands or arms are brought out of water.

5. The action of arms and legs is too rapid and too strong. This action must be slowed down until the floater definitely can feel the water holding him up.
6. The body is too tense, not relaxed.
7. The hand action is one of striking the water rather than of pressure down-ward.
8. The floater believes that his face must be clear of the water at all times. He fails to realize that the face need be clear only at the instant he wishes to breathe.

How to Get Out of Difficulties.—When it happens that the feet sink and the body goes from the horizontal position to one of perpendicular because of faulty technique, carelessness or interruption, any one of the following devices may be employed to return the body to the horizontal:

Four or five applications of the elementary back stroke arm action, with the body straight or arched and the head inclined backward can be used. Success is certain if the breath has not been expelled, but if exhalation has taken place, the strokes must be strong and a greater number will be required.

The position of float is maintained and the knee action is exaggerated, with the legs moving as though they were stepping over hurdles on a bulkhead or the floater were attempting to walk.

The floater takes a full breath, submerges in a turtle float with the back upper-most and the hips level with the head not below. From this position the arms are extended forward and the legs thrust backward to put the body in face down prone float. Immediately, one arm is drawn across the body with elbow bent and without coming out of water; the other arm and hand press down against the water, and roll-over on the back is performed. The head leads the body roll but must not be drawn toward the chest in this action and the leg kick and hand scull must be resumed as soon as the roll-over is completed.

The Vertical Float

This is the position into which most horizontal floaters will gravitate if the skill is performed in fresh water. Beginning with the horizontal float position with the arms extended to the side or overhead (underwater) and the legs drawn up with heels together and knees extended outboard (underwater), with the head back to leave only the face showing, and with the quick exhalation and inhalation of con-trolled breathing. The great majority of floaters will find that the feet immediately begin to sink and the body is soon in a perpendicular position. Hence, instruction in the vertical float has far wider application and utility.

Body Position.—The back is arched, the head is drawn backward to leave only the face above water, and the shoulders are drawn back with arms extended out-ward to the side.

Breathing.—The lungs are kept filled with air; the exhalation is quick and inhala-tion follows immediately.

Arm and Leg Action.—Traditional teaching of this float prescribes that it not be adulterated with leg or arm action. The addition of a hand sculling and leg tread action will, however, relieve strain and make success attainable. The desired end is not to test specific gravity but to provide a means whereby the swimmer can stay afloat; hence, arm and leg action is not only justifiable but advisable. The result is a combination of floating and treading.

Three Common Faults

1. The back is not held in an arched position.
2. The head is not held backward, the top of the head and not the face is out of the water.
3. The arm and leg action is too fast or strong. Only enough sculling and treading should be employed as is necessary to permit relaxation and make breathing normal.

Finning

Finning provides a simple means of propulsion while the beginner is in a back glide or float position. Its value lies in its simplicity and because it may serve as an intermediate state between back glide and elementary back stroke. As an advanced skill, it may be used in surface diving and by competitive swimmers as they do lengths of the pool in flutter kicking practice while in either the face down or face up position.

The Body Position.—This corresponds to that for the horizontal float.

Arm Action.—Beginning with the hands extended alongside of the thighs, the elbows bend as the fingers are drawn up the thighs to the hips, both hands acting simultaneously. At this point, the wrists are flexed and the back of the wrist leads the extension of the hand to a distance approximately 12″ outside of the hip; then the wrist is extended, to present the broad surface of the palm for a press or push backward toward the feet, finishing with the palms against the thighs and elbows straight. The propulsion power of this abbreviated stroke is not sufficient to provide momentum for glide, and, therefore, the arm action is continuous—just as is true of the fin of a fish.

Leg Action.—This may be combined with the hand finning. The flutter, frog or vertical scissors may be used. When either the frog or vertical scissors is employed, and one kick is taken to each double arm stroke, the result is a weak or primitive version of the elementary back stroke.

Sculling

Sculling is a skill of many uses and not difficult to master. This arm action assists in the performance of the vertical float, surface float, surface diving, underwater swimming, back glide, racing back stroke, changing direction, altering body position, and is a vital part of the horizontal float. Performed while the swimmer is on his back, the hand action may provide lifting power only or combined lifting and propulsion power. Competitive swimmers more frequently choose sculling than finning as an adjunct to the practice of the flutter kick.

The Body Position.—This corresponds to that in the horizontal float.

Arm Action.—This begins with the palms at the thighs, thumbs uppermost. The wrist is rotated, turning the palm downward and outward and bringing the little finger to a level slightly higher than the thumb. This presents an angled surface, like that of an airplane wing, which provides lifting power as the hand is drawn to the side and parallel to the water surface. The movement of the hands away from the hips begins while the wrist is being rotated at the thigh. The distance that the hand travels from the side may be anywhere from 6″ to 20″. When full distance is reached, the elbow and wrist are again rotated to turn the palm downward and

PLATE 11. *Sculling*

inward and bring the thumb to a level slightly higher than the little finger. If support is the major objective, the thumb will be very little higher than the level of the little finger as the hand is drawn inward to the thigh. If propulsion is the principal end desired, a full quarter rotation of the wrist is performed and the action then is one of pushing backward and inward, but not downward, with the palm of the hand. The arm action is continuous with no pause as the hand reaches the thigh. It is the wrist and hand that have the major part in this skill but rotation occurs also at the elbow and shoulder and the muscles of the entire arm are brought into play. It is almost universal practice that the hands move outward and inward simultaneously but the action may be so timed that one hand moves toward the thigh as the other hand moves away from the opposite leg. The arm action may be performed with or without bending the elbow.

Treading

Treading popularly is conceived to be a skill in which only the legs are used and the arms are carried loosely in the water with the body in a perpendicular position. Life saving tests require that the hands be held above the water as a measure of real ability. Its greatest immediate values lies in the fact that it emphasizes and develops leg kicks, for it is in the strength of the kick that the average swimmer is deficient. Treading ability will serve two practical ends: First, it provides the means of keeping the head above water when the swimmer is engaged in removing upper garments, preparing clothes for inflation and inflating them;

supporting a shipmate after underwater approach and level; receiving stretcher from ship's side. In short, it is used at any time that the arms cannot be used for swimming. Further evidence of its utility is to be found in the important contribution a strong leg kick makes to the execution of any stroke, in its application in the surface approach, support of a victim, in sustaining the face above oil on the water, and in its usefulness as an adjunct to the vertical float. For all practical purposes, separate treading, floating and sculling will not occur as frequently as they usually will occur in combination.

PLATE 12. *Treading, Using Hands and Feet*

The Body Position.—This is perpendicular, usually with a slightly forward inclination as would be true when clothing is being inflated, but with the head backward when a shirt is to be unbuttoned and removed.

Arm Action.—Although not truly a part of treading, either a sculling or finning arm movement may be added to supplement the kick.

Leg Action.—There are six types of kicks which may be used in treading. In general, the most efficient will be found to be that kick associated with the stroke in which the learner is most proficient. Exception is found in the case of the flutter kick for, although it is most commonly used, it does not prove effective in treading. The leg action of riding a bicycle, described in the explanation of the horizontal float, is frequently chosen. Greatest success will result from the use of the scissors. double scissors and frog kicks. The final method would have the feet alternately describing a circle with knee half flexed, drawing the foot backward to outward to forward to backward again. Actually, the action is that of the frog kick, except that one leg kicks while the other recovers.

The most important consideration to keep in mind is that each of the kicks is not full to the degree found in swimming strokes; they are sharper, narrower and occur more frequently in order to keep the body steadily in position.

PLATE 13. *Treading, One Arm Raised*

PLATE 14. *Treading, Wearing Clothing*

The Dog Paddle

This stroke has been commonly selected as the first to be taught to beginning children. It possesses advantages in that it follows easily upon the prone glide and prone kick-glide. The arm action is not complex and a minimum of emphasis may be placed upon the kick. The beginner may perform it with the face above water.

However, for Naval Aviation swimming the dog paddle has several disadvantages, the main one being that once the beginner has learned the dog paddle it is more difficult to teach him the basic survival strokes, namely, back stroke, breast stroke, side stroke, and overhand stroke.

From the standpoint of time saving and fundamental skills the Navy believes, therefore, in immediately teaching the beginner the back stroke. The main purpose of the Naval Aviation Swimming Program is to teach all aviation personnel how to swim, and in some cases beginners will turn immediately to a dog paddle and thereby gain confidence on their own. In any case, it does provide another method of staying afloat.

The Body Position.—This position, because the head is held above water, is one in which the hips are from six to fourteen inches below the surface with some arch in the back.

The Arm Action.—The arms alternately reach and pull. Starting from full extension of the glide position, the elbow bends and draws to the outside as the hand pulls through to the ribs or chest. Then the wrist is straightened to bring the hand into a horizontal position, and finally the fingers glide out to full extension as the elbow is straightened. The stroking is slow, not hurried.

Leg Action.—The kick is similar to that of the crawl except that the knee bend is very pronounced. The legs work alternately, toes pointed, ankles loose, and with some movement at the hips. Principal power is derived from back lash of the lower half of the leg. The crawl stroke timing of three leg beats to each single arm stroke may be taught from the beginning.

Breathing.—This is not a problem when the stroke is performed with the head held above the water. A more efficient riding position is obtained, however, when a prone position is assumed and the face is placed in water and raised only for inhalation. In this event, the breath is taken at the side and is exhaled under water. If the left is selected as the breathing side, the head turns to the left and is lifted slightly at the same time that the left hand pulls through and the right hand recovers for the next stroke. As the left hand recovers, the face is again turned to the front and into the water. Exhalation will take place just prior to the turning of the head for next inhalation. The swimmer may elect to breathe with every left arm stroke or may inhale with every second or third pull with the left hand. The pull of the right arm is, of course, the key to breathing on the right side.

Six Common Faults

1. The pull does not finish at the chest with fingers leading the extension of the arm. The recovery is made with the entire lower arm pressing forward against the water.
2. The arms come out of water on recovery and slap or pound the water on entry
3. The arm strokes are taken too rapidly and with muscles tensed. The recovery is too short.

4. The leg muscles are not relaxed. The knees and ankles are not loose. The toes may be hooked rather than pointed.
5. The swimmer fails to sense the lift and glide to be derived from the arm in action of recovery and in position of full extension. The swimmer fails to sense the benefit to be obtained from a steady application of power in the arm pull.
6. The kick is too rapid, resulting in muscle tension fatiguing to the legs and back.

CHAPTER IV

Basic Swimming Instruction

During the past decade, it was felt that one should acquire proficiency in swimming in order that he might enjoy the sport as a means of recreation, and, in an emergency, might save his own life. Since no one stroke need be preferred over another, the fastest and the most modern was the popular choice. The emphasis in teaching was upon strokes offering speed, and particularly upon the crawl.

But experience gained in combat has greatly changed the emphasis. Versatility is to be desired, long distance strokes which make minimum energy demands have become musts, special skills to prepare one to meet specific dangers are now considered necessary to everyone and the information which accompanies instruction is of a new and practical nature.

In keeping with this point of view, this chapter lists four basic swimming strokes. These four fundamental requisites of the well trained swimmer, in the order of their presentation, are the elementary back stroke, the breast stroke, the side stroke and the overarm stroke.

PLATE 15. *"With the Greatest of Ease"*

THE ELEMENTARY BACK STROKE

When and Why

Distance.—This stroke is useful when the swimmer is faced with the necessity for swimming a long distance.

Time.—It is advantageous to the swimmer who is aware that he must maintain himself at the water's surface for an extended period of time.

Quiet.—It lends itself to quiet swimming without splash and so permits one to avoid attracting sharks and barracudas.

Vision.—The face-up position permits the swimmer to watch the horizon for ships and the sky for planes and will also permit one, in the confusion of abandoning ship, to see and avoid other men jumping into the water.

Simplicity.—Because it follows the horizontal float in simple progression, the stroke is easily and quickly mastered.

Breathing.—Since the face is out of the water most or all of the time, the breathing problem is minimized.

Progession Carry-over.—The body position is very closely related to that employed in sculling, finning and floating. The body position and kick are easily adaptable for use in the head, hair, chin and clothing carries. Mastery of this position facilitates learning of the inverted breast stroke and other backstroke variations.

Injury Protection.—The thick, resilient muscle structure of the back provides greater protection from injury due to underwater explosions.

Energy Conservation.—The simplicity of the stroke provides that there will be a comparatively greater return from the energy expended. Fatigue is retarded by the regularity of breathing permitted.

Description

The proper starting position will have the body in a back reclining position, the body straight, the feet together, the arms at the sides with the palms turned downward, the hips up, the head up with the ears under water.

From this position the arm recovery is begun. The hands are drawn up the sides as the elbows drop slightly and remain close to the body. The shoulders are pulled back and the chest appears to be forced up.

As the finger tips reach the upper ribs or armpit, the leg recovery is begun. Simultaneously the wrists are rotated to point the fingers outward with the elbows still holding a position close to the body; the heels are drawn up under the body; the knees are bent and angled outward while the toes are pointed in line with the body. Inhale during the arm recovery.

Together, the arms and legs complete the recovery, with the arms extending outward to the pull position, bisecting the 90° angle between shoulder and head lines, and the heels describe an arc from a position inside of the knees to a position outside of the knees, placing the legs in a straddle with the knees slightly bent. The leg action at this point is continuous with that described in the following paragraph. There is no break or hesitation. The legs do not thrust out, hesitate, and then squeeze.

Propulsion power is derived from the simultaneous arm pull and leg kick. The hands are rotated a quarter turn to place the thumbs upward and to face the palms towards the feet. The kick is completed with both legs squeezing together until the

PLATE 16. *First step in arm recovery.*

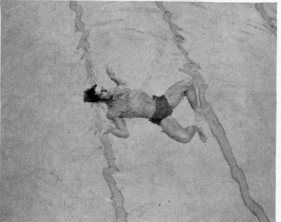

PLATE 17. *Second step in recovery. Wrists have been rotated outward and leg recovery is started.*

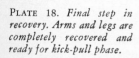

PLATE 18. *Final step in recovery. Arms and legs are completely recovered and ready for kick-pull phase.*

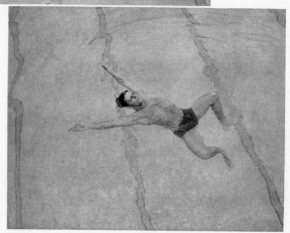

heels touch, and the arms are pulled steadily through to the sides, fully extended throughout the pull with the palms pressing the thighs or facing toward bottom at the completion of the pull.

Exhalation occurs simultaneously with the arm pull and leg kick. Exhale through mouth or nose or both.

At this point it is imperative that the body be kept relaxed and motionless, maintaining the position obtained at the completion of the pull and kick, while the body glides. Then the glide position becomes the starting position and the complete stroke is repeated.

Timing is the remaining element of this stroke. If each part is inserted at the proper instant, the stroke becomes a smooth musclar pattern.

For the Instructor to Check

Common Faults

1. The body is not stretched and kept level in the water.
2. The hips drop below the level of the feet.
3. The knees, on recovery, are not drawn sideward as well as forward.
4. The legs are thrust directly backward from the knees drawn-to-chest position.
5. The recovery of arms and legs is too abrupt.
6. The glide position is not held.
7. The hands are drawn out of water on recovery, or not rotated before extension.
8. The hands scoop upward at the completion of the pull.

It will have been noted that in the description of the stroke, it is prescribed that the arm recovery shall precede that of the legs, and in the drills the recovery of arms and legs is simultaneous. This is because the distance which the arms must traverse is greater than that through which the legs must move. Either the arm recovery must begin before that of the legs, or the arm stroke must be completed after the kick is finished. To start the arm recovery before that of the legs results in greater efficiency and smoother stroking. However, in order to make the drills no more confusing than necessary, the leg and arm recoveries are made simultaneously to count in drills.

Variations

The Inverted Breast Stroke.—This stroke is identical with the elementary back stroke in all respects with the exception that the arm-leg timing differs. There is a somewhat more pronounced overhead extension of the arms prior to the pull and there is a period of glide taken while the hands are in an overhead extended position.

Land drill and water drill procedures are similar to those employed in the breast stroke. On the command "around" the hands pull through laterally from an extended position overhead, parallel to the water surface, finishing at the hips. On the command "up" the arm recovery is begun along the sides followed immediately by the start of the leg recovery. On the command "out" the arms are placed out in full extension overhead and the legs complete the recovery and begin the circular action of the frog kick. On the command "together" the hands are held in the overhead extended position and the kick is completed. This position is maintained during a brief period of glide. On the command "around" the arms are brought down laterally at full extension, finishing with the palms against the thighs. Hold for glide.

The timing in the inverted breast stroke coincides with that of the orthodox breast stroke. A few beginners undergoing instruction in elementary back stroke will by chance fall into the timing of the inverted breast stroke. When this happens, there is no advantage in forcing a change to the elementary backstroke since both strokes serve the same purpose.

Breathing will be easier if the inhalation is taken during the arm pull and the exhalation is made during the kick and subsequent glide.

It should be noted that since the arms are pulled through to the sides, the term "inverted breast stroke" can be misleading.

THE BREAST STROKE

When and Why

Distance.—Because it permits free breathing, vision, long glide and possibility of performance without strain, the breast stroke is of great value to the man who finds himself in the water far from land.

Time.—Varying in type from the orthodox stroke to one performed in almost vertical position, the breast stroke satisfies the demands of an endurance stroke.

Quiet.—Whether it be employed in the crossing of streams, in the jungle.or in waters where sharks are known to be present, this stroke offers a method of quiet swimming.

Vision—It provides, when performed with the head above the water at all times, vision of the water, surface and sky.

Morale.—Men in the water should stay together in a group. A high breast stroke permits bantering, discussion of plan and general conversation.

Breathing.—Since the face may be held out of the water most or all of the time, the breathing problem is negligible. Therefore, the high breaststroke is the easiest form of breaststroke to teach to beginners for they are concerned with coordinating but two movements, the arms and legs, and not three which includes arms, legs and breathing as in the orthodox stroke.

Association with Other Strokes and Skills.—The frog kick is also part of treading, inverted breast, elementary back, life saving carries and underwater swimming. The arm stroke is very short and more pressure is exerted on the water than in the orthodox stroke. It is like treading water only the body is in a less vertical position.

Energy Conservation.—When performed without haste and with full utilization of buoyancy and guide, the breast stroke makes comparatively light energy demands. It is a restful stroke which provides power and reasonable speed, yet conserves energy for swimming long distances.

Against Waves and Choppy Sea.—By holding the head high, vision, direction and breathing are possible. By ducking the head and swimming through waves and breakers, physical punishment is avoided.

In Debris, Oil and Flame.—These strokes allow one to see and avoid debris in the water. This is of extreme importance when a ship has been sunk in heavy seas.

PLATE 19. *The Rough Water (High) Breast Stroke. Beginning the arm sweep.*

PLATE 20. *The Rough Water (High) Breast Stroke. Completion of pull.*

PLATE 21. *The Rough Water (High) Breast Stroke. Ready for the kick and the arm extension.*

PLATE 22. *The Rough Water (High) Breast Stroke. Position of head and arms in glide.*

PLATE 23. *Land Drill for the Kick. Arms in Position*

PLATE 24. *Land Drill for the Arm Pull*

PLATE 25. *Shallow Water Drill. Leg Kick and arm extension completed. The Glide position.*

PLATE 26. *Start of Sweeping Breast Stroke*

The high breast stroke increases the possibility of keeping oil out of the mouth. The sweeping breast stroke offers a technique for clearing a path through the flame of burning oil or gasoline.

Equipment may be carried in pack style on the back or may be pushed in front of the body.

Clothing.—The swimmer who is clothed finds this an easy stroke to use.

Life Saving.—The breast stroke is the only practical method for performing the tired swimmer carry. The high position is advantageous to most constant vision of a victim or other objective. The kick is important in carries and the arm stroke is helpful in surface **diving**.

Description

The proper starting position will have the body in a prone float position, body straight, feet together with legs straight, arms extended in advance of the head with palms down, head either above the surface or lowered with face only submerged. The more the head is raised, the greater will be the depth of the hips and feet below the surface. For clarity, a high head position may be called high breast stroke, or rough water breast stroke. A position with face submerged may be termed low breast stroke.

From this fundamental position, either the high or low breast stroke is begun, the assumption being that the run of the glide has been taken. Just before the run of the glide has been completely spent, the arms begin the backward sweep, moving in an arc and only to a point even with the shoulders. At this point the elbows bend to draw the hands in to the chest, then the hands are extended forward into the glide position. This action is continuous and steady, with the only pause occurring while the arms are extended during the glide. The type of stroke will influence the manner of pulling.

In the execution of the low breast stroke, the palms will be rotated with thumbs down and the pull will be backward, with straight arms. The palms are turned to prone and slightly past as the fingers drop in an arc and are drawn in to the chest, and finally, the hands rotate back to prone and are extended forward into the glide. The action of the hand, through pull and recovery describes an oval.

In the performance of the high breast stroke, greater emphasis is upon the supporting power obtainable from the hands and therefore there is less sideward pull. Attention is directed to the use of arms in front of the chest in contrast to emphasis in the low breast stroke upon a pull at full arm extension. From the glide position, the wrists are rotated to bring the little fingers slightly higher than the thumbs and place the palms in position similar to sculling. The elbows are slightly bent at the start of the stroke and continue to bend in order to keep the hands close and more under rather than abeam of the body. Wrist rotation is slight during the recovery except that the fingers describe the arc, by wrist flexion, as explained for low breast stroke arm recovery. In both types of arm action, the elbows are drawn in close to the ribs during recovery.

Inhalation, in the performance of the low breast stroke, is taken during the initial stages of the arm pull. In the high breast, breath may be taken at any time but it is during the arm pull that inhalation is most easily performed.

PLATE 27. *Leg Recovery in the Water*

Frog Kick.—As the arm recovery is begun and the hands are being drawn in to the chest, the leg recovery is also commenced, slowly and with muscles relaxed. The recovery is completed as the arms reach out to extension. The leg drive is delivered just as the hands reach the glide position. In the first stages of leg recovery, the knees are drawn forward and outward slowly, heels together with toes pointed out.

The legs press backward and outward as the feet whip around in an arc and the action is completed by squeezing the legs together with toes pointed. The feet are held in this trailing position during the glide and until the arms are about to be drawn in to the chest.

Exhalation is performed while the body is in the glide. This permits relaxation and rest.

For the Instructor to Check

Ten Common Faults

1. The body line is not straight. There is an excessive arch in the back.
2. The glide is not held.
3. The arms pull past the line of the shoulders.
4. The arm pull is too shallow or too deep.
5. The knees are drawn up to the stomach on recovery.
6. The knees are not spread as they are recovered.
7. The knees are thrust directly from the knees-drawn-up position of recovery back to the entended position of the glide.
8. The kick is not made a continuous whipping action.
9. The legs drift, rather than kick, together.
10. The breathing rhythm is poor.

Variations

Sweeping Breast stroke.—This is an orthodox breast stroke as far as timing is concerned but it has some variations in the hand movements that enable the swimmer to clear a path through oil and flame. On the extension of the arms, the palms are faced forward with finger tips breaking the surface and on the arm pull the hands skim the surface. This action tends to push debris forward and to the side as the body moves forward.

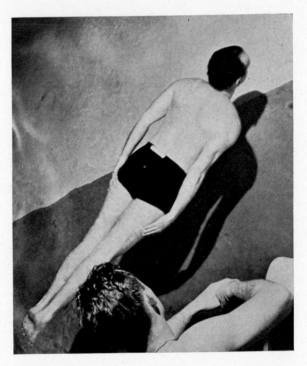

PLATE 28. *Arms to the Sides for the Under Water Breast Stroke*

Underwater Breast Stroke.—The breast stroke is, for most swimmers, the most efficient underwater swimming method. There is no change in kick or timing. The arms are brought all the way down to the sides on each stroke. Better streamlining can be obtained if the swimmer looks toward the bottom, instead of in the direction that he is going, by leading with the top of the head rather than with the forehead. If there is danger of running into debris or a solid surface, however, vision will be more important than a streamlined position.

The Breast Stroke with Vertical Scissor Kick.—This is a variation which not only serves as a means of partially resting muscles used in the breast stroke kick but also holds an appeal for the swimmer who possesses a particularly strong scissor kick. There is no change in arm stroke, body position, breathing or timing. The sole difference rests in the action of the legs which scissor either vertically or diagonally sideways.

THE SIDE STROKE

When and Why

Distance and Time.—This stroke is of value to anyone who must swim for a long distance or for a long time. It may be used exclusively or as a restful change from another stroke.

Quiet.—Because neither the arms nor the feet are out of water at any time, it is a quiet stroke.

Energy Conservation.—When performed easily and without haste, the side stroke permits one to swim with limited expenditure of effort.

Breathing.—In calm water, the face may be kept out of water and breathing is unrestricted. In rough water, the back of the head may be turned to windward and the breath taken to leeward.

Waves and Choppy Seas.—This stroke helps a swimmer slice into the waves, emerging in the trough between the wave and the next. Because the hands and legs are always under water, swells can be ridden without undue effort. For the same reason, it is a useful stroke when clothed.

Progression Carryover.—The similarity of arm stroke action, relates the side stroke to the breast stroke. The over-arm side stroke (or side over-arm) is intermediate to the orthodox side and the trudgen. The complete stroke, or a modification of it, may be employed in underwater swimming.

Equipment.—Since it can be performed without the use of the upper arm, the side stroke permits the use of that free arm to hold and carry a rifle or other article above the water.

Injury.—If an arm is broken or injured in a crash landing, the pilot may swim on the side which will place the injured limb uppermost. The arm is trailed on the surface.

PLATE 29. *Cross Chest Carry with Side Stroke Brings Home Exhausted Swimmer*

Lifesaving.—The scissors kick can be used in the performance of any life saving carry, either as horizontal or as vertical scissors. The same will apply when it is necessary to tow another person who is on debris or a rubber boat.

PLATE 30. *Land Drill for Arm Action of Side Stroke*

Description

The correct starting position will have the body straight and reclining on the side, the feet together and legs extended. The upper arm will be resting on the upper thigh, the lower arm extended forward under water, palm downward. The back and side of the head will be resting in the water, and on the shoulder of the extended arm. The ear will be underwater, the face turned sideward and upward.

This position is held while the run of the glide is taken, and then the lower arm begins its stroke from a position of extension in advance of the shoulder. The pull is carried through to a point nearly to the upper hip.

The legs and upper arm will recover coincident with the completion of the press of the lower arm. The legs are recovered by a flexion of the knees so that the heels are brought up behind. Then the legs go into a stride position, with one leg drawing backward and the other extending forward, both moving in a plane parallel to the water surface.

A swimmer may choose to learn to bring either the upper leg or the lower leg forward. He will choose that method which for him is most natural and efficient.

The upper arm recovers, with thumb inboard, by moving from the thigh to a point adjacent to the lower shoulder. The wrist is then flexed and the hand cupped, ready for the backward press to the thigh. During this action, the lower arm is completing its pull and is drawn across the chest preparatory to extension forward.

The inhalation is taken during the press of the lower arm. Exhalation is performed as the leg kick is executed and during the glide. This is a time for relaxation and rest.

The pull of the lower arm is a sustaining action, designed to counteract the resistance caused by the recovery of the legs. The principal propulsion power is derived from the backward pull of the upper arm and the scissoring action of the legs, both of which actions occur simultaneously.

To complete the leg action from the stride position, the toes are pointed and both legs scissor inward against each other. The instep of the backward leg, and the calf and sole of the forward leg, are the pressure surfaces.

The forward extension of the lower arm may precede, or may occur simultaneously with, the leg scissor and the pull of the upper arm.

PLATE 31. *In the Water Doing the Scissors Kick*

For the Instructor to Check

1. The body is not in a straight and stretched position.
2. The body is not in a position squarely on the side.
3. The glide position is not held.
4. Both arms pull through simultaneously.
5. The arm recovery, rather than the press, is accented.
6. Upper arm reaches too far forward causing the face to be submerged and the body to roll.
7. Legs are drawn up too far forward or too far to the rear on recovery making the kick move offcenter and causing the body to go to the right or left.
8. Legs are opened too forcibly on recovery.
9. Lower arm is pulled behind the body causing the body to assume a prone position.
10. Lower leg is dropped too low on recovery making the body lose horizontal position.

Variations

Side Stroke with Flutter Kick.—A few swimmers with a weak scissor kick and a strong flutter kick, will prefer to use the latter. This will be particularly true in like saving carries when one hand is employed in the performance of a carry and an increased demand for propulsion power is placed upon the legs. Except as this variation is used as a speed stroke, it is to be considered as a sign of weakness rather than a sign of strength.

Side Stroke with Frog Kick.—This variation is another adaptation of stroke to strongest kick and will most frequently be found to be useful by swimmers performing a life saving carry. It will also be found that those who have just mastered the breast stroke, may tend to use the frog kick in the side stroke. The frog kick has undeniable power and the use of it in the side stroke is not severely open to criticism. However, it is essential that all swimmers learn more than one type of

PLATE 32. *Drill for Scissors Kick; Upper Hand on Hip*

kick, each of which places particular demands upon certain muscle groups and, at the same time, rests other muscles.

The Side Overarm Stroke.—One major difference distinguishes the side overarm from the *orthodox* side stroke. In the former, the upper arm is brought forward above the water on recovery. Further variation may permit the upper arm to reach farther forward for the catch, the body to roll somewhat toward the stomach to enhance vision in the direction of progress, and the breath to be exhaled through the mouth or nose under water.

Side Stroke with Double Kick.—This variation differs from the orthodox side stroke only in that, in addition to the kick normally timed with the pull of the upper arm, a second kick is given with the pull of the lower arm. In other words, there is both a leg recovery and kick during the pull of each arm. The glide which follows each kick is of very brief duration and great strength is required.

THE OVERARM STROKES

When and Why

In Danger Area.—This stroke, because it necessitates that the arms be brought out of water on recovery, is tiring to the average swimmer and therefore is of particular value only when bursts of speed are essential. The area close by a sinking ship must be left quickly to avoid being rolled or forced under by the suction. Parts of the ship which may break loose under water and come rocketing to the surface are real hazards. Occasionally a ship may be drifting onto a swimmer who must escape on the lee side, and only a speed stroke will enable him to move faster than the ship.

Rescue.—A speed stroke is often needed to reach a drowning shipmate before the man has disappeared.

In Breeze.—Light articles like rubber boats, life jackets and some forms of debris are blown quickly across the surface by a breeze. Recapture of these articles may mean the life of the pilot. At such times, a speed stroke is essential.

Enemy Attack.—The man who finds himself in the water along with members of the enemy may not choose to engage in water combat. Escape will demand use of a speed stroke.

As a Substitute.—If, for reasons of darkness, weeds or lack of time, the use of surface dive and underwater swimming is impractical, the overarm stroke may be the procedure chosen to cross a stream under fire, land on a shore or escape enemy strafing.

Currents.—Whenever it is necessary to make progress against a current, a stroke must be used which will enable the swimmer to move ahead faster than the current can carry him back.

Ship Rescue.—Every moment that a ship lies motionless while it picks up survivors is a moment of danger. Men who can get quickly to the side of the ship are more likely to be rescued.

Against Fish.—The flutter kick creates commotion and splash which helps to discourage sharks from attacking. Used either on the back or in face down position, the action is one of an up and down thrash of the legs. This same splashing will help attract the attention of pilots of rescue planes.

The Crawl Stroke

This is a stroke which is as American as the "Spirit of '76." It is still the best stroke to use when speed is an important factor. Begin the stroke by pushing off, chest down, from the side of the pool. Make the body as long as possible with arms and legs extended. Start with the kick. Kick from the hips with a loose ankle and knee action as if there were no bones in the legs. Make the kick a good, vigorous up and down movement, depending upon the speed and the number of strokes taken.

Most swimmers breathe from the left. With this assumption, coordinate the head, shoulders and arms smoothly, reaching with the right and left arm alternately. The elbow should be high and the shoulder loose to enable the swimmer to reach forward. Get a grip on the water, press downward, and bring the arm through to the thigh.

Raise the head so that the waterline is on a level with the eyes. Inhale every

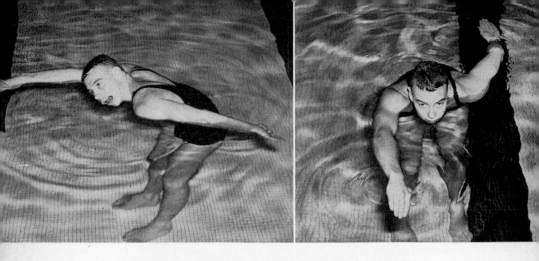

PLATE 33. *The Crawl Stroke—perfection of coordination. timing and rhythm are necessary to swim the world's fastest stroke.*

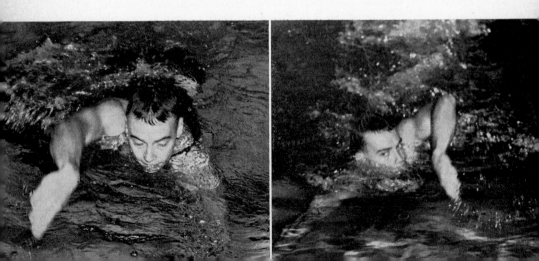

stroke as the head is turned to the left side. Exhale completely as the head is turned forward. Do not turn the head too far backward when inhaling as this causes the body to roll. No two men swim the crawl stroke exactly alike. It is essential that each swimmer strive for a natural reach, pull, and follow through. Proper timing of the arms, feet and breathing results in a perfect rhythm, which makes the crawl stroke the ultimate goal of every beginner.

For the Instructor to Check

Ten Common Faults

1. The body is not in a level and stretched position.
2. The arms fail to complete the recovery to a point directly in front of the shoulders or head.
3. The arms fail to press downward during the first part of the stroke.
4. The arms zig-zag back and forth during the pull.
5. The arm pull is not carried through to the thigh.
6. The breathing is poorly timed.
7. The head is turned too far backward for a breath and the breathing action is jerky and abrupt, not even and sustained.
8. The kick is too loose, with excessive knee bending.
9. The kick is too tense and narrow.
10. There is a body twist at the hips on every arm stroke.

The Trudgen Stroke

The trudgen is a stroke that has brought many a sailor home. Supplanted in recent years by the crawl, it has received but scant instructional attention. However, as an intermediate stroke between the side overarm and the crawl, it is reasonably fast, steady and not so tiring to the average swimmer as is the crawl.

Fundamentally, the trudgen is a stroke performed with a single scissors kick and alternate over water recovery of the arms. The body position is similar to that of the crawl except for a pronounced roll onto the breathing and kicking side. The mechanics of arm recovery are essentially the same as for the crawl, the kick basically the same as for the side stroke. If a brief glide is held following the execution of the kick, breathing is made easier.

PLATE 34. *Trudgen Stroke—Old in Form but Ever Dependable*

PLATE 35. *Trudgen Kick and Arm Pull*

If a swimmer chooses to turn on the right for intake of breath, the performance techniques will be as follows. Beginning with the swimmer in prone float position with right arm extended forward and left arm trailing at the left thigh, the legs will be trailing. While the body is in face down position, the left arm begins its overwater recovery. Coincident with the recovery of the left arm, the right arm begins its pull and the leg recovery is performed, with the right leg drawn up in the scissor position. As the left arm moves past the left shoulder and toward full forward recovery and extension, the body is rolled to turn the face to the right, the right arm completes the pull through, the scissor kick is delivered. The action of the right arm and right leg is so timed that the hand will have pulled almost through to the knee as the kick is executed. Inhalation is taken while the body surges high in the water as the result of the kick and the right arm pull.

Either immediately, or after a brief glide, the left arm begins the pull through and the right arm recovers over the water, reaching a degree of extension varying between that of the side overarm and that of the crawl. At full extension of the right arm, the face is either submerged or held above the water, but in either case is turned into a forward position. Exhalation is performed during the pull of the left arm and during the first stages of the pull of the right arm.

The above description has specified that the stroke be performed with a scissors kick. It must be noted, however, that many swimmers have used and preferred the frog kick.

If the swimmer elects to turn toward the left for the intake of breath, the words "right" and "left" must be transposed in the above explanation.

Variations of the Trudgen Stroke

The Trudgen with Double Kick.—This stroke is basically the same as the orthodox trudgen, except that the body has a more definite prone position, rolling to both left and right as one kick is delivered with each arm stroke.

The Trudgen-crawl.—If a trudgen kick is delivered as the hand on the breathing side is pulled through, and if two or four flutter kicks are performed as the opposite hand pulls through, the result is a combination of trudgen and crawl strokes, appropriately called the trudgen-crawl. This is a transitionary stroke and was used in the days before the crawl stroke was perfected and when the continuous flutter kick was considered too difficult.

CHAPTER V

Supplementary Strokes and Skills

THE RACING BACK STROKE OR INVERTED CRAWL.

When and Why

Speed.—The inverted crawl provides an alternate speed stroke which a man may use to get away quickly from the suction area of a sinking ship or to remove himself from the line of enemy fire.

Vision.—Although this stroke presents the possibility that the back of the head may collide with floating debris, the position on the back permits a man to see and avoid others jumping towards him. He can also swim out of the way of debris which may be belown into the air by explosions.

Immersion Blast Injury.—The inverted crawl provides a position of greatest protection against the effects of immersion blast, at the same time permitting swimming speed.

Breathing.—If the water is not rough, the position with the face above water enables free breathing action.

Against Sharks.—The inverted crawl permits a swimmer to create splash and commotion to frighten away sharks.

Alternate Stroke.—Muscles can be rested by changing strokes. The inverted crawl serves as an alternate speed stroke.

Between Swells.—When the swimmer has to watch each approaching wave as he swims in the trough between swells, and yet has need for speed, the inverted crawl stroke will give him the necessary position for both vision and speed. As a comber or whitecap breaks over him, he turns and heads into the wave. With the passing of the comber, he again tucks and resumes a position on the back.

Keep Direction.—A back stroke swimmer, like an oarsman, fixes his eyes upon a point aft and holds his direction constant. The inverted crawl permits him to keep to the course.

PLATE 36. *Rhythm, Relaxation and Timing*

Description

This is a stroke requiring perfect rhythm, relaxation, and timing. If the swimmer feels relaxed and the stroke looks effortless, the chances are that it is a correct back stroke. An abrupt, jumpy motion of the arms and legs is proof that the stroke is not executed properly.

The proper starting position is on the back with the body in a slight sitting position, with arms overhead about four or five inches from the ears. The legs are straight and almost together, with toes pointed. The head is inclined slightly towards the chest with a double chin effect.

From this position of riding on the middle of the back, the alternate stroking of the arms begins. To start the first arm pull, the palm of the hand is turned outward for the catch; the straight arm is then drawn to the side of the body at a depth of about fourteen inches. Avoid pulling too deeply. It is an even pressure of the hands all the way through. At the completion of the pull, the wrist is placed in a position which permits a final backward push, and the hand is drawn toward the thigh. As one arm finishes, the other begins. There is no difference between the pull and the push. They merge into one complete, even motion. The arms must be completely relaxed on the recovery. The rotation of the shoulder girdle, elbow,

PLATE 37. *Kick from Hips—loose Ankle and Knee*

and wrist raises the little finger outward and turns the palm of the hand downward toward the surface of the water. The arm is held at a position of full extension as the hand describes an arc in order to reach the water. This sweep of the arm may swing sideward and forward just clear of the water in an action simulating the recovery of an oar. This latter style, of course, requires more strength.

If a momentary glide is to be held, the wrist will be straight at the finish of the arm recovery. If the pull of the arm is to begin immediately, the wrist should be flexed and the palm turned out for the Catch. The point at which the hand enters the water will be determined primarily by the degree of rigidity of the swimmer's shoulders. A loose jointed swimmer may place the hand in the water directly in advance of the shoulder; the average swimmer cannot do so without pronounced body roll. The hands of most swimmers will enter the water well outside of, and at a point fifteen to twenty inches in advance of, the shoulder.

PLATE 38. *The Kick Is Upward and Backward*

The kick is from the hips with a flip of the instep upward and backward, resulting in a kick of about fourteen inches. The ankles are loose and the toes are pointed inward. The knees are flexed and permit the instep to lash upward and backward during the accent of the kick. Timing of the leg kick will be three kicks to each arm stroke.

For the Instructor to Check

Seven Common Faults

1. The hips are permitted to sink excessively.
2. There is too much shoulder dip and body lunge on the catch.
3. The elbows are not straightened for the catch.
4. The arm pull is too deep.
5. The palms are faced upward during recovery of the arms.
6. There is an excessive bend in the knees.
7. The leg kick is too tense and narrow.

UNDERWATER SWIMMING

When and Why

Escape from strafing is made possible.

Oil and Flame.—The safest way to avoid oil and flame is swimming underwater because a man escapes those dangers while he is below the surface.

Ditching.—The pilot, crash landing in water, may be forced to swim underwater to escape from his plane.

Crossing Streams.—The pilot forced down in hostile territory may have need to cross streams underwater to avoid being seen by the enemy.

Abandoning Ship.—The ability to swim underwater is extremely important after a jump from the ship's deck. The swimmer who emerges at the spot of entry may be injured by others whose jumps follow his own. He must swim away from the ship underwater and surface at a safe distance.

Falling Debris.—The man who has abandoned ship can swim underwater to protect himself from falling debris and flaming oil.

With Life Saving.—Underwater swimming is a part of the surface approach and is related to the lifesaving breaks.

With Surface Diving.—Surface dives performed to retrieve objects under the surface and to plunge through or escape under breakers, are usually followed by underwater swimming.

Description

Breathing would not seem to be a part of underwater swimming and yet it is one of the most important factors to be considered. This is because the swimmer anticipates the needs and demands of immersion and fills his lungs before he swims.

The underwater swimmer surfaces because the need to breathe becomes so insistent that the demand must be obeyed. The strength of the demand is determined by the amount of carbon dioxide in the blood.

Carbon dioxide in the blood is removed, via the lungs, by exhalation. Normally

PLATE 39. *Underwater Swimming—Class Instruction*

a state of homeostasis, or body balance, is maintained. Enough carbon dioxide remains in the blood to stimulate the respiratory center to cause the breathing muscles to draw in air and expel it. That balance can be altered by a deliberate effort to do so and the underwater swimmer, anticipating the coming submersion, removes much of the carbon dioxide by forced breathing.

Forced breathing simply consists of the act of forcibly inhaling and exhaling as rapidly as possible. These must be deep breaths. The action can be continued to a point where dizziness results, but the underwater swimmer does not need to alter the body balance to that extreme. The number of breaths should be between 10 and 18. The submerged swimmer feels no desire to breathe until carbon dioxide has accumulated to a normal degree, and he may still continue his progress until the blood becomes over supplied with it. He is thus enabled to swim at least half again as far as would otherwise have been possible.

Fear, resulting from tension, may keep a fairly good surface swimmer from staying under water longer than 6-10 seconds during which time he may swim two or three strokes. Have him attempt some forced breathing followed by sitting on the bottom in shallow water. With but little practice he will soon be holding his breath 30 seconds. Explain to him that he should be able to swim 50 ft. underwater in that length of time, although swimming will take more oxygen than merely sitting on the bottom. Have him try swimming for distance in shallow water first if fear is causing his failure. Try to divert the attention of the swimmer to some factor such as counting strokes, counting seconds or watching for markings on the bottom of the pool. They should try to swim a certain number of strokes such as 8 or 10 and not to hurry any of them. The stroking should never be hurried and a glide should follow each stroke.

There are any number of strokes or combinations of strokes from which the underwater swimmer may make a selection. The breaststroke is most commonly used. It is by far the best adapted for such swimming although each swimmer may prefer the stroke which he does most proficiently on the surface. If a swimmer is very poor in underwater swimming and he is using an unorthodox stroke, it might be best to teach him a version of the breaststroke and have him practice it in shallow water. If he has a good frog kick it should be the orthodox stroke or the stroke with a full arm pull, and a glide at that point. The breaststroke arm movement may be used with a horizontal scissors, vertical scissors or a flutter kick in place of the frog kick. The side stroke may be used in orthodox fashion, with a double arm pull or with a flutter kick in place of the scissors kick. Even dog paddle may be used with a longer arm stroke. Some men swim faster and more easily with kicks alone or with a combination of kicking and finning.

A swimmer may have good strokes and not be able to remain submerged. If he cannot remain under in fresh water more trouble can be anticipated in salt water swimming. Submersion for the underwater swim is done by surface diving feet first or head first. The entry must be sharp and leveling off for the swim must not be done until the body is well under the water. Th ehead must be kept down and the stroking must be done with the hands pushing back and against the surface. If the head is down the feet will be higher than head and the kick will drive the body down slightly. The rise to the surface should be sharp if the swimmer is under flame or heavy oil. This can be done by drawing the legs under the body and throwing the head back to look for the surface. In the case of strafing, ditching, or abandoning ship, the rise can be made gradual by raising the head and pressing down on the water through the stroke.

For the Instructor To Check

1. Leveling too soon on the surface dive.
2. Inability to remain submerged because the hands are pressing down.
3. Stroking too fast and not utilizing the glide.
4. Inability to swim straight, probably due to the use of an unorthodox stroke.
5. Failure to exhale, causing tension. Several strokes lost.
6. Taking one deep breath before sumerging instead of several forced breaths.
7. Failure to keep the head low enough.

ELEMENTARY DIVING

When and Why

Confidence.—The swimmer who has not learned to make a head first entry into the water is not yet fully confident of his ability.

(a) Try the First Dive from Edge of Scupper

(b) Bend at Knees and Look Down at the Water

(c) Roll Forward, Keeping Arms Straight

(d) Enter Water Not Too Far from Edge of Pool

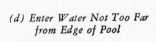

PLATE 40. *Elementary Diving*

Progressive Carry Over.—Elementary diving is closely related to surface diving and plunge diving.

Recreation.—Diving is an established recreational skill.

Description

The instructor will find elementary diving easy to teach. Most men should acquire the necessary techniques within five minutes. It is only necessary that they understand what they are to do, and then do it.

Elementary diving can be taught most easily and quickly if the procedure is one of the presentation of a series of steps arranged with each step slightly more advanced than the preceding one. If the beginner is to learn to dive within five minutes, he must not hesitate before the performance of each step; the techniques must be explained and he must immediately execute them. (See Plate 40)

THE PLUNGE DIVE

When and Why

Confidence.—The acquisition of this ability contributes to confidence in the water.

Glide.—The position in which the body must be held as it glides through the water is based upon the same principles that make an application of gliding important to the correct performance of swimming strokes. The plunge dive serves to enhance perfection in the glide.

Progression.—It is but a short step from plunge dive to racing dive.

In Surf and Waves.—The plunge dive teaches the stretched and streamlined body position essential to efficient piercing of waves and breakers.

Description

This technique for entry into the water represents the stage next advanced beyond elementary diving. The objective of the diver who uses it is to achieve distance quickly and to emerge in position to begin swimming immediately.

The general method of performance, points which the instructor should stress in a presentation of this skill, will include:

1. The crouched starting position.
2. The arm action and shoulder lift.
3. The extension of hips, knees and ankles. The spring.
4. The position of the body in the air.
5. The entry into the water.
6. Holding the glide.
7. Surfacing.

The instructor must point out that in some respects the performance of the plunge dive differs from that of the racing start. The point of entry into the water is not as far removed from the bulkhead or take-off point; the body is more sharply angled downward, and the entry into the water is cleaner. Because of the angle of entry, the body is bent forward in an even arc, and the depth of the dive is greater. Finally, the swimmer surfaces in a more leisurely manner, riding out the glide before stroking is begun. The drills presented for the racing start may, with the minor modifications noted above, be used by the instructor for drill in plunge diving.

SURFACE DIVING

When and Why

Strafing.—Diving underwater will protect from strafing.

Retrieving.—This skill helps one to find lost articles or to rescue a shipmate.

Oil and Fire.—Surface diving permits escape under oil and fire.

PLATE 41. *Bend at Waist and Swim Downward*

Ditching.—Surface diving may precede underwater swimming as men escape from a sinking plane.

Debris.—Falling debris and jumping men may be avoided by submerging.

Life Saving.—The surface dive is essential to the underwater approach.

Description

Head First Surface Dive with Tuck.—To begin this type of surface entry, the body is in a prone position on the surface. The first action is to take one complete stroke and arm pull. As the hands reach a point even with the shoulders, the head is inclined downward and the body is drawn into a tucked position, with the hips and knees flexed and the heels drawn up toward the body. As this action takes place, the arms pull through almost to the thighs, instead of drawing in to the chest in the performance of an orthodox breast stroke arm recovery.

Immediately the hips and knees are straightened above the water and above the remainder of the body, and the palms are turned toward the head and the hands are scooped toward the face from a position at the sides.

The breast stroke arm movements are performed to complete the submersion, the body is then leveled to a horizontal position and the underwater swim is begun.

Head First Surface Dive with Pike.—This form of entry differs from that performed with tuck only in that there is no bend in the knees. The body bends only at the hips. As the submersion is begun, the body doubles into a jack-knife position. To complete the submersion, the hips are straightened to extend the legs upward with feet together and toes pointed.

Submerging Feet First.—The entry is begun with the body in a vertical position in the water and with the palms at the thighs. The wrists are then rotated to turn the palms outward and the hands are drawn sideward and upward with the arms at full extension. At the completion of this action, the body will be completely submerged and the arms will be at full extension overhead. The hands complete the submersion by sculling with the fingers pointing upward toward the surface.

BOBBING

When and Why

As a Surface Dive.—When a number of feet first surface dives are made in succession, they may serve the same purposes as were listed under WHEN AND WHY for Surface Diving.

As a Preliminary Skill.—Performed in shallow water, and combined with breathing drill, simple bobbing helps to develop watermanship. As an advanced skill, it further enhances this development.

In Oil and Fire.—Bobbing is the standard procedure for progressing under oil and fire, and to emerge in flame of moderate height and obtain a breath.

Carrying Equipment.—This skill enables one to carry heavy weights in water varying from six to ten feet in depth.

Description

Simple Bobbing.—This practice accustoms the beginner to the water. The chilly swimmer may also employ it as a device to warm himself somewhat.

It is simply performed. The swimmer takes a breath, submerges in a tuck

PLATE 42. *Going Down, Feet First Entry*

position in shallow water, exhales, regains a standing position, inhales and submerges again. This procedure is repeated a specified number of times in quick succession.

PLATE 43a. *Elementary Bobbing. Going Down!*

PLATE 43b. *Bobbing. Coming Up!*

Advanced Bobbing.—In deep water a vertical position is assumed. The hands are extended outward from the sides and just under the surface of the water. The palms are turned downward. The legs are drawn into a position of readiness to deliver a frog or scissor kick.

Simultaneously, the hands are drawn sharply to the thighs and the legs execute the kick. All of the body above the hips emerges above the surface and a breath is taken when the highest point is reached. As the body begins to sink, the wrists are rotated to turn the palms outward, and the arms are brought sharply outward and upward into an extended position overhead. A hand sculling action completes the immersion.

When the desired depth is reached, the body is drawn into a tuck position, with the hips slightly higher than the head. Immediately the arms and legs are extended to place the body in a prone horizontal position from which underwater swimming is begun.

After normal progress underwater, the swimmer is ready to emerge for another breath. As he approaches the surface, he tucks slightly to place the body again in a vertical position. He then extends his arms so that the hands may break the surface, and by striking in all directions, splash away the oil or flame on that spot. The starting position is then assumed, but with the head entirely underwater and the arms extended sideward at a depth of approximately twelve inches below the surface.

For bobbing where the bottom may be reached, submerge with the body inclined backward, push off with the body inclined forward.

CHAPTER VI

Competitive Swimming (Basic)

No attempt will be made in this manual to present a specific program to apply to the training of varsity team men. The essence of good coaching is the ability to recognize individual differences and to prescribe varying training routines according to individual needs. In general, training methods will be the same; specifically, methods will differ as the individual differs.

GENERAL PROGRAM FOR TEAM TRAINING

The program for the training of the Team swimmer may be divided roughly into four phases. The length of time to be devoted to each stage will depend upon the total time available. If time is extremely short the phases must be telescoped.

First Phase

First Stage of Pre-season Conditioning
1. Warm-up. Light kicking. Bobbing. Slow swims for 50 or 100 yards. Arm and body bending movements on pool deck or beach.
2. Relaxation drills on deck and in water. Shaking, slumping.
3. Easy swimming for form.
4. Distance swimming for endurance.
5. Learn or perfect essential skills.
   (a) Starts
   (b) Turns
   (c) Perfection of strokes
   (d) Necessary dives for divers

Second Phase

Second Stage of Pre-Season Conditioning
1. Repeat drills 1 and 2 for first phase.
2. Drill on the quicker and smoother performance of starts and turns.
3. Swim laps, kicking only. Swim laps, using arms only.
4. Swim short sprints. Divide the men and swim continuous shuttle relays for from 10 minutes to one-half hour, depending on size of group.
5. Increase the length of distance swims. Better swimmers may go one mile.
6. Begin establishing the sense of pace. Every swimmer must know how fast

PLATE 44. *Competition May Be Conducted Anywhere*

he must swim to cover a given distance within a certain time. In a pool he should know the pace for a 15, 18 or 22 second lap, and be able to swim and hold that pace constant.

7. Sprint a distance slightly less than or slightly in excess of the chosen event. Sprint the shortened distance to build speed. Sprint the lengthened distance to build stamina.

8. During the final stage, the swimmer competes against the watch. Both he and the coach must know the speed of which he is capable.

Third Phase

Maintenance of Competitive Peak During Season

1. Repeat drills 1 and 2 listed for first phase.
2. Short Sprints.
3. Occasional time trials to increase pace.
4. Concentrate on correcting harmful faults discovered during competition.
5. Work for continued improvement in form, relaxation and power.

Fourth Phase

Tapering Off—Post Season

1. If the swimmer has no desire to continue swimming for pleasure, the season has been too long or too severe. No athlete should bring himself to the peak of condition and then abruptly stop exercising.
2. Introduce water polo, water basketball and water safety skills.

Suggestions to Coaches

When Sending Swimmers into Competition

1. Have the men follow their normal habits as much as is possible.
2. Do not let the men eat for from 3 to 4 hours before competition.
3. Use pep and fight talks sparingly. Instead, talk individually with swimmers.

Suggestions to Pass on to the Swimmers

1. Never start a race without first taking a complete warm-up.
2 Relax in the water. Shake the muscles. Loosen up. Bob in shallow water.
3. Watch for your event. Give yourself time to walk leisurely to the starting block.
4. Note the position and lane in which the best opposing swimmer will be.
5. Watch the starter. Don't be caught flat-footed.
6. Swim your own fastest pace, but know where your opponents are.
7. Be sure your turns are fast and good.
8. Swim completely into the finish. Finish hard. Don't drift.
9. Swim lazily through one or two laps to help the muscles to recuperate.

Essential Skills for Competition

The inexperienced competitor loses the race at the start. Lack of arm whip, spring of the legs, proper body position in the air, correct entry into the water, glide and coordinated emergence from the water can mean a handicap of 15 feet or more. The well trained swimmer will, on each turn in an enclosed course, gain two or three seconds advantage over the untrained performer because of quick spin and strong shove-off. These skills must be acquired by the competitive swimmer.

PLATE 45. *Racing Start*

Starts from the Deck

1. Starting Position
   (a) The knees are bent in a crouch, feet directly under the hips, body inclined forward, weight well forward on the balls of the feet, head up, the arms in front of or behind the body.
2. The Arm Action (Three types)
   (a) The arms are held in one-half extension forward. At the starting signal the hands flick forward to full extension.
   (b) The arms are held in one-half extension forward. At the starting signal the hands move in approximately fifteen-inch circle, upward, outward, downward and inward. Spring of the legs and the shoulder rise and fall are timed with the action of the arms.
   (c) The hands are held behind the hips, with the arms at full extension and with the palms turned inward or upward. At the starting signal, the arms are quickly brought downward and forward to full extension in front of the head.
3. Completing the Start
   (a) As the hands whip into extension forward, the body leans off balance and the knees straighten in a spring, the head is lowered between the arms, the body plunges out and enters the water with the head slightly lower than the feet. Avoid a pike or extreme arch.

   The kick is not begun until the momentum resulting from the dive is half spent. The body then planes gradually upward, propelled by the kick. The first arm stroke is completed as the body surfaces. Breast stroke dives should be deep and the swimmer should continue under

(a) Preliminary Position

(b) Arms and Chest High on "Go"

PLATE 46. *Back Stroke Start*

water, with the arms stroking through to the hips, for a distance of approximately fifteen to twenty yards.

Starts for Backstroke

1. The Starting Position
   (a) The swimmer faces the bulkhead, hands grasping the gutter, eyes looking straight ahead, with knees or knee doubled up and the soles of the feet pressed against the bulkhead.
2. The Start
   (a) At the starting signal the arms pull the body high in the water and then are thrown back overhead. The legs straighten, the back is arched and the body is propelled across the surface to enter the water at a slight downward angle. The body is then straightened, the hands are inclined slightly upward, the kick is begun and the body angles toward the surface. Just before the body surfaces, one arm is pulled through to the side and recovers as the other arm pulls through.

   If the race is an elementary back stroke, both hands will pull through together to start the stroke.

Start for Underwater

1. The Starting Position
   (a) The competitors are lined up at the end of the pool, with backs to bulkhead, hands reaching backward under the shoulders and grasping the gutter or gunnel. The body is inclined forward, the knees are tucked and the soles of the feet are placed for the shove-off.
2. The Start
   (a) At the starting signal the swimmer takes a breath, releases his double grip on the gutter, drops his hands in front of his face and pushes his arms to full extension forward.
   (b) The body is allowed to immerse except for the hips and then the shove-off is performed by a vigorous extension of the hips, knees and ankles.

Racing Turns

1. For the crawl stroke there are two types of turns; the closed turn for sprints, and the open turn for distance.
   (a) The Closed Turn: Swim in close with the palm of leading arm touching the bulkhead. Pull around with the trailing arm, swing the hips, toss the head in the direction of the turn and spin the body fast. Plant both feet against the bulkhead with a good knee bend. With hands in front of chest shove off vigorously, and with a strong kick plane to the surface. Don't come to the surface too abruptly. Take advantage of a long deep breath.
   (b) The Open Turn: Similar to the closed turn with the exception that the body goes into the turn while on the side permitting your forearm to grasp the gutter or railing. The body turns as before but twists slightly on the shove-off in order to bring you back on an even keel.

2. For Breast Stroke and Underwater Swimming
   (a) The Closed Turn: Competitive rules for breast stroke require that both hands shall touch simultaneously and that the turn shall not be anticipated. Swimmers should be instructed to do as follows:
   1. Both hands touch at the same time. Momentum and kick carry the body into the bulkhead. The elbows bend and are drawn in to the sides.
   2. The legs are drawn up in a tuck. The head ducks in the direction of the turn. The body is bent and twisted at the hips in the same direction. The fingers of both hands push away from the bulkhead to spin the body.
   3. The feet are placed against the wall with knees flexed. The arms are pushed out to full extension. Shove-off well under water, glide and begin the stroke, angling gradually to the surface.
   (b) The Open Turn: This differs from the underwater touch turn only in that:
   1. The hands grasp the gutter.
   2. The body is pulled partially out of the water by flexion of the arms.
   3. The body is turned and tucked before sinking back under water.
3. For Backstroke (Inverted Crawl, and Elementary Backstroke)
   (a) The Backstroke Flip Turn: At a little over arm's length from the wall the leading arm is thrown backward directly behind the head and downward so that it hits the wall about one foot below the surface of the water. The hand hits with the palm against the wall and fingers pointing approximately toward the bottom of pool. At the same time the head is thrown back and downward. This motion of the head and arm produces a lunge into the wall which puts the head and shoulders about 1½ feet below the surface. At the same time the legs are drawn up in a loose tuck, but legs together. The spin is then made. The head and shoulders are below the water and legs go over the top. The spin is made pivoting on the shoulder of the arm which contacted the wall. The feet are thrust against the wall below the depth of the head and shoulders so as to be inclined toward the surface. The legs are then straightened and after a slight glide the kick is brought in to bring the body to the surface. Just before breaking the surface one arm is pulled through causing the body to shoot to the surface and the swimmer immediately picks up the stroke with the other arm.
   The turn is a half somersault and then a spin pivoting on one shoulder.
   (b) For the Elementary Back Stroke: Touch with either hand and turn in the direction you touch. For example: if the touch is made with the right hand, turn in that direction. After the glide is taken, pull both arms downward to the side and resume stroke.

For the Coach to Check

Nine Common Faults

1. The leading hand touches the bulkhead and then the trailing arm is brought

forward, crossing over the top of the leading arm and also is placed against bulkhead. (In crawl stroke touch turns.)

2. Coasting into the turn.
3. The push-off is attempted when the body is too far away from the bulkhead.
4. The body is kept straight rather than tucked when the spin around is performed.
5. The trailing arm is not used in sculling or scooping action to facilitate the spin around.
6. The swimmer performs the push-off before his feet and body are set in position.
7. The arms are not placed in extended position before the push-off is performed.
8. The swimmer fails to get an adequate breath before or while making the turn.
9. The kick is not strong enough on the push-off.

ADMINISTRATION OF A SWIMMING MEET

Interest in competitive swimming can be easily developed, but it can be killed by a few meets that are poorly administered. Spectators, officials and participants can be brought to a point of disgust if the meet is not carefully planned. No meet should be run off unless the coach is prepared to give careful attention to detail. Better to have no meet at all, than one poorly conducted.

Suggestions on Meet Administration

1. *Arrange the competition* well in advance and work with the opposing teams to set the date, time, place and events. Determine the rules to govern the competition.

2. *See that the meet is advertised,* by means of radio, activity bulletins, the ship paper, metropolitan papers, posters, announcements, and a posted schedule of a series of meets.

   Keep the public relations officer informed and work through him.

3. *Secure the Necessary Officials:*

   (a) Notify or obtain the services of these men well in advance of the meet day. Inform them of their duties, how they should dress and what time they should be on hand.

   (b) Almost any man can be trained to perform these duties, if experienced officials cannot be obtained. Start early to instruct and develop officials from among the men available.

   If few men are available, one official may be assigned to two or more duties. The referee, for example, may also act as starter, judge of turns and head diving judge.

   (c) The following officials should be obtained:

   1. *Referee*—He should be unbiased and should be recognized as well as informed on swimming rules and meet administration.

2. *Starter*—Do not assign this responsibility to an amateur. He must know how to time the start, calm the swimmers and get the men off to an even start. He should be a quick thinker who can act to call back a poor start.

3. *Clerk of Course*—This official makes or breaks the meet. He must know his job, keep the events rolling in quick tempo, know the events and entries and have the competitors on the mark for each event by the time that the starter is ready.

4. *Timers*—These men must be carefully selected if record times are expected or if qualifiers for final races will be chosen by individual time performances. There should always be at least three timers; one to be designated as head timer and who will determine the official time. If finalists are selected by individual performance, there must be one timer for each lane in the preliminaries.

5. *Finish Judges*—There should be at least one judge to pick each scoring place winner and the next non-scoring place. One should be designated as head finish judge.

6. *Judges of Form and Turns*—They must know the rules and be quick to disqualify if a rule is definitely broken by a competitor. In many meets this responsibility will fall to the referee and judges of the turn will not be needed.

7. *Diving Judges*—These officials must be trained and instructed in what to look for and how to judge. There should be 5 or 7 judges, with the highest and lowest award disregarded in scoring. If both teams agree, one, two or three judges will be sufficient.

8. *Scorer*—He must be adept and accurate in dealing with figures. He keeps the official score and the official entry form. He should have one or more assistants to make additional copies of the score sheet.

9. *Diving Scorer*—By means of a diving computation table, this official maintains a running account of scores for each diver. He should be able to announce the final result within four minutes after the last dive is performed. An assistant should be provided to check the computations. This official may be the same person who scored the swimming events.

10. *Announcer*—He must be able to speak distinctly with or without the aid of a public address system. He should be colorful and be able to put drama into the meet by his descriptions, tone, manner and emphasis. He should announce the events, entries, present records for the event and tell who is leading during the race. He should announce the place winners, the winning time, and note any new records.

11. *Head Diving Judge*—He will usually serve in the capacity of diving announcer. He will, before competition starts, briefly explain the dives that must be performed, the method of scoring and request no applause until the dive has been scored. He will announce each diver and dive. As the diver returns to the surface, the head judge blows a whistle, the diving judges flash their awards and the head

judge calls out the award of each judge so that the diving scorer may record them. He will announce the result as soon as possible after the completion of the event.

4. *Arrange for the Following Additional Assistance:*

(a) Designate some person to keep an unofficial score on a backboard, visible to all spectators and competitors.

(b) Designate clerks to collect the slips from the finish judges and timers and take them to the announcer and then to the scorer. If entries are made by event, rather than completely before the start of the meet, two runners will be used, one to go to each coach to obtain entries for the next event.

(c) Assign some person to the equipment room to check valuables and to issue lockers and towels.

(d) Select assistants who will be comparable to high school or college athletic managers. One will stand by to serve any request of the opposing coach. Others will see that all equipment is on deck, prepare the score board, fix the floating lane markers, arrange the individual name plates, etc.

(e) A pool engineer to close the gutter drains, raise the level of the water and bring it to the right temperature. If an indoor pool, he should regulate room temperature to suit spectators.

(f) An electrician to stand by the public address system and to set up any flood or spot lights which may be used.

5. *Arrange Accommodations for Opponents:*

(a) Arrange meals and rooms for the team.

(b) Provide a time when teams may practice.

(c) Assign a locker to each man. Print the names of the men on strips of tape and affix to the lockers. Provide towels and soap.

6. *If the Meet Is a Championship with Three or More Teams:*

(a) Call for entries to be in at least one day before the preliminary heats

(b) Schedule a meeting for coaches before the preliminary heats.

To scratch men who will not swim, draw for heats and lanes.

All drawings are posted for participants to read.

(c) Schedule a meeting following the preliminary heats, to draw for lanes for the finals.

7. *Prepare the Necessary Blanks and Forms:*

(a) The official meet score sheet.

(b) Entry blanks. One sheet which will provide for all entries, or slips for each event.

(c) Slips for place judges and timers.

(d) Information sheet for announcer. Listing the events, records, entries and how points are scored.

(e) Diving score sheets.

(f) Name plates for each swimmer.

8. *Have Necessary Equipment Ready:*

(a) This will include starting gun and blank shells if available, whistles, finish line, stop watches, clipboards, pencils, diving flash cards, starting blocks, scoring table, public address system, phonograph and records, and the national ensign on a standard.

9. *Administering the Meet:*

(a) Start on time; ask the officials to report 20 minutes early and to register on a check list.

(b) Permit competitors to warm up in the water.

(c) All swimmers return to the locker rooms while the announcer introduces the officials and describes the meet.

(d) The teams return to the pool. They remain on the deck.

(e) Raise or otherwise display the American flag with appropriate ceremony.

(f) The announcer introduces the coaches, captains and teams.

(g) Place the names of the competitors in the first event in standards at the ends of the lanes. Start the meet.

(h) Include, during the competition or after the meet, some specialty stunt, clown diving, clothing inflation, etc. Give these specialists a proper introduction.

(i) Announce the meet results. Summarize briefly.

(j) Give copies of the official score sheet to the public relations officer.

THE SPORTS PROGRAM

The swimming program will provide racing opportunities for some, but it is in the Sports Program that competitive swimming is made available to the greatest number. By means of contests scheduled between battalions, squadrons, companies, classes and platoons in swimming meets and in relay carnivals, extensive oppor-

For: Scoring in
      Swimming

SPORTS PROGRAM

_____ VS _____   DATE _____
(SQUADRON)   (SQUADRON)

100 METER SIDE STROKE	SCORE		TIME	SCORE
1.		1.		
2.		2.		
3.		3.		
200 METER FREE STYLE			TIME	
1.		1.		
2.		2.		
3.		3.		

FIG. 1. *Summary of Meet*

tunities are created for participation in this phase of training. Competition for cups or trophies will further stimulate interest and enthusiasm.

The Swimming Program will not endeavor to draw every available swimmer into competitive racing. This deficiency will be covered by the fact that provision is made in the instructional classes for testing, for competitive games and for relay races.

General Organization

There may be one coach in charge of the Sports Program or sports may be under the direction of the Senior Athletic Officer. In any event, one person will be the Officer in Charge and the person to whom the task of administering the swimming Sports Program has been delegated will be responsible to that Officer in Charge. The plan of administration in swimming, the method of scoring, the general conduct of competition and the type of records kept and submitted should conform to the general plan for all sports. Clearance in all matters should be obtained from the Athletic or Sports Program Officer-in-Charge.

Administrative "Musts"

1. Set a precise time when muster is taken, when practice starts, when entries must be in and when the first event starts.
2. Plan practice periods carefully and definitely. Post the plan for the day and inform the coaches how they will be expected to conform and assist.
3. Keep a complete record of the results of all competition. Have constantly at hand the meet results, individual places won, points scored and the race records.
4. Instruct all coaches thoroughly in officiating methods and procedures. Indoctrinate them with an appreciation of the importance of flawless officiating.
5. Provide an opportunity for coaches to appeal decisions and interpretations of rules but impress upon them the thought that constant bickering destroys the spirit of good competition.

Planning the Practice Periods

1. *The Nature of the Practice Period Will Depend upon a Number of Influencing Factors:*
   (a) The previous experience and training of the swimmers.
   (b) The size of the pool or swimming area.
   (c) The number of swimmers.
   (d) The number of coaches. The number of teams assigned to each coach.
   (e) The temperature of air and water.
   (f) The amount of additional space available for land talks, motion pictures, etc.

2. *The Programs Should be Varied.*

   Selections may be made from the following:
   (a) Warm-up. Five or ten minutes kicking.
   (b) Instruction by members of the swimming staff in:

WATER POLO - ENTRY BLANK

SQUADRON:	COACH:		DATE:
NAME - 1st TEAM	POSITION	NO.	NAME - 2nd TEAM
	LF	1.	
	RF	2.	
	CF	3.	
	LG	4.	
	RG	5.	
	G	6.	
		7.	
		8.	

FIG. 2. *Team Entries, Water Polo*

1—Stroke techniques
2—Starts and turns
3—Competitive strategy

PLATE 47. *Squadron Team Practicing Starts*

4—Reasons for disqualification
(c) Demonstrations by coaches or superior swimmers.
(d) Time trials at ⅓, ½, ¾ or full distance.
(e) Time trials in which each swimmer must be tried in an event in which he has not previously been timed.
(f) Relays—Free style, medley, carry and underwater.
(g) Distance swimming.
(h) One lap sprint swimming. Men are sent down the pool in waves, and at intervals of 30 feet apart.
(i) Cross-pool shuttle, medley and kicking relays.
(j) Cross-pool drills in starts, turns and strokes.
(k) Individual instruction given on deck by coach as he meets with his entire team personnel.
(l) Team time trials in each event for places on the team. Team time trials to classify new men.
(m) Continuous cross-pool relays for conditioning.

Events for Sports Program Competition

1. *The events will vary* according to such influencing factors as the size of the pool, the number of swimmers and the amount of time available.
2. For the most part, the events should be those which will give further practice in those skills taught in the instructional program.
3. *For swimming meets,* both dual and championship, the events may be chosen from the following:
   (Arrange distances to suit pool measurements)
   (a) Elementary back stroke—75 to 100 yards.
   (b) Breast stroke—75, 100, 150 or 200 yards.
   (c) Free style (any stroke)—two or three races—50, 100, 200 or 220 yards.
   (d) Underwater race—maximum distance of 60 feet.
   (e) Life saving carry race—50, 75, or 100 feet.
   (f) Swimming clothes—50, 75 or 100 yards.
   (g) Relay races:
      1—Medley relay—4 men on a team. Elementary back stroke, breast stroke, side stroke, and free style—100, 200 or 400 yards.
      2—Free style relay—4 men on a team—100, 200 or 400 yards.
4. *For relay carnivals,* the events may be chosen from among those listed for swimming meets or from the following:
   (a) Rifle carry—2, 4, 6 or 8 men to a team—Each man swims 50, 100 or 150 feet.
   (b) Rubber boat tow relay—50, 100 or 150 feet per man.
   (c) Obstacle relay race—75 or 100 feet per man.
   (d) Life saving carry—Each man performs a different carry—50, 75 or 100 feet per man,
   (e) Life ring or rope tow relay—50, 75 or 100 feet per man.
   (f) Kicking relay—with or without kickboard—50, 75 or 100 feet per man.
   (g) Relay with ankles tied together; with wrists tied together in front—50, 75 or 100 feet per man.

PLATE 48. *Varied Competition as Attested by Record Board*

(h) Relay wearing life jackets—50, 75 or 100 yards per man.

(i) Stretcher carry race—75, 100 or 150 feet per team.

(j) Inflate clothing, place victim on the clothing and transport 75, 100 or 150 feet. Three swimmers and one victim on each team.

5. *To develop life saving skills,* a competition similar to the following may be **scheduled:**

(a) Cross Chest Carry.

1—Partner about same weight required. Contestants dive from end of pool, swim to victims at opposite end, make under water approach and carry victims back to start.

(b) Head Carry.

1—Same requirements as Cross Chest Carry, only using surface instead of underwater approach.

(c) Rescue for Speed.

1—Same requirements as Cross Chest Carry, only any style approach may be used and any carry except the Tired Swimmer may be used.

(d) Tired Swimmers Carry.

1—Contestants dive from end of pool. Swim to opposite end of pool using breast stroke. Victims to be about four feet away from bulkhead facing wall. Contestants will get victims in position and shove off from the bulkhead. Swim two lengths of pool with victim. At

PLATE 49. *One Arm Towing Race, Sports Program*

shallow end will be a suspended line five feet from end of pool. Any turn may be used inside this line.

(e) **Surface Dive Race.**

1—Contestants dive from shallow end of pool. Swim two-thirds the length, make three surface dives, retrieving one weight each dive. All weights to be placed on deck at deep end edge of pool.

Dividing the Pool for Competition and for Practice

Where length and breadth are sufficient, the pool may be divided by lines permitting competition and practice across the pool.

(1) On practice days, one or two teams may be assigned to each area. If two teams are assigned to one area, they may practice at the same time or alternately.

PLATE 50. *Six Inter-Squad Teams in Competition*

(2) On meet days, one meet will be conducted in each area. One set of officials will be assigned to each area. One starter will start the same event for all six meets at the same time.

(3) If it is possible to obtain only a few officials, or if the pool is less than 60 feet in width, the racing events will be conducted lengthwise rather than cross-pool. Only one race will be conducted at a time in a narrow pool, except that 2, 4, or 6 relay teams may compete at once.

PLATE 51. *Finish of Clothes Race*

Rewards

Recognition of meritorious performance is a stimulant to improvement and increased effort on the part of the participant. Three examples are given. Others may be devised.

(1) The names of winners of all events are read to all competitors at the close of the meet. If time permits, the names of all place winners can be read.

(2) The name and time for these performers who establish new records is posted on a record board. Note of these performances is made in the activity paper.

(3) The flag of the winning squadron is flown from the Sports Program mast. The pennant of the winning squadron in swimming is displayed at the swimming pool or a cup is awarded the winning team.

CHAPTER VII

Water Polo and Other Games

Aquatic games, contests and relays play a prominent part in building confidence and developing team work. They provide a means of relaxation from strain; they contribute to the development of advanced water skill; and they assist in the maintenance of a superior physical condition.

PLATE 52. *Water Polo*

WATER POLO

The Object of the Game*

When possible, the goals should be in the form of a box with all but one side enclosed by wire or twine mesh. The open side will have the dimensions; three feet high, ten feet wide and one foot deep. In the absence of an official goal,

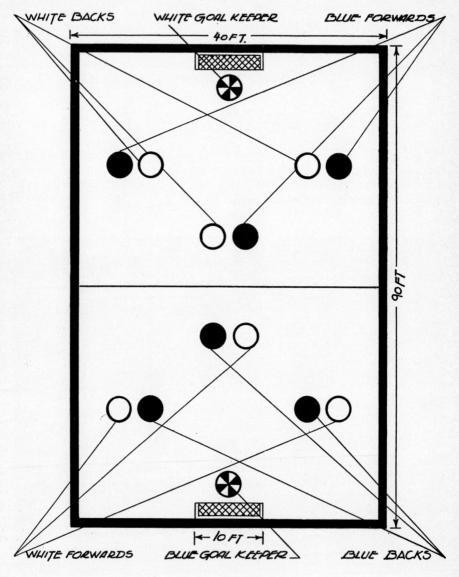

FIG. 3. *The Players*

* For complete rules and hints on Water Polo, see the National Collegiate Athletic Association Official Swimming Guide or the Amateur Athletic Union Swimming Rule Book.

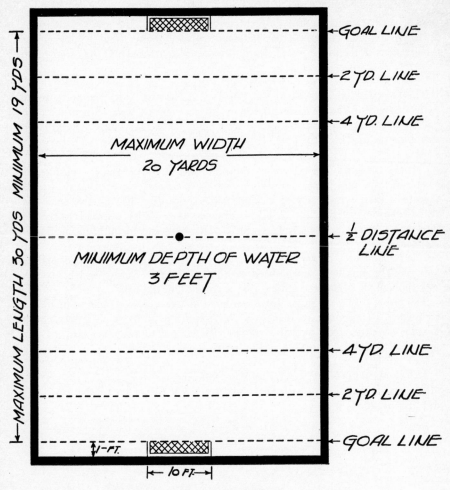

FIG. 4. *Field of Play*

a board may be substituted or a space designated on the bulkhead at both ends of the playing area.

Each team attempts to score by throwing or forcing the ball through or against the goal of its opponent. To accomplish this, the ball is first advanced by passing or dribbling until one player is able to flip, throw or swim the ball past his opponents. The final barrier will be the defending goal tender and he will attempt to intercept the ball and pass to one of his own teammates.

Each team consists of seven players. There are three forwards, three backs and a goal tender. (Fig. 3)

Necessary Equipment

The minimum essentials for play are a ball and two areas designated as goals; referee's whistle; and a black flag and a white flag.

Confusion will be avoided if each player wears a numbered polo cap, the head-gear of each team to be of a different color. The caps of the goal tenders are also distinctly colored. The game may be played in lake or ocean but a pool which has the divisions of the playing area clearly marked, will add much to the competition.

Basic Skills

The fundamental position of the player is the lay-out. With the body in a near horizontal position at the surface, he is able to start quickly. From this prone position he may swing upward using the hips as a hinge, at the same time using the breast stroke or scissors kick to lift himself well out of the water to catch or intercept a pass.

Starting combines the actions of the arms and legs in a quick explosive effort. This is as important in polo as it is in track or basketball. To perform it, the player executes a sharp scissor or frog kick and takes short, digging arm strokes. It is used at the beginning of play and as play is resumed after a goal is scored, to break into position, to evade an opponent, to reach a free ball, and to pursue a breaking opponent.

The Fundamental Strokes Are Three in Number.—The over-arm stroke (usually the crawl) is employed when speed is required in maneuvering or when pursuing an opponent. It is also the stroke used for dribbling the ball.

The breast stroke is a sustaining action used to keep one in a position of readiness, and which permits one to maneuver without losing sight of the play. The back stroke with either frog, scissor or flutter kick is used to evade a guard, to make a shot from back layout position, and to enable the player to see the play while moving away from it.

Lifting the Ball.—This method may be performed in three ways.

The first and simplest method is when the player places his hand under the ball and lifts or scoops it upward.

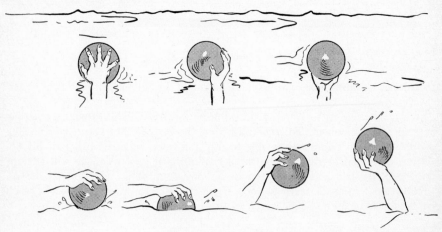

FIG. 5. *Lifting the Ball*

PLATE 53. *Water Polo Skills*
(a) Dribbling; (b) Catching; (c) Ball Handling; (d) Getting Set; (e) Passing; (f) Guarding.

The second is termed the "rolling pickup." To accomplish this, the player places his hand, with the fingers widely spread, on the top of the ball. The wrist and arm then rotate to roll the hand under the ball, sideward and downward, and then the ball is lifted.

To perform *the third* type of pickup, the hand is placed on top of the ball, a short and quick downward push is applied, and the ball bounces up out of the water as the wrist flexes back to place the hand under it.

Passing.—The ability to handle the ball and to pass determines the quality of individual player or team. These points must be remembered:

1. Get height above the water. Keep the throwing arm free.
2. Get full weight of the body behind the pass if needed.
3. Get purchase on the water with the free hand, use it for balance.
4. See your target. Don't throw blindly.
5. Be able to pass from all positions; front layout, back layout, and vertical treading.
6. Be able to use a variety of passes: looping, long, inverted U and bullet.
7. Be able to pass from scooping pickup. Be able to pass with receiving and passing combined in a continuous motion.
8. Pass the ball so the receiver can catch it easily. Avoid putting a spin in the ball. Use "soft" passes whenever possible. Pass directly to the receiver if he is free, ahead of him on the water if he is swimming, and pass so he must reach for it if he is guarded. Accuracy is the prime essential of passing.
9. Pass the ball with the hand held close to the head and with the palm facing the point of aim.
10. Keep the fingers spread.

Scoring Shots May Be Made from Varying Positions:

1. From back layout while on your back and in possession of ball. Tuck quickly, kick, and throw.

PLATE 54. *Anybody's Ball*

PLATE 55. *Scrimmage*

PLATE 56. *A Good Reach*

2. From front layout. Steady the shot with the under-water hand. Roll slightly onto the side if necessary.

3. From position high out of the water.

Catching or Receiving goes hand in hand with passing. Poor passing means poor receiving. These points must be remembered:

1. The receiver must get height above the water.

2. He must be able to receive and pass in one motion and before losing his height.

3. Reach to the side, up or back to make a catch but never reach toward the throw; let the ball come to you.

Dribbling is next in importance to passing. A player dribbles by pushing the ball forward in the pocket formed by the head and the two arms, and by using the over-arm stroke. The dribbler always must be alert to the playing situation. He must know not only who is ahead and beside him but who is behind him as well, and must be ready to pass to a teammate anywhere. The following points should be remembered:

1. Learn to dribble while swimming straight, zig-rag, slowly, at full speed, and with change of pace.
2. Keep the ball in position so you can get immediate control of it in order to flip, pass or throw.
3. Watch for a team-mate who is breaking into position to score.

Guarding.—A skillful back will keep the opposing forward on defense. He can do this by playing in front of, or at the side of, the forward and then outreaching him to intercept passes and transform the play for his team from defense to offense. In some situations the guard will have to play in back of his opponents.

The Players and Their Positions

The backs should be the best players on the team, and of the three, the center back should be the most skillful. A quick-thinking, fast breaking back will start the plays that result in scores. These points must be remembered:

1. Learn and practice "switching," to insure that all opposing offensive men are covered.
2. Start with a dribble but do not attempt a shot until deep in the scoring zone.
3. Watch your forwards. One may be in better position to score than you are.

The forwards will do most of the scoring but are dependent upon the backs to set up scoring plays. These points must be remembered:

1. Must be expert in all scoring shots, and must be skilled receivers of passes.
2. Must be constantly aggressive.
3. Must be alert and ready to "switch" if a back has lost his forward in setting up a play.

The goal tender has the task of intercepting all scoring throws made by the opposing forwards and backs. He must be alert to the location of the ball and the positions of all of the players, and must shift position in anticipation of the development of each scoring play. He must be aware of the positions of his own team-mates in order that he may immediately get the ball to one of them after an interception.

He will play the greater part of the game in the fundamental layout position but he must possess a very strong kick to enable him to quickly get height in front of the goal.

Suggestions on Teamwork

1. Work as a unit. Forget individual scoring.
2. Set up plays by dribbling and passing.
3. Be alert to team work situations. A trailer should follow the dribbler. The

PLATE 57. *Circle Drill*

dribbler should look for a forward who is a potential scorer. Be ready to "switch."

4. Know the strengths and weaknesses of your own team members.
5. Drill on plays until the movement of men is synchronized and the performance of skills is perfected.
6. Use a blackboard to study your own plays and to analyze the play of opponents.

Officiating

These points are to be noted:

1. The officials must know the rules and should read the "Hints for Guidance of Water Polo Referees" to be found in the official A.A.U. Swimming Handbook.
2. The officials must keep the game moving and must keep it under control.
3. The better the official, the less conspicuous he is.
4. Players can be trained to become satisfactory officials. Moreover, officiating will give them a better knowledge of the game and will develop leadership.

The rules in brief.

1. It is an ordinary foul:
   a. To tackle an opponent or to interfere with him in any way unless he is *holding* the ball.
   b. To hold the ball underwater when tackled.
   c. To handle the ball with two hands at the same time (excepting the goalkeeper).

The penalty for an ordinary foul is that an opposing player is permitted to make a free throw to a team-mate.

2. It is a willful foul:

   a. To deliberately hold a player, by the leg or suit, who is swimming toward the ball.

   b. To deliberately change position after the referee has blown the whistle to stop play, and before the ball is again in play.

   c. To deliberately take up a position within two yards of opponents' goal line.

The penalty for a willful foul is that the offending player must leave the game until a goal has been scored. A player who has been willfully fouled within four yards of his opponents' goal line, is permitted a free throw directly at the goal, when a whistle signal is given by the referee.

PLATE 58. *Navy Ball*

NAVY BALL

Navy ball is a game to be taught before the swimmer makes an attempt to master the more intricate rules and strategy of water polo. The game possesses very positive value as a means to relaxation from strain and as a means to enhance the development of aquatic endurance.

Because the rules are few and a minimum of skill is required, instruction in Navy Ball should precede the introduction of Water Polo. Care must be taken that play does not degenerate into roughhouse because few rules are imposed.

Rules for Navy Ball

1. Each player wears a numbered polo cap.
2. The number of players on each team may vary from seven to twenty.
3. Floating lane markers, 40 feet apart, may be used to limit the side boundaries.
4. The game is started with all members of both teams in the water. Each man must be touching the bulkhead at his own goal line.
5. To start the game, the official throws a polo ball into the center of the playing area.
6. One point is scored when the ball is touched to the opponents' goal.
7. An opponent may be tackled when he is within five feet of the ball.
8. When the ball goes out of bounds, the referee throws it back into the center of the field of play.
9. The goal dimensions are 4½' long by 1½' high.

WATER GAMES

Cage Ball or Push Ball

The game is played with a cage ball varying in diameter from 30″ to 60″. There may be from four to 40 players on a side. The object of the game is for each team to attempt to push the ball against the goal line of its opponent. The game may be played in shallow water, in deep water, or partially in both deep and shallow water. The following rules may apply:

1. If the area is part deep and part shallow water, the teams must exchange goals after each score.
2. A set number of goals may declare a winner, or the game may be won by the team which scores the most goals within a set time limit.
3. The size of the goal can be adjusted to the number of players and to the size of the playing area.
4. The game is started by the referee, who tosses the ball into the center of the playing area when he sees that all players are in contact with their own goal line.
5. A goal shall be scored when the ball is held momentarily against the goal area.

Water Baseball

The game is played with a hollow ball with a diameter varying between 6″ and 8″. There may be from seven to 14 players on a side. The game may be played with either four or three bases; modification permits the elimination of second base. The object of the game is the same as in baseball. The game may be played in deep or in shallow water, at a beach or in a pool. The following rules may apply:

1. The batter and catcher stand on the deck, or in shallow water on the beach. The pitcher is in the water.
2. The basemen and fielders may or may not be required to stand on the deck. At a beach, they will stand in the water.
3. Bases in a pool are made by draping a towel over the gutter. At a beach, any anchored smooth edged float may be used.
4. For indoor play, first and third bases are approximately 30 feet from home base.
5. The batter strikes the ball with his open hand. He may dive into the water to begin his swim to first base.
6. The batter is permitted only one strike. A foul ball puts the batter out. To be a fair hit the ball must strike the water. In other respects, indoor baseball rules apply.

Water Volleyball

The game is played with a regulation rubber or leather water polo ball or with any hollow ball from six to eight inches in diameter. As many players may participate as the size of the pool will allow. The object of the game is to make the ball strike the water on the opponents' side of the net.

1. Regulation volleyball rules apply. Modification permits the ball to be caught

and thrown, but not held. Modification may also permit the participants to hold their playing positions for five points, so that there will be a minimum of delay caused by rotation after point is scored.

2. The height of the net above the water should be between three and five feet.

Water Basketball

The game is played with a regulation rubber water polo ball or with any ball from six to eight inches in diameter. Regulation size blackboards and baskets are used. Pails, waste baskets or boxes may be used as goals if there are no regulation baskets.

PLATE 59. *Water Basketball in Chest High Water*

Five is the ideal number of players on a side, although two or three may play on a side in a game in which both teams score at the same basket. The following rules may apply:

1. Semi-official

A player may walk or swim with the ball. A player in possession of the ball may be held under water until he releases it. Piling on is not permitted. A player who is not in possession of the ball cannot be tackled until he is within five feet of it.

2. By Official Basketball Rules

A player in possession of the ball may not take more than two steps, although he may swim with or dribble the ball as in water polo. A player may not be tackled, but must be guarded as in basketball.

A guarding foul allows the offended player two free throws. If any player grasps the bulkhead while either guarding or scoring, the opposing team is awarded one free throw. If a player dives or jumps from the deck, one free throw is the penalty.

Free throws in a deep water game are made from a point five feet from the basket. In shallow water the distance is ten feet.

3. With Two Basketballs

Play with more than six on a side will make the game rough. This may be partially avoided by using two balls in the game. Play stops when a goal is scored by either team with either ball. One ball is awarded to each team to start play again.

Tag

The number who may play this game is limited only by the amount of space available. The object of the game is for each player to avoid being tagged by "It," and when tagged to pursue the others in the game. These rules may apply:

1. *Standard Tag.*—A player is not permitted to tag the man who last tagged him. To escape pursuit, a player may not run on the deck. A player may not go around the corners on the deck, he must jump into the water from the side deck and climb out again onto the end deck. The same rule applies to the crossing of diving boards.

2. *Poison Tag.*—A player must hold one hand to the part of the body on which he was tagged.

3. *Cross Tag.*—Any player shall, by diving or swimming between "It" and the player then pursued, take the place of the player pursued until another swimmer crosses between "It" and himself.

"Thar She Blows"

The only equipment required is a whistle. Any number may play. The object of the game is for any player to locate the whistle on the bottom of the pool, come to the surface, and blow three blasts before being forced under water by other players. The following rules may apply:

1. To start the game, all men stand on the deck with backs to the pool. A whistle is thrown into the water by the referee or instructor, the starting signal is given, and all players take a breath, turn, and dive or jump into the water without hesitation.

   Each player swims underwater looking for the whistle, and on each occasion that he emerges for a breath he is ready to dunk any other player who may have found the missing object.

   If a player fails to blow three blasts before being pushed under water, the game may be started anew or that player may be required to submerge and drop the whistle on the bottom.

Running the Blockade

The object of the game is for each player to attempt to be the last one captured. These rules may apply:

1. One player is made "It" and is stationed amidship between port and starboard decks. All other players are on one side of the pool. Each time that the referee blows his whistle, all players must jump or dive in and swim to the opposite side of the pool.

   "It" tries to catch one or more swimmers as they endeavor to get past him. To catch a player on the surface, "It" needs only to tag him, but a player caught under water must be forcibly brought to the surface.

   Each player caught joins "It" in attempting to capture the other remaining players, until but one remains.

Water Dodge Ball

Two teams with an equal number of players are chosen. The object of the game is for each team to endeavor to have fewer of its players hit by a rubber ball within a set time limit. The ball should be from six to eight inches in diameter. The game may be played from either a line or circle formation. The former makes a faster game. The following rules may apply:

1. Team "A" players tread water or stand in the center of the pool. Half of the players of team "B" are by the port bulkhead and half are by the starboard bulkhead.

   Players of team "B" throw the ball at players of team "A", back and forth across the pool.

   At the end of the time limit, a count is made of the number of players of team "A" who were hit and eliminated. Then the two teams exchange positions for a similar period of time.

Circle Passing

The players are grouped into two or more teams. Each team is given a ball. The object of the game is to pass the ball around the circle as many times as possible within a set time limit. The team making the most passes is the winner. Modification permits heavy objects or balloons to be used instead of balls.

King Pigeon or Elimination

All contestants sit on pool side with arms wrapped around their knees. At the starting signal, all jump or dive into the water, swim across the pool, climb out on the far side and assume the starting position on the opposite side. The last man to resume position, drops out. One contestant is eliminated each time until only one remains.

Horse and Rider

Each player has a partner. One acts as the horse and the other becomes the rider, sitting on the shoulders of the horse. The horse wraps his arms around the rider's legs. On the starting signal, the horses try to maneuver the riders into favorable attack positions. Each rider attempts to unseat opposing riders. A rider is unseated and out of the contest when his head is submerged. No player may be a rider unless his fingernails are clipped.

The contest may be either a team competition or an elimination free-for-all.

Ping Pong Contest

The players are all seated on the pool deck edge at any point. Ping-pong balls or corks are thrown into the pool, the number to be equal to or greater than the number of players. At the starting signal, all players jump or dive into the pool, catch a ball or cork with the teeth and without the use of hands, and then return to the starting position. If the contest is conducted as team competition, the two teams will be seated on opposing sides.

Retrieving Contest

Two teams equal in number are chosen or designated. The players on one team stand at the pool side facing the bulkhead. The players on the opposing team take up a similar position on the opposite side. An equal number of two types or colors of non-buoyant objects are thrown into the pool. Each team is told how many objects, and of what type, it must recover.

On the starting signal, the men about face and jump or dive into the pool, endeavoring to find the objects to be found by that team. The team which is first assembled at attention on the deck, with the correct number and type of objects piled in front of it, is the winner.

Poison

This is a shallow water game but may be played in deep water by good swimmers. The players either join hands to form a circle or each person places one arm around the shoulders of each adjacent player. In the center of the circle there is a floating ball or person. The object of the contest is for the players to force one of their number to be drawn into contact with the floating object, and thereby eliminated from the group. As each player is eliminated, the circle is re-formed and the signal to start is again given. The last player remaining in the circle is the winner.

Bombardment

Two equal teams are formed. A rope is suspended across the center of the playing area. A number of polo balls are thrown to the teams, each starting with an equal number of balls. Each team tries to keep all of the balls in the territory of the opposing team. The winning team is the one which has the fewest polo balls on its side of the rope when the playing time is up.

Direct Hit Elimination

The players are restricted to a small playing area. One player starts with the ball in his possession and attempts to hit any other player with it. Any player struck by the ball is eliminated. Any player may retrieve and throw the ball. The last player remaining is the winner.

Shipmate Support

Two equal teams are formed, each team to have an even number of contestants. The players on a team arrange themselves in pairs, one to be the shipmate, the other to be the rescuer. All players enter the water and at the starting signal all rescuers support their partners by treading water. The team having the greatest number of active rescuers at the end of the time limit is the winner.

Abandon Ship

The members of the class are assigned to either of two teams, both teams to be equal in number. The instructor holds a stop watch. To start, one team is lined up at the base of the jumping platform. At the signal, the members of that team climb the ladder and jump into deep water as rapidly as possible. The team which abandons ship in the shortest time is the winner.

Getting Aboard

This contest is the same as Abandon Ship except that the contestants start from in the water and must climb a line or cargo net to the jumping platform. Time is stopped when the last player climbs on the platform, but preceding players must descend to the deck, to avoid overloading the platform.

This contest is made more difficult if the swimmers wear life jackets.

RELAYS

Points for the Instructor to Keep in Mind

1. Attempt to have all competing teams equal in number and nearly equal in ability.
2. Explain the object of the relay in detail.
3. Explain just what must be done.
4. Disqualify immediately any man who departs from the rules or instructions.
5. Judgment must be exercised in the selection of relays. Choose those which are suited to the interests and abilities of the group. Do not repeat the same relay to the extent that the swimmers tire of it.
6. Relays may be built around almost any of the skills taught in the training program.

Grab Bag Relay

Pants, shirts, raincoats, rubber boots and similar articles of clothing are stowed in bags. One such bag is placed at the end of each lane. The lead-off men swim one length, put on the clothing, swim back to the starting point and remove the clothing. The next men on each team put on the clothing, swim the length and return. Each member of the team repeats the procedure. There should be not more than six men on a team in order to reduce the time element.

In and Out Race

Each member of the team must swim to a rubber boat, climb in, get out, swim back and touch off the next man on his team.

Ball Dribbling Relays

Each man dribbles a polo ball for a length or width of the pool and return. Modification will permit races in which the ball is carried between the knees and between the ankles, swimming with arms only.

Towel Carry Relay

A towel, which must be grasped by one corner only, is used instead of a baton.

Retrieving Relay

Every odd numbered man retrieves an object from bottom. Every even numbered man returns the object to its original position.

Rifle Carry Relay

A broomstick, length of iron pipe, or a wooden rifle may be used. The rifle must be held clear of the water.

Kicking or Kickboard Relay

Each member of each team must kick one length or width of the pool using a flutter, frog or scissor kick, as specified by the instructor. Shuttle formation will be best.

Life Ring or Rope Relay

Arrange the men on each team in shuttle formation, but with two men ready to start for each team. One man tows the other by means of a kickboard, life ring, towel or line, for a length of the pool. The rescuer then becomes the victim for the next man on his team. This procedure is repeated until every man has been both rescuer and victim.

Life Saving Relays

Use any one of the standard carries. Follow the same procedure outlined for the Life Ring or Rope relay.

Underwater Swimming Relay

Arrange the members of each team in shuttle formation. The men may start with a dive, jump or push-off, as specified by the instructor. Each man swims one length or one width.

Medley Relay Races

Each member of a team swims a different stroke. This may be modified to require that each member of the team swim three widths and on each width he must use a different stroke.

CHAPTER VIII

Standards of Achievement: Tests and Testing Procedures

It is important that the program of swimming instruction for beginning and advanced swimmers should have continuity throughout. As the swimmer moves from one lesson to the next, he should face problems which become progressively more difficult. Not only should the methods of organization and the nomenclature be of the same pattern, but also the syllabi. Every skill will be introduced at some point in this continuity and by means of review at successive times they will be developed and perfected.

PLATE 60. *"Did I Pass the Test?"*

TESTING

A moderate amount of testing with procedures carefully planned, provides an indispensable part of any instructional program. Poorly devised and administered, tests may defeat the purpose for which they are designed. If the testing is too frequent and too severe, the results may be destructive to the program.

Reasons for Testing

Such a measurement may be of value for several reasons. It provides a means to determine to what extent essential information has been retained. It serves to check teaching efficiency. It will, at the same time, make for improvement in teaching efficiency, because, as faulty technique is shown, the instructor is moved to improve his methods to insure more adequate presentation. Measurement provides concrete standards or objectives to be attained and will be a means of motivation to the cadets in their daily practice.

In the well planned training program, swimming ability is measured primarily for reasons of diagnosis and classification. As each incoming group is tested, deficiences are found to exist or particular abilities are apparent. The level of instruction at which a group will begin is determined by the information obtained from an analysis of the test results.

Efficiency of instruction demands, also, that all swimmers be classified within a group according to individual ability. Each man's test record provides the simplest basis for such classification.

Governing Principles

There are a few essential principles which apply to the construction and use of tests. The tests must, of course, measure adequately what they are designed to measure. They must be brief and still serve their purpose. They must be easily administered and scored. They must require limited explanation. They must be sufficiently comprehensive to include the major points of emphasis. The tests should be arranged in a logical progression, both with respect to the individual parts of a single test and with respect to tests of successive classification. Although some measurements may be constructed on the basis of time or distance, others which seek to determine the quality of form demonstrated must depend upon subjective judgment. Subjective judgment is not always reliable.

At present, written swimming tests are used in some naval aviation training. Their aim is to re-emphasize the instructional points advanced concerning form, techniques, rules and specific war-time skills.

Among the factors to be taken into consideration are the following:

1. A number of parts of one or more tests may be given simultaneously, with cadets routed from one testing station to another.
2. Directions for giving tests must be given clearly. Each cadet should know for what he may be disqualified.
3. To test too many men at one time results in confusion.
4. Cadets who are sick or on watch should be given an opportunity to make up the work later.
5. Follow standard procedures in all testing throughout the program. Don't improvise.

PLATE 61. *Group Testing, Five Minute Float*

THE SWIMMING TESTS

As planned for Naval Aviation Cadet Training Program.

D Test

1. Swim, tread or float for five minutes.

C Test

1. Swim 80 yards using each of the following strokes ¼ of the distance in the order named: breast, side, elementary back, and overarm strokes.

B Test

1. Swim 200 yards using each of the following strokes ¼ of the distance in the order named: breast, side, elementary back, and overarm strokes.
2. Carry subject 20 yards using Tired Swimmer Carry.
3. From a surface dive, swim 20 feet underwater.

A Test

1. Carry subject 20 yards using any carry except Tired Swimmer.
2. From surface dive, swim 50 feet underwater.
3. Demonstrate "mouth to mouth" and "back pressure arm lift" method of Artificial Respiration.

4. Jump from 10 ft. height and swim 50 yards wearing shirt and trousers.
5. Swim half mile, or swim continuously for 40 minutes.

AA Test

1. Swim 880 yards wearing shirt and trousers.
2. Carry subject 100 yards, any carry except Tired Swimmer Carry.
3. Demonstrate in deep water releases from front and back neck holds. Follow up each release with cross chest carry to nearest point.

AAA Test

1. Swim one mile.
2. Tow or push a subject on improvised float 220 yards

Maintenance Check (Officers)

1. Swim 440 yards in 15 minutes every two months.

MINIMUM REQUIREMENTS

Naval Aviation Training Program

Officers

B Test Minimum plus Artificial Respiration

Cadets

Flight Preparatory Schools and War Training Centers	C and D Required Train for B Test (No Tests are to be Officially given at War Training Centers)
Pre-Flight Schools	B and A Required
Primary Flight Training Stations	AA Required and Triple A
Intermediate Flight Training Centers	Water Survival Check-Out.
Operational Flight Training Stations and Fleet Air Centers	Maintenance Test Required once every Two Months

Fundamental Considerations in Administering All Tests

1. Plan the test procedures thoroughly.
2. Before giving any test, give careful and thorough explanation. Demonstrate what must be done.
   List the faults that will cause the cadet to fail the test.
3. Assemble all necessary equipment before starting a group test.
4. Wherever subjective judgement is required, set your standards in mind and then be consistent.
5. No cadet may officially pass a test except that he be tested by an officer of the swimming staff.
6. Have posted at all times an explanation of all tests.

The Flight Preparatory School Tests

Organization

The "D" and "C" swimming tests are to be given to every cadet as soon as possible after entry into the Flight Preparatory School, and before the start of instruction. Any cadet who fails to pass both of theses tests must attend the "subsquad" classes until he is able to satisfy the test requirements.

The size of the pool and the number of instructors will determine the rapidity with which the tests can be administered; but a period of from 30 to 45 minutes should be sufficient for the testing of 50 men. Arrangements should be made to have two platoons report to the pool every 30 or 45 minutes on the test day.

Do not combine the two tests into one. Arrange the men in small groups.

General Suggestions

1. Encourage cadets to make a good showing.
2. When you ask men who cannot swim, to step out, do so in a kindly, understanding manner. Do not make fun of them.
3. Have all of your staff in neat and appropriate gear.
4. For each man who does not pass the "D" test, note the reason for his deficiency: "Gets Cold Quickly," "Nervous Type," "Afraid of Water," etc.

The "D" Test

The Test: Float, Tread or Swim for 5 Minutes.

PLATE 62. *Float, Tread, or Swim Five Minutes*

Specific Provisions.—The cadet may float, tread or swim any stroke or combination of strokes. The cadet may not surface dive, receive assistance from another, grasp the bulkhead, or shove off from bottom or bulkhead. The entire test must be passed in deep water.

Suggested Procedures for Administering the Test.—1. Have equipment at hand; include muster sheets, test sheets, whistles, stop watches, pencils or pens, clip boards, and pole or line for rescues.

2. Require all men to take a thorough soap shower and rinse off suds.
3. Form the men in a single column on the deck around the deep water end of the pool. Face them toward the pool. Take muster.
4. Introduce the members of your staff.
5. Explain the test and demonstrate the possible methods to use. Explain subsquad obligations to those who fail.
6. Request any men who cannot swim, to fall out and report to the recorder.
7. Seat the remaining men on the pool side and require them to slip into the pool when the starting signal is given.
8. Record the names of those who do not pass the test. Explain subsquad obligation to those who fail.
9. At the end of five minutes, assemble the successful men on the deck around the shallow area of the pool for the "C" test instructions and demonstrations, after recording that these men have passed the "D" Test.

The "C" Test

The Test.—Swim continuously for 80 yards, demonstrating correct form in the elementary back, breast, side and overhand strokes. Each stroke is performed for 20 yards.

Specific Provisions.—Use the breaststroke for the first 20 yards, the side stroke for the second 20 yards, the elementary backstroke for the third 20 yards and the overarm stroke for the final 20 yards.

The breastroke must be performed with the frog kick; body position must not be faulty; the arms must not be stroked past the level of the chest; the kick and pull must occur separately; breathing must be free; and the glide after each kick must be apparent.

The sidestroke must be executed in orthodox manner, with underwater recovery of the upper arm. The kick may be a true or a reverse scissors but may not be flutter or frog kick. Body position must be on the side and not on the chest. The glide must be clearly held after each kick.

The backstroke must be swum with frog kick; the arms must recover along the ribs; the arm reach must be full; body position must not be faulty; and there must be a glide between strokes. The inverted breaststroke may be substituted.

The overarm stroke may be trudgen or crawl. The stroke must be coordinated and performed in such a manner that the swimmer has no difficulty in breathing.

Disqualification may result from incorrect form, swimming the strokes in incorrect order, resting on or shoving off from bottom.

For turning, the cadet may use an underwater push-off with hands and feet.

Suggested Procedures for Administering the Test.—1. Form the men who have passed the "D" Test in a single column on the deck around the shallow end of the pool.

2. Explain and demonstrate the stroke techniques and test procedures.
3. Form the men, in alphabetical order, in a column on the deck, and facing lane #1.
4. Start the men at 30 foot intervals. They may start with jump or shove off from bulkhead.
5. Each cadet starts down lane #1 using the back stroke, returns in lane #2 with the breast stroke, swims down lane #3 with the side stroke, and finishes in lane #4 with the overhand stroke.
6. Withdraw any cadet who employs incorrect form in any stroke—do not wait until he finishes.
7. Require the men to stay in the water after completion of the swim until directed to leave the pool by the ladder, one at a time. Those men who pass the test have this fact recorded as they leave the pool.

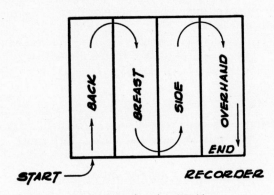

FIG. 6. *Procedure for "C" Test*

THE PRE-FLIGHT SCHOOL TESTS

Organization

The "B" Test should be given to every cadet as soon as possible, after the cadet enters the Pre-Flight School, and before instruction begins. The weak swimmers must be discovered and assigned to subsquad practice classes.

Quickly determine how much time is required to administer the test to a platoon. Then arrange to have platoons report to the pool at this time interval on Test Days.

The parts of the "A" Test are to be given during class instruction periods.

General Suggestions

a. Make testing procedure precise and orderly.
b. Keep the cadets completely under control. Avoid informality.
c. Have equipment ready. Have procedures planned.
d. Inform every cadet as to whether he has passed or failed.

The "B" Test—Part One

The Test.—Swim continuously for 200 yards, using the breast, side, back and overarm strokes.

Specific Provisions.—a. Each stroke is used for 50 yards and in the order listed above.
b. The test is started by a dive and surfacing immediately.
c. The form must be good. (Glide, timing, correct action of legs and arms.)
d. The cadet must not take hold of the bulkhead except for turning and must not touch bottom with the feet.
e. The cadet may push off the bulkhead in turning.
f. Swimming past a slower swimmer is permitted.
g. Infraction of any one of the above will disqualify the swimmer.

Suggested Procedures for Administering.—1. Small Pool (not having 8 lanes).
a. Swim the cadets in a circle pattern. (See Figure 10.)

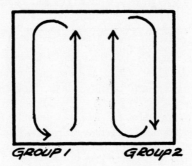

GROUP 1   GROUP 2

Fig. 7. *Testing in a Small Pool*

b. Assign maximum number of men to each pair of lanes.
c. Start men at 10 or 30 second intervals.
d. As each group finishes the test, send in another group.
e. The finish point and points for changing strokes will vary with the length of the pool. The point at which these changes are to be made must be clearly explained.
f. Group number one will start in lane #3 and return in lane #4, continue down in lane #3, return in lane #4, etc.
g. Group number two will start down lane #2 and return in lane #1, continue in lane #2, return in lane #1, etc.
2. Large Pool—8 lanes possible, of at least 75 feet in length. (Lengthwise or cross-pool.)
a. Form the cadets in an alphabetical column on deck and facing pool, in lane #1.
b. Have at hand two prepared alphabetical roster lists.
c. Start men at 10 or 30 second intervals. Each man swims down lane #1, returns in lane #2, down lane #3 and finally returns and finishes in lane #8. (See Figure 11.)

d. Finish points and points where strokes are changed will vary with the length of the pool. If stroke changes are necessary in midpool, explain clearly just where the change is to be made. A rope suspended across the pool may help.

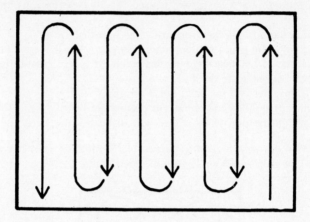

FIG. 8. *Testing in a Large Pool*

Start two watches at the same instant and use one of these to take finish times. Subtract starting time from finish time to obtain time consumed in swimming. (Figure 10.)

3. Large pool—8-28 lanes and 2-7 instructors possible. Pool of at least 75 feet in width. A method permitting more exacting check on swimming form.

a. Prepare test sheets with names arranged in groups of four.

b. Arrange the cadets on deck in groups of four to correspond with arrangement on test sheets. Each instructor has an equal number of groups assigned to him to test.

c. Assign one instructor to each four lanes.

d. Each instructor starts one group at a time. Each swimmer holds to one lane, does not swim in any other lane.

Name	Starting Time	Finish Time	Elapsed Time	Form	Pass
Acorn	:10"	5:10	5:00	x	x
Adams	:20	4:30	4:10	no	no
Allen	:30	5:07	4:37	x	x

FIG. 9. *Form Sheet for Testing*

The "B" Test—Part Two

The Test.—Perform a Tired Swimmer Carry for 60 feet.

Specific Provisions.—a. The cadet is required to perform the Tired Swimmer Carry for a distance of 20 yards, no time limit.

b. Either the frog or the vertical scissor kick may be used.

c. The dog paddle arm action or the flutter kick will not be permitted.

d. Proper instructions to the victim must be given.

e. Disqualification may result from incorrect form, receiving assistance from the victim, or failure to complete the full 20 yards distance.

Suggested Procedures for Administering.—1. *Small Pool*

a. Have all names on test check sheet.

b. Form the group into one rank, count off by 4's.

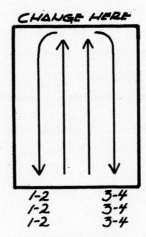

Fig. 10. *Tired Swimmer Testing, Small Pool*

c. Line up in number columns, on deck facing the pool.

d. Start each pair at 10-20 second intervals.

e. Number Two carries Number One down center lane.

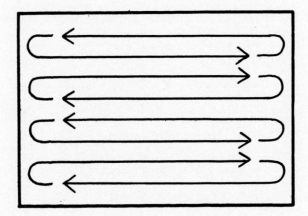

Fig. 11. *Across a Large Pool, Carry Test*

    f. Number One carries Number Two returning along the bulkhead. (Figure 12.)

    g. Number Three carries Number Four down the center.

    h. Number Four carries Number Three returning along the bulkhead.

2. *Large Pool*

    a. The small pool procedure may be used.

    b. Count off to number corresponding to even number of lanes available. If the pool is 65 or more feet wide, the test may be administered across the pool. (Figure 14)

The "B" Test—Part Three

The Test.—From a surface dive, swim 20 feet underwater.

Specific Provisions.—The cadet must be clearly under water for the entire distance.

Suggested Procedures for Administering.—1. *Small Pool*

    a. Send men across the pool in flights of 5-10.

    b. Designate point for dive—20 feet from far bulkhead.

    c. Take the names of those who fail.

2. *Large Pool*

    a. Send men across pool or down length, in flights.

The "A" Test—Part One

The Test.—Tow a person of own approximate weight by any carry, except Tired Swimmer Carry, for a distance of 60 feet.

Specific Provisions.—a. The victim must not provide assistance.

b. The face of the victim must not be submerged by the carrier.

c. The carrier must show correct form.

d. One carry must be used throughout, except that the chin carry may be used to level the victim for 5 strokes at the start of the carry.

Suggested Procedures for Administering.—The procedures suggested for Part 2 of the "B" Test apply equally well for this test (Figure 13).

The "A" Test—Part Two

The Test.—From surface dive, swim underwater for a distance of 50 feet.

Specific Provisions —The body must be entirely submerged for the entire distance.

Suggested Procedures of Administering.—1. *Small Pool*

    a. Send the men down the pool in flights of 5-10.

    b. Suspend ropes across pool on water surface at start and finish unless finish is at end of pool. (Figure 15)

    c. Start the flights at 10-20 second intervals.

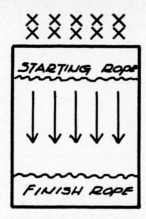

FIG. 12. *Underwater Swimming, Small Pool*

2. *Large Pool*

    a. The flights may be sent down the length of the pool, or across the pool. (If pool is 60 feet or more wide.)

The "A" Test—Part Three

The Test.—Demonstrate correct performance of the "mouth to mouth" and "back pressure arm lift" method of Artificial Respiration.

    Specific Provisions.—a. A correct demonstration of the method of lifting the victim out of the water and turning the victim from back to prone position, must precede the respiration.
    b. Both timing and form must be correct.
    c. He must have some knowledge of shock and its treatment.
    d. Disqualification may result from lack of attention to head position and comfort of the victim, or lack of form or timing.

    Suggested Procedures for Administering.—a. Form pairs by counting the men off by Two's.
    b. Assign each pair to a place on the deck.

The "A" Test—Part Four

The Test.—Jump into the pool from a 10 foot height, swim for 50 yards, wearing shirt and trousers.

    Specific Provisions.—a. Clothing—shirt front and shirt sleeves buttoned, trousers buttoned, shirt tucked in trousers. A belt is optional but recommended.
    b. Underwater push off with hands and feet is permitted.
    c. The cadet must not touch bottom.

Recommended Procedures for Administering.—a. Form the cadets in alphabetical column on the deck with head of the column at jumping tower.

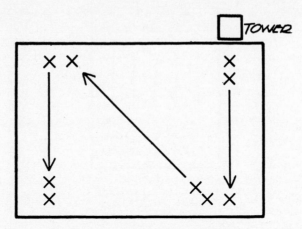

FIG. 13. *Jump and Swim with Clothes*

b. After jumping, the men form into a single line pattern, in groups of from 5-8.

c. Weak swimmers should be permitted to swim without forming a single line.

d. Men in line are 18-24 inches apart, swimming with sweeping breast stroke, as in swimming through flames.

The "A" Test—Part Five

The Test.—Swim continuously for ½ mile, using any stroke or combination of strokes. If pool arrangements make the distance swim impractical, 40 minutes of continuous swimming may be substituted.

Specific Provisions.—a. The bulkheads may not be grasped by the HANDS ON THE TURNS.

b. Underwater shoveoff is permitted.

c. The feet must not touch bottom in shallow area.

Suggested Procedures for Administering.—1. *Small Pool*—(lengthwise) *Large Pool*—(lengthwise or cross-pool).

    a. Form as many groups as there are paired lanes.

    b. Equip each swimmer with a numbered cap.

    c. Provide a checker at one end of each pair of lanes.

    d. Keep record of each lap swum and inform the cadet.

    e. The men in Group Number One, swim down lane #2; return in lane #1, swim down lane #2, return in lane #1, etc.

    f. Each group follows the same general pattern, in the two lanes assigned to it.

    g. Do not overcrowd the groups.

THE PRIMARY FLIGHT TRAINING TESTS

Organization

No pre-instruction testing is done. The three parts of the "AA" are administered during the instruction periods.

General Suggestions

(See general suggestions for the administration of tests in the Preparatory and Pre-Flight Schools.)

The "AA" Test—Part One

The Test.—Swim 880 yards, wearing shirt and trousers.

Specific Provisions.—a. Shirt and trousers, no shoes or neckties. Belt optional. Shirt sleeves down, shirt and cuffs buttoned, shirt-tail in.

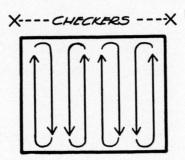

X- - - - CHECKERS - - - -X

FIG. 14. *Lanes for Long Distance Swimming*

b. Turns must be made with touch hand under water.
c. No resting.

Suggested Procedures for Administering.—See and use the procedures suggested for the one-half mile swim in the "A" test.

The "AA" Test—Part Two

The Test.—Perform a life saving carry for 100 yards.

Specific Provisions.—a. Any carry is permissible except the Tired Swimmer Carry.
b. The cadet may change from one carry to another.
c. Turn must be made without holding on to end of pool or resting on bottom
d. Complete control must be maintained throughout carry.

Suggested Procedures for Administering.—See the procedures suggested in the "B" Test Tired Swimmer Carry, or the "B" test 200 yards swim.

The "AA" Test—Part Three

The Test.—Demonstrate, in deep water, the releases from the front and back Neck Holds.

Specific Provisions.—a. Break each hold once, with victim's head turned to left and to right in front strangle.

    b. Repeat with victim's right and left arm uppermost in the back strangle.

FIG. 15. *Breaking Holds in Water*

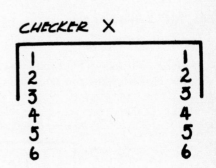

FIG. 16. *Alternate Plan for Breaking Holds*

    c. The victim must be leveled after each break.

    d. No assistance may be given by the victim.

Suggested Procedure for Administering.—a. Line up cadets in the deep end of the pool, grasping the bulkhead.

    b. Group into pairs.

    c. Take pairs in order—all others must stand by holding position at bulkead.

An Alternate Procedure.—a. Count off up to total in rank.

    b. Each man, after passing, applies holds to the next man in number order. Number Two breaks holds of Number One; Number Three breaks holds of Number Two; Number Four breaks holds of Number Three.

The Intermediate Flight Training Tests

Organization

There will be no pre-instruction testing. The parts of the "AAA" test will be given during the class instruction periods. These periods must of necessity be flexible and it will rest with the instructor to determine on which days the tests fall.

The "AAA" Test—Part One

The Test.—Swim One Mile.

Specific Provisions.—a. The swimming must be continuous.

    b. An underwater push-off may be used on the turn.

    c. The cadet may not touch the bottom with his feet.

    d. Any stroke or combination of strokes may be used.

Suggested Procedures for Administering.—In order to expedite the testing of large groups of swimmers over long distances at the same time, the installation and use of lane lines in the following manner is recommended.

1. Have each alternate lane line ends fastened 3 to 4 feet under water at the end of the pool. The lane line thus will be supported by the floats on the surface and the ends of the lane lines will be submerged for a distance of 10' to 15' from the ends, thereby permitting the swimmer to turn at the end of the pool without crossing over or under the lane lines.

2. Each swimmer wears a numbered polo cap. No other cadet assigned to that pair of lanes has the same number. At the start, an interval of 15'-20' is allowed between swimmers and each pair of lanes is filled to capacity on that basis. The instructors check each swimmer at the conclusion of each lap. If a swimmer wishes to overtake a slower swimmer, he will pass him on the right, in the lanes, and remain close to the lane thereafter. By this procedure, the instructor can exercise control over the traffic in the pool and can keep a tally of the number of laps swum by each cadet.

The "AAA" Test—Part Two

The Test.—Tow or push a person who is on an improvised float, for 220 yards.

Specific Provisions.—a. The choice of float will include the kick board, life ring, inflated clothing and floats of similar type.

b. The subject may not assist the carrier.

c. Turns must be made without grasping the end of the pool and without touching the bottom.

d. The carrier must not lose control of the subject.

Suggested Procedures for Administering.—The procedure suggested for the one mile swim will apply in the administration of this test.

THE OPERATIONAL FLIGHT TRAINING AND FLEET TESTS

Organization

Because the personnel at these stations and centers will vary widely due to kind and amount of previous swimming instruction, the testing program will show wide divergence. Little is known of the degree of ability possessed by many men who will attend the instructional periods. It is therefore suggested that the "D" and "C" tests be administered during the first drill to those men whose record does not show that these tests have been passed.

The administration of the Maintenance Test is an additional responsibility assigned to these stations and centers. It will be given as a part of one instructional period and also may be administered during the recreational swimming hours. The importance of this test is obvious and the instructor is charged to provide ample opportunity for everyone to take it and to pass it.

General Suggestions

See General Suggestions for Administration of Pre-Flight and Flight Preparatory School Tests.

The Maintenance Test

The Test.—Swim 440 yards in 15 minutes every two months.

Specific Provisions.—a. The swim must be continuous.

b. Any stroke or combination of strokes may be used.

c. Any type of turn or push-off is permitted except that the swimmer must not grasp the bulkhead to rest and he may not stand on bottom in shallow area.

Suggested Procedures for Administering.—The procedures recommended for the "A" one-half mile swim or the "AAA" mile swim will apply in the administration of this test.

NAVAL AVIATION SWIMMING CHECK-OUT TESTS

Fundamental Considerations

1. The Check-Out tests are designed to test more specifically the techniques acquired during instructional periods. Each test is based upon essential skills; skills every Naval Flier should possess.
2. The Check-Out tests skills—singly and in combination. Attempt is made through them to instruct the cadets to perform the skills in series as they will occur under battle conditions. Thus a continuity of action is learned.
3. These tests must be administered with the same forethought and care as is devoted to the administration of the Naval Aviation Swimming Tests (D.C.B. etc.).
4. These tests should enter into grading or rating of the cadet at Pre-Flight Schools. The cadet must be present during instruction periods in order to pass them. Failure to pass lowers the grade or rating.
5. Follow the general suggestions listed for the administration of Naval Aviation Swimming tests at Preparatory and Pre-Flight Schools.

THE PRE-FLIGHT SWIMMING CHECK-OUT TESTS

Checkout No. 1—Jump from 10 foot height, tread water, make head entry surface dive, and swim 30 feet underwater.

Checkout No. 2—Jump from deck height, swim overarm one length as from sinking ship, elementary backstroke one length to protect self against explosion injury, pair-off and perform Tired Swimmer Carry (one length per man).

Checkout No. 3—Jump and make life saving approach from deck height, perform surface dive, retrieve victim from bottom, level, and carry one length (not Tired Swimmer Carry) and support victim for one minute.

Checkout No. 4—Jump from 10 foot height clothed, form line with 4-6 other men, swim 50 yards with sweeping breast stroke, remove shirt and inflate it by two methods, and remove trousers and inflate by two methods.

Specific Provisions.—The specific provisions to govern these checkouts should be drawn up by the Head of the Swimming Department, to conform to performance techniques taught in instructional periods.

Suggested Procedures for Administering.—The procedures for administering can also be drawn up, using the methods suggested for the Naval Aviation Swimming Tests.

The Primary Flight Training Swimming Check-out Tests

Checkout No. 1—Swim under water 25 feet, wearing shirt and trousers.

Checkout No. 2—One-quarter mile swim.

Checkout No. 3—Demonstrate treading water for 5 minutes (hands alone 1 minute, feet alone 1 minute, hands and feet 3 minutes)

Checkout No. 4—Demonstrate fireman and saddle back carries.

Checkout No. 5—Demonstrate separating two people.

PLATE 63. *Cockpit Drill*

Checkout No. 6—Board a rubber boat; help another person aboard.

Checkout No. 7—Swim 50 yards wearing a life jacket.

Checkout No. 8—Climb and descend cargo net, Jacobs Ladder or line.

The Intermediate Flight Training Check-out Tests

Check-out No. 1—Cockpit Falls or "Drops"

Suggested Procedures for Administering.—a. Using a model cockpit without engines, instruments, wings or tail assembly, suspend cockpit above water. Pilot and model are then submerged below surface.

b. Within 15 seconds the pilot must clear himself from the plane.

c. At the end of 30 seconds, the cockpit is quickly drawn up out of the water to avoid injury or drowning.

d. The cockpit floor will be meshed to permit water to drain out or fill up as the case may be. The cockpit will be furnished with the customary seat and safety belt. The pilot at a given signal will be dropped from varying positions from which escape is possible, into the water.

e. The pilot then will:
  1. Release his safety belt. (Hood is normally open for any landing.)
  2. Launch life raft and salvage the parachute if possible.
  3. Get out of plane.
  4. Climb into life raft.
  5. Inflate rubber life jacket, if necessary to keep afloat.
  6. If the pilot is forced under water and has extricated himself from the plane, he may pull the toggles to release the gas charge in the rubber life jacket, to bring himself to the surface as quickly as possible.

Check-out No. 2—Life Raft

Suggested Procedures for Administering.—1. Give a land demonstration to include method of operation, inflation and mechanics of raft operation (latest model available).
2. Illustrate the use of mechanical features contained within kits; knife, line, whistle, pump, fishing kit, reflector, etc.
3. Placing raft into use. Following normal release of gas into life raft.
  a. Pump up seats. Leave pump attached, valve closed.
  b. Demonstrate the proper use of oars. Washers in proper position so oars may not be lost.
  c. Demonstrate how to use control valves in pumping.
  d. Secure all loose articles in the raft to prevent loss if the raft is tipped over.
  e. Tip over the raft by the proper method to avoid being detected by strafing planes. Hold on to the seats beneath the tipped over raft. Breathe air in pocket formed by seats.
  f. Right the raft and climb in again. Bail out the water.
  g. Row 100 yards.

Check-out No. 3—Parachute Jump

(Suspended above water, wearing Rubber Life Jacket)

Suggested Procedures for Administering.—1. In a swinging action the cadet will extricate himself from his parachute within a limited time as follows:
  a. Release leg harness snaps.
  b. Release chest snaps. Hold straps together although unsnapped.
  c. Release himself for fall by raising arms overhead.
2. Inflation of the life jacket following a fall into water.
  a. Pull toggles on life jacket to inflate.
  b. Deflate life jacket (to avoid detection and permit pilot to swim underwater where necessary—strafing, oil, fire, debris).
  c. Submerge feet first, swim underwater for a distance of 25 feet.
  d. Inflate life jacket by mouth.
  e. Swim to end of pool or fifty yards.
3. A minimum of three jumps in good form.

THE NAVAL AVIATION SWIMMING TEST CARD

This card is issued to the individual swimmer and is his personal possession. The person to whom it is issued will deprive personal satisfaction from it and may also make it unnecessary for him to retake a test he has already passed. This card does not replace the official jacket record. Additional reasons for the use of this card:

1. The cadet can always produce evidence that he has passed certain tests.
2. The cards stimulate interest in the tests.
3. It is a record form for use at Operational Stations and Fleet Centers.
4. It provides a compact picture of the entire swimming program.

Where and to whom the cards are given:

1. They are issued by instructors at Intermediate and Operational Bases only.
2. The cards may be issued to any men in the Naval Service who satisfactorily pass tests as prescribed in the syllabus.
3. No person is eligible to take any one test until he has proven that he has passed or can pass the preceding tests.
4. When a person passes a test, the officer in charge will sign the card and fill in the person's name, and include the data required.

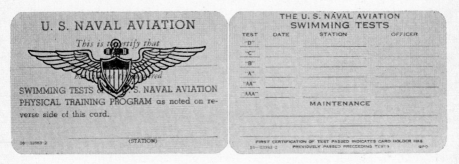

A. Front   B. Back

PLATE 64. *Naval Aviation Swimming Test Card*

CHAPTER IX

Competitive Swimming (Advanced)

COACHING SUGGESTIONS

Swimming Candidate Qualifications

It is never safe to ignore any swimming candidate on the basis of pre-determined qualifications. Any attempt to select a good swimming prospect on the basis of his physique alone is absurd, since no one body type has predominated in swimming up to this time. All other factors being equal, a good, large bodied athlete is usually better than a good, small man. However, many other factors must be considered. A large man may be "heavy" in the water while the smaller candidate may be very buoyant. Muscle and bone structure differentials must be taken into consideration.

There are certain physical qualities that are of material aid to a swimming candidate. In general, the athlete with a long, smooth and loose, muscular structure is better adapted than the candidate with a heavy and tight, muscular body. Buoyancy of the body, other than that caused by excess fat, is a great asset. Large, broad feet and hands along with loose ankles and wrists are usually helpful.

Temperament plays a major role in the development of any athlete. This is particularly true in competitive swimming. Great swimmers are made, not born. A candidate must be willing to work hard and regularly. He must be willing to follow instructions explicitly, and must also be willing to sacrifice a great deal of time to practice, while constantly keeping his body in perfect condition through various elements of guided training. He must have the desire to excel, and the willingness to "pay the price" in becoming a greater competitor.

Conditioning and Training

Conditioning through training is the process whereby the body is brought to a state of physical readiness for tests of speed and endurance with a maximum of efficiency, but without harm to the competitor's body. The young coach should establish his own rules of training, which, coupled with good spot judgement, will enable him to condition his swimmers in line with his objectives.

Conditioning and training will mean sacrifice on the part of any competitive swimmer. The selling of this thought to his swimmers is a major problem for any coach. Greatness in swimming cannot be attained without complete concentration, training, practice and conditioning.

Physical Examination

Every swimming candidate should have a complete and thorough physical examination, PRIOR to any try-outs or work-outs. This must be done in protection of the candidate, the coach and the institution involved. No candidate should be permitted on the squad unless he is completely cleared by a medical examination.

Diet

The diet of any swimmer should be given careful consideration. Eating habits differ with each individual. Food agreeable to one swimmer may not agree with another. Foods that disagree with a swimmer's stomach must be avoided at all costs.

In general, plain, wholesome well cooked foods of the type habitually used by a candidate are best for that particular individual. No food should be eaten from three to four hours before a meet, or heavy work-out. Food prior to that time, on the day of a contest, should not include heavy pastries, fried foods, heavy foods, condiments, or beverages such as iced liquids, coffee or strong tea. Fruits and vegetables are excellent. Orange juice and honey mixture can be used during meets; depending upon individual reactions.

Regularity

Regularity of all daily routine habits should be established for eating, sleeping, evacuating, work-outs, etc.

Sleep

Sleep rebuilds the body energy from day to day. It must be given primary consideration, must be at regular habitual hours, and should range from eight to ten hours each night.

Elimination

Proper diet, rest and regularity of habits should regulate this function. Constipation is often started by passing up elimination at the natural time. Liquids and foods with roughage qualities will assist these processes.

Illness

Sickness can ruin a good season for any competitor. It can usually be avoided through common sense. The worst enemy of the swimmer in this respect is the common cold, and precautionary measures should be taken.

These colds can be kept at a minimum if the following precautions are observed by swimmers:

1. Have a cold prevention injection before the season begins.
2. Drink plenty of fruit juices and water.
3. Dress sensibly and do not go out of doors before drying and cooling off carefully.
4. Avoid becoming overtired. Get plenty of rest and sleep, at regular hours.

Weight Chart

A daily weight chart should be kept of all competitors during the entire season. A sudden drop of weight, especially later in the season, may be indicative of approaching staleness from overwork, or of approaching illness.

Conditioning Exercises

Exercise should be a regular phase of the swimmer's training routine. It is an important factor in increasing body efficiency through the building up of strength, muscular tone and looseness. Many swimmers are underdeveloped in the early stages of their career. Individual weaknesses cannot be corrected by swimming alone.

Exercises should be prescribed to correct each candidate's particular weaknesses. Other routines should be utilized as a general squad conditioning media. These squad exercises should be such as to lead to general looseness and strength particularly in those muscles used in deep breathing, timed breathing, arm pull and leg kicks. Stretching exercises should be used to loosen the areas of the ankles, crotch, shoulder girdle and the backs of the legs.

Pre-season exercises should become progressively more extensive until actual water work-outs are begun. This extensive use of exercises should continue until the meet season begins. At this exercises should be limited to the limbering up process prior to entry into the water work-out. This should be continued throughout the season.

TRAINING LIMITATIONS—SEASONAL PERIODS

A swimming candidate may be in excellent condition, generally speaking, but may be unable to swim any distance without undue fatigue. This usually indicates that he has had very little recent swimming experience, or that he has recently been actively engaged in another sport. In either case he is unable to relax in the water, is tight or is using muscles in a manner that is of little value in competitive swimming.

Many coaches agree that a swimmer should not engage in other sports to or during the swimming season. The development of certain muscles areas and the usage of those muscular groupings varies with different sports. Some sports practically eliminate an athlete from becoming a great swimmer. Swimmers may become so loose that they cannot perform efficiently in other activities.

Keeping up interest and enthusiasm for the entire season is a difficult problem, unless there is satisfaction from improvement or unless the swimmer is a competitor in the championship class. Workouts should be carefully planned to keep interest at a high level.

Each season should involve at least four phases of emphasis in training. Emphasis on particular elements of training should vary during the Pre-Season, Early-Season, Schedule-Season and The Tapering off-Season. Each coach will have his own particular problems in this regard. However, there should be about six weeks of Pre-Season drill, six to eight weeks of Early-Season drill, followed by the period of the Schedule-Season, and then two to three weeks of the Tapering off-Season. If the first meet is scheduled for early January, practice should start twelve to fourteen weeks previously; about the first of October.

Pre-Season Drills

The objectives of this period are:
1. To attain conditioning through prescribed exercises
2. To correct strokes

3. To determine squad personnel
4. To start building stamina and endurance
5. To learn and improve auxiliary skills

Conditioning through exercise was discussed earlier but since it does become part of the regular, training workouts some additional discussion is in order. All members of the squad need the benefits that are derived from this type of conditioning. Generally speaking the younger candidates and those who have done little exercise, other than swimming, will need strengthening exercises, while the older men and those who have engaged recently in other sports need stretching exercises. The exercises should be taken at the beginning of the workouts and before the pre-swim shower is taken. The amount should be limited at first, with gradual increase.

When the men report for the first practice sessions there will be all degrees of abilities in the group. Naturally the men who need help most will be those with less experience. A great deal of this period should be devoted to bringing these men along to the level where they can be trained with the rest of the squad if they possess the natural ability to make competitive swimmers. These men should be given instruction in all strokes and not allowed to specialize until they have tried all of them. They should not attempt to swim more than a length until they can do these strokes satisfactorily. This does not mean perfection. When they have learned the front crawl, back crawl and breaststroke in this manner, it is safe to have them swim medleys. These medleys should be short at first with a gradual increase in numbers, followed by an increase in lengths swum. When enough endurance is built up so that they are able to swim 300 to 400 yards in any stroke without stopping, separate drills can be introduced which will aid the arm stroke and leg kicks. Arm drills can be practiced by simply standing in a half crouch in shallow water, with the use of a belt, with the use of swim cans, or by simply tying the legs together and depending on buoyancy. The kick drills can be conducted with kick boards, without any support, or by hanging on the bulkheads. Breathing drills should be used several times in these workouts. Swimming all strokes will not affect the execution of any one stroke and the variety offered may be just enough to relieve boredom. The experienced swimmers should undergo some of the same type of swimming, for they may need correction. Ofttimes during summer months one of them may have developed skills which will make him valuable in additional events.

When this period is completed the makeup of the squad will have been determined, barring sickness and academic failure. The coach should have ample time to observe all candidates swim and can decide whether they have any future in competitive swimming. He should have a fair idea as to which strokes they are best adapted. Many men will eliminate themselves at this time through lack of ability or unwillingness to work. If they quit of their own accord, after the coach has worked with them and encouraged them, he is well rid of them at this early stage, before they have gained a place in his plans for the year.

Stamina and endurance must be built up during this period. A great deal of distance swimming or some swimming coupled with water games will do this. Water polo is very popular and its advocates insist that it does help to eliminate the monotony of this period. The experienced swimmers should engage more in this type of conditioning, expecially if there is some good competition available. As the swimmers improve their strokes and as distance is increased, stamina is developed.

Distance swimming does not infer swimming a mile crawl without stopping but it means swimming a distance totaling a mile which might be broken down into the three different strokes plus some kicking and stroking drills. However, there should be little or no rest between changes.

Work on auxiliary skills should be started at this time. This includes starts, turns, and takeoffs. The inexperienced swimmer will need much work here and preliminary work can be started at this point. These type drills can be practiced when the entire squad is present and working at the same time. Width-way swimming in the pool may be utilized at such times.

Early-Season Drills

The objectives of this period are:
1. To continue conditioning process
2. To bring stamina and endurance to a peak
3. To continue stroke instruction
4. To stress added auxiliary skills
5. To introduce pacing
6. To place men in proper events
7. To afford practice under meet conditions
8. Body building program.

Perhaps these drills could be added to the first period. Yet it is at this point in the training program that the squad will be able to start working out as a unit, both because they will all be able to take the same workout physically and because the personnel of the squad will be fairly well determined. If the squad is too large or the pool too small special groups can work out together.

Conditioning exercises should be lessened during this period but they should not be discontinued. The men will know their own routines well and this phase of the workout should not take long.

Stamina and endurance will be increased mostly by swimming during this period. Again it is not necessary to swim long distances in one particular stroke, but there can be two or three strokes included and certainly there should be a breakdown and kicking and stroking drills included. At the close of this period the swimmer should have reached a point where any type workout, within reason, can be handled without harm. One to two miles should be covered each day and there should be as little rest between parts of the workout as possible. Some of the kicking drills should be done in sprint tempo.

Stroke correction will continue during this period but there should be less of this to do than previously. At the close of this seasonal period corrections should be practically minimized and no drastic changes should be attempted during the meet season for several obvious reasons.

Turns and starts should be practiced and near perfection should be the goal. The starts should be executed with the proper commands and a gun for the signal as often as possible. The starts should include the glide and at least two or three strokes following the glide. If the starts are attempted across the pool the turns can be included. In this manner many can be attempted without unduly tiring the man. At the end of this period, when the team is fairly well established, relay takeoffs can be practiced. A good drill for this is to have the squad divided into several relays and have each man swim one length and keep the relay going long enough so that each man has had several one length swims. Keep them in medley relay order.

It is during this period that pacing is introduced. This is the process whereby a swimmer distributes his endurance so that he achieves the greatest speed over a given distance. He must learn how to distribute his efforts over a given distance even in these drills; otherwise swimming distance will do him little good. He might swim 600 yds free style, through 500 yds of which he loafs, and then sprint the last 100 yds. He may be just as tired or more tired when he finishes than the swimmer who does it faster but who swims at a more even rate. A 440 yard swim is a good arbitrary distance for a swimmer to attempt in order to learn pacing. A set time should be prearranged with time splits for the laps and the swimmer with the aid of pacing devices should attempt to negotiate the distance in that time. These pacing aids may be special mechanical devices or simply cards (diving cards) which are flashed at the end of each lap. For example if a four is flashed that may mean 44 seconds for the lap. He can slow down or speed up depending on the prearranged times set for each lap. As soon as he proves that he can swim the distance in a given time with the aid of cards or a pacer he attempts it without such aids. The next step is to lessen the time, which means increased speed. Be careful not to increase the speed so much that he cannot make or barely make it. Only after repeated lowering of times should he reach a peak where he cannot swim any faster. At this point other standard competitive distances can be attempted in the same manner. This type of training should help the inexperienced and the distance swimmers most as far as their races are concerned, but it will aid in building endurance and stamina in a sprinter with the result that the so called sprinter discovers he is a good distance man as well. There are several pacing machines that have been developed by leading coaches. The principle is similar to the use made of a mechanical bunny at dog racing tracks.

Placing men in their best events will follow closely with the pacing technique which has just been discussed. It will separate sprinters from the distance men and middle distance men. The number of events that each is capable of swimming in a dual meet will be determined during the meet season and should be tested under meet conditions. Condition and the power of recuperation are important factors.

Practice meets should be set up at the close of this season for the purpose of testing the men under actual meet conditions. Many will swim faster with a watch on them and with no competition, while others will prove to be better competitors and outstrip those with faster time trials. In addition the coach will find out who can come back fast enough to swim the relays in the early meets. These meets can be between the freshmen and the varsity or between two equally matched squads made up of the varsity men. The meet should be run exactly as a duel meet and with the same time allotment. At least two such meets would be beneficial before the first regular dual meet of the season.

The Schedule-Season

The objectives are:
1. To develop speed
2. To improve auxiliary skills
3. To maintain stamina and endurance
4. Interval training

5. To reach and maintain peak performance

6. To maintain team morale

This is the "payoff" phase of the swimming season. In many respects it is the most interesting, yet it can be the most difficult and trying for the coach. The pressure will be felt by the athletes as well as the coach. The psychology practiced by the coach may prove to be the most important single factor. The experienced coach will definitely have an advantage, and the coach with an experienced squad should profit because of the previous seasons he has worked with the same swimmers.

Speed, the number one objective, wins races and subsequently wins meets. The swimmer should learn a great deal about pace, and should be capable of judging his own abilities over a given distance. The competitor, at this stage, should take careful stock of himself and try to analyze his own weakness and strength. He should be given periodic time trials, followed by a thorough analysis of each race to determine why it was too fast or too slow, as the case might be. With a meet on Saturday the time trials should be held on Wednesday.

Minor stroke corrections can still be made and much stress should be given to turns, starts, and takeoffs. The makeup of the relay teams should be fairly well established by now. These relay men should practice takeoffs in the order that they swim in the relays. Each man has his own peculiar habits and his teammates should know these and be able to compensate for them. The day before meets is the best time for an extensive practice on such skills, although some time should be allocated for this at least two or three times during the week. Stamina and endurance should have now reached a point where the maximum performance can be expected without harming the swimmer. There must be no letdown that will change this condition. The workouts must be sufficiently strenuous to maintain condition and yet not be too strenuous so that the men become overworked and eventually stale. Distance swimming should not be as regular as it was in the earlier stages of training, but certain days should be set aside for this type of workout. With a Saturday meet coming up, Tuesday and Thursday are suitable days for distance practice.

Peak performance should be reached at the beginning of the championship meets. It may have to be maintained for from one to four weeks, depending on the order of the meets and the classification of swimming in which the team is engaged. Younger swimmers will reach a peak faster and lose it sooner than more experienced swimmers. Loss of weight, apparent loss of interest, a sudden drop in performance, and intense irritability or nervousness are signs to heed if a complete letdown is to be avoided. Staleness is the word that is usually descriptive of the above conditions. Poor competition or lack of competition will cause a loss of interest and a gradual letdown in performance. Overwork or sickness will be evidenced by loss of weight, sudden drop in performance, and extreme nervousness. Whatever the cause, each swimmer will have to be treated individually. For this reason the coach may make some mistakes with a first year swimmer that can be eliminated the second year.

Maintaining team morale during the period of competition presents many problems. If the schedule has been made with foresight, the green team should have easier meets at first to build up confidence. It should also have fewer meets. A veteran team with talent should be given a tough schedule with real challenges all season. A weak schedule may ruin such a team. Individual team members who are mediocre should be given opportunities to compete, but not so regularly that they forget the team score comes first. The topnotch swimmers will have ample opportunity to compete in the championship meets, while during the dual meet season they should be made to subordinate themselves to the best interests of the team. If it is a poor season from a team standpoint, many more problems will arise. A pep talk by the coach to the entire team will seldom help, for such talks should be given individually and to the men who need them. Many men are high strung in the beginning while others become so during the season. A private talk will iron out more troubles than a general talk to all the men.

Competitive Phase

The previous section defines one way of conditioning. A more modern method, used by some outstanding teams, is the Fartlek type (Swedish for *speed play*)—fast-slow, fast-slow at early stages. The feeling now is that a man can only burn out from the neck up. The body must be strong and able to stand the pain of training; the more pain the swimmer can stand, the better his efficiency.

Getting Ready for Meets

Schedule lots of clock work, and repeats—25's or 50's for sprinters, 100's and 200's for middle distance men—during the whole work out period. There must be many repeated distance swims at a pace equal to or faster than race pace.

High School vs Prep Swimmers

The only difference between a high school and a college swimmer is two to four years in age—one can work just as hard as the other.

Tapering off-Season

The objectives of this period are:
1. To taper off physical condition
2. To rebuild lost confidence
3. To experiment with men in different strokes and events.

At the close of the championship or regular season, the swimmers should be in top condition. It is considered a harmful practice to suddenly stop exercising without a tapering off period of two to three weeks. If the swimmer is not reporting immediately for some other sport he should continue swimming. Most of the men will enjoy it, for the tension is off and the workouts will not be as formal.

During the season some of the men may have decided that they are better fitted for some other event or events but because there was no time to experiment they were not given a chance. Graduation may be leaving holes in the ranks. This, therefore is the ideal time to start finding someone else for these spots. Those who participated but little during the season can be given more attention, thus the spade work for the next year has begun.

BREATHING

The preliminary drills can be carried out with the body in a vertical position, hands grasping the gutter or standing in water that is just deep enough so that the head can be raised for inhalation. The exhalations should all be done under water through the mouth or nose. The head or face should come to the surface just as exhalation is completed. As the face emerges a quick inhalation is made through the mouth with all of the body under the water excepting the head. The head should then be submerged immediately, to at least the eye level. The body position for these drills can be changed so that the breast strokers and free stylers positions approximate those of their actual swimming positions.

It takes added muscular strength to inhale when the body alone is submerged and similarly to exhale when the face and body are in the water. These drills exercise the proper muscles and allow the coach to check carefully for faults. Holding the breath too long before exhalation is started is a common fault which may cause a loss of rhythm. Correction of this is essential when the breathing is being synchronized with the rest of the stroke.

These drills can be executed at the beginning of practice, after certain strenuous parts of the workout and at the end of the workouts. It should always be done following races, or time trials, and should be continued until the breathing returns to normal. Inexperienced swimmers will want to scramble out of the pool and sprawl out on the deck.

Breathing in Free Style Sprinting

Forced breathing is excellent for all swimmers before the start of the race. This is especially true of sprinters. Forced breathing is done by taking several deep inhalations followed by deep exhalations and should be done while the swimmers are back of their marks awaiting the starting signals. After the swimmers take their marks breathing must be normal and the breath is held during the dive and glide. This gives added buoyancy to the body. The number of breaths to be taken during the race will differ although in a fifty yard sprint one breath should be sufficient for the first length. On the return length one or two breaths should suffice. Attempting to hold the head too high or the hips too low may cause tenseness in breathing. No attempt should be made to take a breath on the first stroke after coming out of a turn. The body is usually too low in the water. This may result in either a slight loss of rhythm or a deviation in direction which may be disastrous to a sprinter.

Races of 100 yards are considered sprints, but due to the added distance the breathing is slightly different. Forced breathing should be done before the race and the breathing during the first length (25 yards) is about the same as in the first length of the fifty yard sprint. Usually two breaths should be taken on this length instead of one and on the second length it is common practice to breath every other stroke. During the last two lengths the breathing is regular and done with every stroke.

Breathing in Free Style Distance Swimming

Forced breathing should be done prior to the start. Breathing should be done with each stroke. All distance swimmers should master breathing on either side as there will be many opportunities to use this added skill during a race. It may be necessary to spot a close rival when he is on the blind side or near the close of a race when there is danger of being outsprinted by swimmers on either side. The head should ride somewhat lower than in sprinting and it may take slightly longer to catch each inhalation. This means there will be a longer pause with the head turned but since the entire stroke is slower there should be no loss of power or deviation in rhythm. Proper body alignment can easily be changed if the head is not recovered soon enough. It must be recovered before the arm on the breathing side is carried forward, or the catch of the opposite arm will be affected and a body roll will be introduced that is detrimental to the kick and the forward movement through the water. Distance turns in these events should allow for extra large breaths. This aids buoyancy and breathing.

Breathing in Breaststroke Races

In Breaststroke the face should be held high, near the surface in a glide position and lifted easily for breathing. Breathing can come at the start of the pull or at the end of the kick as desired. Easy exchange of air is the best action for distances of 200 yards. Breathing every other stroke, or every third stroke, for 100 yards or less is probably best.

Breathing in Backstroking

Competitive backstroking presents some difficulties in breathing due to starts and turns. There are fewer other difficulties than in any other type of competitive swimming. At the start of the race when the body is in a glide position and submerged water will run down the nasal passage unless some preventative action is taken. The same problem is present when flip turns or pushoffs on the turns are attempted. Exhalation should be done slowly, and continuously. This will keep water from entering. There is danger of some loss of buoyancy should exhalation be finished too soon.

Breathing should be regular in all races. Exhalation must be done through the nose and inhalation must be done through the mouth. The face is above the surface but no occasional attempt should be made to breath through the nose. A little drop of water in the nasal passage can ruin a race under such circumstances. Flip turning when a swimmer has a cold can aggravate a sinus condition to the extent that serious complications may follow. Some backstrokers use a nose clip to avoid this circumstance.

There is no necessity for rolling or bobbing the head. The head is part of the keel that keeps the body even and smooth. The head should be kept in a position with the chin slightly tucked except on the pushoffs and at the finish of a race. At those times the head is streamlined between the arms.

THE FRONT CRAWL STROKE

The front crawl is the most popular stroke among competitive swimmers. It has more variations than any other stroke. In competitive circles it is often called "Free Style." This name was given it because many of the events on the competitive program are called free style events, meaning that any style may be used. Since the front crawl is the fastest stroke it has always been used in these events. The front crawl stroke receives more attention than other strokes. Its popularity can be traced to two factors. First, it is the fastest of all strokes. Second, more than half of the events on the competitive program call for free style. Therefore, the demand is greater for front crawl swimmers.

Each time a group dominates the field their style is copied on the general assumption that they have improved the stroke. The recent 1949 National Outdoor A.A.U. Meet produced such a situation when the Japs dominated the distance and middle distance front crawl events. It is true that better coaching has improved mechanics in swimming as well as have better training methods. Times will continue to be lowered as long as the swimmers can be made to realize that no record is out of grasp.

The Leg Movements, Front Crawl

The kick employed in the crawl is an alternating, rhythmical up-and-down movement of the legs that is generated from the hips. It is called the flutter kick but this is almost a misnomer, for the action of the legs is not a flutter nor a shimmy but more closely resembles a shallow bicycling movement. The action of a fish tail is similar except the movement is lateral and there is no alternating movement such as the two legs produce.

The six beat kick is used almost exclusively today, although a few use the four (4) and eight (8) beat kick. A six (6) beat kick means that there are three (3) up beats and three (3) down beats for each complete arm cycle. The six (6) beat kick seems to synchronize more easily with the arm stroke at varying speeds. There must be some bending at the knees. The ankles are kept very loose and appear to have a floppy motion. The dept of the kick will range from 15 to 25 inches, depending somewhat on the size of the swimmer and the length of his stroke. The kick should be deep enough so that the feet do not come out of the water excepting the heels. The feet will have a tendency to come higher in sprinting than in distance swimming. However, if they are too high traction will be lost.

Most of the power in the kick comes from the upbeat, as the action of the knee joint allows for more movement in the upbeat than in the downbeat. The power comes from pushing the water backwards over and under the legs and feet and not from squeezing it out between the legs, as was formerly thought. The action is generated in the hips and moves to the feet where the ankles furnish the final drive to send the water backward. Herein lies the value of large feet with loose ankles since they serve as the paddles, determining how much water will be pushed back and with what force.

If the feet are large and the ankles are loose there still must be strength in the legs to give them the necessary whip. Thus, time must be spent in building up the legs. The first kicking drills should be conducted with the swimmer hanging on the bulkhead. If after some correction the movements are fairly accurate, drills can be given with or without a kickboard. In the latter drill the swimmer may fin with his hands to enable himself to breathe more easily. Regardless of which drills are used, the position of the body should approximate the regular swimming position as closely as possible. If the ankles are tight they can be stretched with prescribed exercises to make them more supple. Sprinting lengths with the kickboard is helpful. A sprinter can stroke no faster than he can kick. It is beneficial for crawl swimmers to do some back crawl kicking during workouts.

The Arm Movements, Front Crawl

The arm stroke is the most controversial action in the entire stroke. There are many variations in the arm recovery. Since this phase of the stroke is executed above water it is easy for others to observe and emulate.

At the completion of the propulsive action of the stroke the recovery begins with the elbow breaking the surface first. As the elbow is lifted the forearm and hand emerge from the water with a slight outward swing. The palm is turned upward at first, but as the forearm and hand swing forward with the elbow fixed, the palm is turned outward. This gives a little added elevation to the elbow without raising the shoulders. The hand and forearm swing forward until the hand reaches a point opposite the head, at which time the entire arm reaches for the entry point in the water. The arm is not fully extended when the hand enters the water, for the elbow is kept higher for effective catch purposes. The palm is still turned slightly outward as contact with the water is made but it should be turned down as it slips into the catch position. It is not necessary that the fingers be together during the recovery but they should be closed as they enter the water.

The angle, as the hand slips into the water, marks the point in the stroke where the sprint crawl and distance crawl differ. The sprinters make a sharp angle on the entry and the catch is made sooner with no glide at this point. In the case of the distance swimmers there is a shallow angle between the arm and the water and a hesitation follows which allows the body to ride on the glide. The sprinter gets to the propulsive action of the stroke faster and so he strokes faster. The distance swimmer will ride lower in the water unless he gets a ride out of the stroke before the catch is made. The sprinter will ride higher regardless, because he has enough speed to keep his body high in the water.

The hand enters the water straight out from the shoulder. The catch is made when the hand has reached a point about six (6) inches under the water. Up to this point the distance swimmer has placed some pressure on the water but the sprinter very little. The hand is slightly depressed as soon as the hand is in a position to exert pull instead of pressure. The elbow should be pointing outward while the hands are turned in slightly. In this manner the broadest part of the forearm as well as the hand is being used in the pull. As the arm reaches a point under the shoulder the elbow is flexed more with a slight feathering of the hand and the push phase of the stroke takes over. The flexion at this point relieves the shoulder joint of a great deal of strain, as the leverage is better and the muscles that are brought into play are in better position to do the work. The tightening that often comes in the shoulders is due, usually, to too straight an arm pull. The push phase of the stroke continues until the arm is almost in line with the hips. If it is continued too far the body will be forced too low making recovery more difficult.

At no time in the stroke should the hand be whipped through the water. There should be a feeling that the hand has a hold on the water and it should continue to hold that water as the body passes over the hand. The hand should be slipped in the water on the entry and not smashed on the water.

Body Position, Front Crawl

The body should be as high and as flat on the water as possible. This does not mean the head and shoulders are high and the buttocks low. The buttocks should break surface. There should be no rolling of the shoulders with the arm pull and no lunging forward with the shoulders on the recovery. There must be a conscious effort to keep the hips high. The downbeat of the thigh will help some. Arching the back too much will affect breathing and place the body in a poor riding position. The head position should be such that the water will strike about eyebrow height when the face is in exhalation position. Inhalation should be done by turning the head to the side as the arm on the breathing side finishes its propulsive action and the other arm has made its catch. If the opposite arm has not made its catch there will be a tendency to ride on this arm and the shoulder will drop, with the arm executing a pull that is too wide. The chin should not be tucked nor the head dropped on the movement to exhale; instead the head is just turned and a breakwater is formed which enables the mouth to take in air in an easy manner. No matter how slow the stroke may be the head should not be held too long on the side for inhalation. Instead the inhalation is done quickly and the face is placed back in the water in the position of exhalation immediately, but smoothly.

Timing the Stroke, Front Crawl

Timing pertains to the ability of the swimmer to maintain the same ratio between the arm stroke and the leg kicks at varying speeds. This factor does not become a problem until speeds are attempted that are different than the one employed at the time the stroke was learned. When the swimmer wants to go faster he cannot speed up the arm stroke and the leg kick without regard for timing and expect to get adequate returns for the amount of energy expended.

It is easier to have good timing at slower speeds. That is why it is better to swim two thirds speed in the early season. Pacing will help the timing but the swimmer should not be pushed too fast.

If the stroke is to be speeded up the arm stroke must be shortened. That means the glide is eliminated. It is not easy to speed up the kick to a certain point after the limit of the stroke has been reached. As soon as the kick ceases to be a whip-like motion because of acceleration, it loses its effectiveness.

Faults to be Checked:

1. Ankles and knees are too tense
2. Hips too low
3. Reaching too far on the recovery
4. Accentuating one phase of the kick beat too much, especially the downbeat
5. Holding the head to the side too long on breathing
6. Pulling through with too straight an arm pull
7. Riding the glide too long in sprinting
8. Hand too near the surface when pressure is first exerted

THE BACK CRAWL STROKE

The competitive program lists the swimming events in the backstroke events but no particular stroke is designated. Since the back crawl is the fastest stroke on the back it is the only racing backstroke used today. At present there seems to be more agreement on correct backstroke form than there is in other competitive strokes. When it is swum correctly it is a very smooth stroke, appearing to be effortless. The breathing is much simpler except for the start and turns. The arch of the pull does not afford as much power as can be generated in the front crawl stroke, hence the differences in times.

The Leg Movements, Back Crawl

The leg kick is much the same as that used in the front crawl stroke except it is inverted. Power is derived in the same manner and the same beat is recommended as for the front crawl stroke. The action starts in the hips, the knees should bend enough to give the whiplike motion, the ankles should be kept loose and the feet should be toed in on the upbeat. The feet should not break the surface. The knees should not break the surface on the unbeat for when they do the feet are not lifting and pressing against the water. The knees are bent at the start of the up-beat but they are straightened to give the feet the necessary whip. The depth of the kick will be determined by the position of the body on the water.

The kick may be practiced by swimming on the back with the arms extended over the head and the hands clasped. This is a good exercise for one who is having difficulty keeping his hips high enough. The other method of practicing the kick is simply to hold the arms at the side while kicking on the back. The front crawl kick should be utilized in practice, with a few lengths devoted to the use of a sprint rhythm. Turns should be practiced while doing the kick lengths.

The Arm Movements, Back Crawl

There are slight variations in recoveries and in the propulsive phase of this stroke. The arm recovery starts as the hand and arm are lifted from the water. Some swimmers still lift the arm with the elbow locked but the majority bend the elbow slightly. Bending the elbows allows the water to drain off the hands and arms and it relaxes the upper arms more than the straight arm recovery. The palm is turned outward as the arm is swung outward and backward while the wrist and hand remain relaxed. The last part of the recovery should be smoothly speeded up so that the entry can be made promptly. This gives the shoulders some lift when the body rides with this arm. Avoid the jerkiness that can arise at this point. The hand should be angled downward from the wrist at the time of the entry and a short glide should follow. Many swimmers make the entry with the palm facing downward because they feel they can ride and glide better than when the palm is turned outward. It may be more difficult to refrain from starting the catch in the former style, thereby affecting the timing, but the hand is in a better position for the catch. The entry is made at a slight outward and forward angle from the shoulder. Swimmers, however, who have tight shoulder girdles will be unable to reach back very far forward without throwing the body off balance.

The pull starts with the wrists flexed slightly in order that the initial pull will be applied as a force in making the body forward. A common fault is to start the pull before the hand is completely in the water. Speeding up the recovery and making the entry with the wrist turned down will make the swimmer conscious of the position of the hand in relation to the water. The start of the pull should not be deeper than three or four inches. As the arm pulls through it deepens until at the end of the stroke it may be eight or ten inches below the surface. The arms should be kept straight throughout the stroke. A weak, long armed swimmer may experience some difficulty. The wrist should not be flexed after the arm reaches a point in line with the shoulders.

A variation of the style described in the last paragraph utilizes a bent arm pull The entry is made about the same, but when the arm reaches a point in line with the shoulders the elbow is flexed and the arc becomes smaller. This allows the arm to be pushed through the water faster, and gives better leverage. The stroke is shallower than the other style since the elbow cannot be flexed without dropping it. This necessitates the plane of the push being higher. This stroke does help long, weak armed swimmers, especially when they become tired near the finish of a race.

Body Position, Back Crawl

The body should be kept as flat as possible with a minimum of rolling of the shoulders. The hips should be high but not so high that the kick has no depth with its effectiveness lost. If the hips are too low the body will be pushing water from the hips to the shoulders and create too much resistance. If the arm recovery is fast enough the shoulders will be flat on the water and the body will slip over the water with much less resistance. To high an arm recovery will cause the shoulders to roll excessively.

The position of the head is very important. It should be anchored. It is a fixed part of the long axis of the body and it should not vary. Some swimmers will bob it up and down while many will roll it from side to side. The chin should be tucked slightly so that the swimmer can see his feet. If it is tucked too much some difficulty in breathing may be experienced. Sometimes the head is raised in order to raise the hips or to reach back farther in order to reach the wall for a turn or finish.

Timing the Stroke, Back Crawl

Timing in this stroke should not be too difficult as one less factor is present. There is no breathing with the face in the water. The same rhythm is used as is used in the crawl stroke. When the stroke is smooth there should be no halting at the finish as often evidenced by a sculling movement. This is done to adjust the timing but a better way to adjust is by gliding, following the recovery. The stroke may be too fast, the kick too slow, or the entry too wide; if so the pull will finish ahead of the kick. The arms should not be held too long at the side at the completion of the pull nor should the recovery be too slow. One hand should be taking hold of the water as the other finishes its drive. Sometimes the kick is too shallow and the arm stroke is not completed in keeping with the rhythm. The propulsive action is not completed until the arm or hand is pressed against the side. If the stroke is shortened the hips should be dropped and the kick lengthened.

Faults to be Checked:

1. Lifting the knees so that they break surface
2. Holding hips too high
3. Failure to keep the head in a set position
4. Recovering too slowly
5. Sculling at the end of the stroke because of poor timing
6. Carrying arms too high on recovery
7. Rolling the shoulders and stroking too deep
8. Head held too far back
9. Attempting to place the hands too far back in relation to the shoulders
10. Failure to relax arms on recovery
11. Legs and ankles too tense

THE BUTTERFLY STROKE

The breaststroke and butterfly were classified as the same stroke for many years, even though they were fast losing any similarity they might once have had. Realizing that limits had to be set for each stroke in order to eliminate this "medley" within a stroke, the NCAA and AAU decided to recognize both strokes and to establish rules for each.

The frog kick may still be used in the butterfly stroke, or it may be alternated with the dolphin kick, although none of the top "butterfly swimmers do this. When the stroke was making its debut, many "flyers" were unable to complete a race without resorting to the frog kick since this was much less strenuous. At the present time practically all "flyers" have attained the conditioning and technique which enables them to go all the way with the dolphin kick.

This butterfly or dolphin (dolphin if the dolphin kick is used) is the infant among competitive strokes. Its origin can be attributed to Dave Armbruster, retired coach of swimming at the University of Iowa. Crawl swimmers are able to execute this stroke well as there is a decided likeness to the crawl stroke in many respects.

The advent of this stroke meant a realignment of the medley relay and the individual medley. Each event has a fourth leg with the butterfly leg holding third spot in the medley relay and the lead-off spot in the individual medley.

The regulations governing the execution of the strokes are the same for both the AAU and the NCAA although the wording may be slightly different in the two rule books. Briefly, the regulations are:

1. Arm recoveries must be made over the water, together, simultaneously and symmetrically.

PLATE 65. *The Butterfly Stroke*

2. The body must be kept perfectly flat on the breast and both shoulders must be in line with the water (no side stroking).
3. All movements of the feet must be executed in a simultaneous manner. This includes dolphin and frog kick, and this phase of the regulation makes it possible for the "flyer" to use either type kick.
4. On turns and finishes, the hands must touch simultaneously on the same level with the shoulders in the horizontal position.
5. The swimmer is not limited on the number of kicks that may be used on the start, on the pushoffs from turns, and for each arm stroke.

The Dolphin Kick

The dolphin kick is executed about the same as the crawl kick except the legs do not alternate but work simultaneously. It should be pointed out that the two-beat kick (two kicks per arm cycle) has been found to be best suited to this stroke. Since the stroke is in its infancy, it is possible that a new ratio might be developed and prove superior. Although there are fewer kicks per arm cycle than in the crawl stroke, more whip is put into each kick, and the kick is faster than the flutter kick used in crawl.

The starting position of the legs will be with both legs straight and in line with the body. The first movement of the legs should be to raise the feet which bends the knees and brings the feet to or above the surface slightly. The down beat follows immediately, and the legs are straightened with a strong whiplike action at the end of the press downward. This down pressure forces the hips up and the position of the legs in relation to the hips makes a 30-45 degree angle. The pressing down and backward movement of the water forces the body forward, and it should be pointed out that the down beat does give more propulsion forward than does the upbeat. The ankles should be loose and relaxed in which case they will be toed in slightly, and this affords the feet greater surface for contact with the water. The legs will be kept fairly close together although they may relax some and the knees may spread on the upbeat and then close on the downbeat.

The hips move up and down through the action of the legs and propulsive action moves from the feet to the hips and on to the shoulders which is the one part of the body that remains in a fairly constant position in the water at all times.

The kick can be practiced with a kick board or without, depending on the individual. The beginner will have a tendency to bend the knees too much on the upbeat and they will not press nor whip the feet downward enough.

Arm Movements—Butterfly

The arm recovery demands that the shoulder girdle be loose and relaxed. The arms are recovered out of the water by rotating and carrying them high enough to clear the water. The elbows emerge from the water first and the hands follow with the palms turned slightly backward. The arms are carried around to the side with the palms almost facing downward, hands relaxed and elbows straight but not stiff. As the arms swing by the shoulders, the elbows are slightly bent and the hands should enter the water in front and in line with the shoulders with the elbows still bent and in a position higher than the hands. As the hands slip into the water, no attempt should be made to hold them motionless, but they should slide out to the side a short distance and then they are pressed and pulled in towards the body. This is the spot in the stroke where the timing is either gained or lost, and this sliding movement of the hands can be the determining factor. The stroke describes a shallow "S". The top of the "S" is where the hands slide to the outside and then they are pulled in towards the body until they are ready to release their hold on the water at which time they turn out and emerge from the water.

The hands should not be smashed on the water although they enter more forcibly than in the crawl. This hurry is necessary because the body may have a tendency to sink on the arm recovery phase.

When the hands start pressing on the water, the elbows are still bent slightly, and the hands should be about four to six inches under the water. As soon as they are deep enough, the hands will start the pull toward the body, and the body will move over the hands where the push phase of the stroke takes place. As the hands near a position under the shoulders, the elbows are bent more thus reducing the arc of the pull and increasing leverage. In addition, the bent arm pull presents the broad part of the forearm which increases the surface for engaging the water. The push or final phase of the stroke should not extend too far as the wrists must relax in order to take unnecessary strain off the forearms. At the finish of the push phase, the wrists relax and the hands release the water thereby allowing the elbows to break surface at the side for the start of another recovery.

Nothing is gained when the hands are pushed through too far. Fatigue is certain to set in from over tensing the wrists.

Too much pressure of the water at the beginning of the catch will cause the body to bob, and this can be eliminated by sliding the hands outward and downward as soon as they enter the water.

Timing of the Butterfly Stroke

The timing in this stroke is difficult for the beginner to learn. Unless the kick, arm movement and breathing are synchronized, the stroke is tiring and inefficient.

There are two kicks per arm cycle, and the first kick comes just as the hands enter the water; this action moves the body over the hands in a manner that makes the catch much easier. The second kick comes midway through the arm stroke at the point where the arm pull is under the body, and propels the body forward and upward which action makes for an easier arm recovery over the water. The kicks should be about the same with no undue emphasis on either.

The timing can be learned more quickly if the swimmer is advised to kick very little or not at all and then execute the arm pull. After trying this procedure, gradually add the kick to acquire timing that feels very natural and easier.

Avoid stopping the hands on the water following the recovery as the swimmer will find it very difficult to get going. It is better to move the hands from the moment they enter the water until they are lifted for recovery.

Breathing in the Butterfly Stroke

The breath should be taken as the "flyer" is in the first part of the arm pull which is actually the press phase. The kick has just pushed the body up on the water, and the pressure of the hands on the water has raised the head and shoulders enough so that at this precise moment, the entire body is higher on the water than at any other time. In the act of breathing, the face is raised quickly and the breath is taken.

Breathe by raising the face forward, not sideward. Side breathing can very easily become illegal if the swimmer is tired and one shoulder lags behind the other.

Breathing patterns should be set up for each race, and conditioning will be the final factor determining whether the "flyer" follows them. In the 100 meter or 100 yard race, the "flyer" can use almost the same pattern as the free styler, which means taking as few breaths as possible on the first half and then alternating in the last half. If he breathes every other time in the 200 meter or 200 yard race, it will give him an advantage.

Faults to be Checked

1. Not whipping the feet downward enough at the end of the down beat.
2. Breathing too often.
3. Stopping the hands upon entering them in the water instead of keeping them moving.
4. Pressing downward too hard on the water when the hands enter the water.
5. Attempting to move the hips up and down instead of allowing the kick to move the hips.
6. Breathing on the side instead of breathing in front.
7. Failure to bend the elbows on the pull.
8. Not relaxing the wrists enough at the end of the push.

CONVENTIONAL OR ORTHODOX BREASTSTROKE

In this stroke starting position is full extension of the body, arms, and legs. Propulsive power of arms and legs come at alternate times. Skill in the stroke depends on timing and coordination. The run of the body or glide is the result of power applied. So for competition one must find best results from experimenting, long glide, short glide, or no glide for best timing. Glide or body position should be close to the surface. Arm pull is deep and powerful backward and downward keeping ahold of the water as long as possible without loss of rhythm and forward run of the body.

The leg kick is probably the most important propulsive part of the stroke. Rules state, "feet shall be drawn up, the knees bent and apart. The movement shall be continued with a rounded outward sweep of the feet bringing the legs together. Up and down movements of the legs in the vertical plane are prohibited. All movements of the legs and feet must be simultaneous, symmetrical and in the same lateral plane."

The amount of outward sweep will vary with the individual. There should be forward progress all the time. If there is a great amount of up and down movements of the body there is a loss of efficiency somewhere in the stroke and a close look by a coach should be undertaken.

Faults to be Checked

1. Kicking too wide and too slowly.
2. Failure to complete kick.
3. Exerting too much pressure near the surface.
4. Bobbing the head too much for breathing.
5. Hands too tense on recovery.
6. Keeping the arms too straight on the propulsive phase of the stroke.
7. Allowing the hips to sink too low.

STARTS

A good start from the starter's standpoint means that every swimmer has had an equal chance to get off his marks. To do this a starter must use a slow start and each man must be motionless and balanced. This constitutes a "flat" start which is the fair one.

The swimmer's objective is to get off his marks first and to get out the farthest when the gun sounds. The swimmer with the fastest reaction time will get off his marks the fastest providing all other things are equal. The swimmer with the most spring, harnessed with good mechanics, should get the most distance.

Swimmers should be acquainted with the starting commands. The swimmer should rehearse these starts often under a set-up as near actual racing start conditions as it is possible to have. The start for each of the strokes will be described separately.

Starts, Free Style

When a starter asks the other officials if they are ready, each competitor should be behind his own marks, but only a short step away so that he can take his marks promptly without losing his balance. He should be doing some deep breathing at this time, especially prior to the sprints. At the command "Take-Your-Marks" the swimmer must step quickly but not hurriedly to the edge and place his feet so that they are gripping the edge of the starting box or pool, as the case may be. He should not take his eyes off his feet until they are firmly set. The feet should not be too far apart, with the weight evenly distributed from heel to toe. The feet must be under the body. Two styles of body position will be described at this point.

In the first style the body bends at the waist, knees are flexed slightly, arms hang loosely, and the head is raised in a position to look down the pool. As the gun

PLATE 66. *First style discribed*   PLATE 67. *Second style described*

sounds, the arms describe quick outward half circles as the knees bend in preparation for the spring. The extension of the legs and the forward thrust of the arms (last half of arc) come simultaneously. The head remains up for a short time in order to maintain some height and then it is dropped to a position between the arms in the final stages of the flight through the air, just prior to water entry.

In the other style the swimmer takes his marks and places his feet in the same position as in the first style. The position the body assumes is different. The knees are bent more, the head is lowered and the arms are swung backward and upward. The body is in more of a jacked position. When the gun sounds the knees are extended and the arms swing forward with no preliminary windup. This style is a little faster but the rhythmical flexion and swinging of the arms may give additional momentum in the first style described. Following the takeoff the actions are the same, including the entry.

The body should be straight with no arch as the arms and head contact the water first. Upon entry the hands must exert additional pressure on the water; otherwise, the force of the contact with the water will cause them to bend upward and the entry will lose the desired knife-like quality. The body slips into the water in a very shallow dive. There should be no attempt to start kicking until the momentum from the dive is such that it can be made stronger by kicking and stroking. The first stroke should be such that it will not cause the body to rise too quickly. There should be no attempt to breath on the first stroke. The hand does not have to be out of the water when the first stroke is taken but by the time its recovery is ready the body should be high enough to lift the arm without resistance from the water above it.

Faults to be Checked:

1. Too far from the marks and too slow in taking them on proper command
2. Feet spread too far apart
3. Arm drive started too late causing an arched position
4. Arm drive started too soon causing a jacked position
5. Failure to hold head up on first phase of flight
6. Hands not together upon entry into water
7. Kicking in air or water too soon causing unnecessary friction
8. Failure to exert pressure on water at time of entry
9. Pressing down too much on first stroke
10. Breathing on first stroke

Starts and Turns in the Breaststroke

The Breaststroke must be swum on the surface. Following the start and each turn, one arm-pull and one leg kick may be taken under water, but some portion of the contestant's head must break the surface of the water before another stroke is started.

Some experimenting must be undertaken to get the swimmer up and underway to comply with the rules. The depth of the dive will vary with the swimmer depending on the run of the stroke. One should not come "dead" in the water or come up like an elevator but should on finish of the arm-pull and leg kick come up and out on the surface of the water in a running moving movement ready to apply full force for the first surface stroke.

Faults to be Corrected on Starts
1. Same as first 6 listed in the Free Style events.
2. Diving too shallow or too deeply.
3. Remaining under the water too long; thereby creating too great an oxygen debt.
4. Not pulling all the way through on underwater stroke.

Starts, Butterfly

The start for the butterfly race is the same as the start in the free style events. The angle of entry, the stretch and glide should extend the same length of time depending on the momentum of the flyer. The flyer should start the kicking just as the free styler does, and the number of kicks to be executed before the arm pull depends on the individual. Most flyers will take at least two strong dolphin kicks before starting the arm pull which does afford the arms some relaxation.

It must be borne in mind that all arm recoveries must be made above the water, so following the first arm pull, the recovery must be above the water. The body should be on the surface if the dive is executed correctly, and there is no problem in getting the arms over the water cleanly.

The hands should slide into the proper catch position which is slightly to the side and under water four to six inches. If this isn't done, the driect downward press on the water will cause the flyer to bob too much.

Faults to be Corrected
1. Same as first six listed in the free style events.
2. Keeping arms extended straight in front instead of sliding them slightly to side.
3. Breathing on first stroke.
4. Pressing down too forcibly on water on first stroke thereby causing bobbing motion.
5. Bending the knees too much on the first kick instead of whipping them downward forcibly.

Starts, Backstroke

The backstroke start differs from the others because it is executed entirely in the water. The competitors should be in the water in ample time to check the starting surface of the wall. When the starter asks the swimmers if they are ready, they should grasp the starting holes, rail, or gutter as the case may be, and place their feet against the wall. The swimmer should still be relaxed, and not until the starter gives them the command "Take-Your-Marks," should the final stages of preparation be made. This consists of placing one foot above the other with the top foot about six inches under the water. The feet are spread apart, the same as in the free style start, front crawl. This position prevents undue slipping and gives better balance. The arms are flexed and the body is drawn close to the gutter.

When the starting gun sounds the arms are simultaneously thrown backward over the head to a position in line with the extended back. Knee extension followed by ankle extension comes directly after the arm throw. These combined actions should raise the hips above the surface so that a dive is actually made backwards into the water. This start is not a push or shove backwards through the water. The head should not be kept back too far. As the body settles into the water, the head should not be pointing backwards and downwards or the entry will be too deep. The body should be under water in a shallow dive. The glide should follow until momentum has decreased to the point where the kick and stroke will assist rather than retard forward motion. The kick should start after the glide, and in turn be followed by the arm stroke. The single arm pull is best. The rise to the surface will be less abrupt. The other arm should be kept in the water. The first arm pull should be fast giving the body a sense of shooting out of the water into swimming position.

Faults to be Checked:

1. Starting the leg drive too soon, thereby not allowing the body to rise above the surface.
2. Allowing too great an interval between the arm throwback and the leg extension, causing the body to go straight up and stall.
3. Holding the head back too far, causing the dive to be too deep.
4. Failure to throw the arms back far enough, causing the hips to drag.
5. Pull not strong enough on the first stroke.
6. Faulty position of feet on start.

Starts, Relay

The relay starts should receive a great deal of attention even though they differ from the regular starts only in takeoff timing. A relay start is legal as long as the feet of the takeoff man are in contact with the pool's edge or starting blocks at the instant any part of the body of the incoming touch-off swimmer touches the wall. This means the takeoff swimmer can start his preliminary movements before the incoming swimmer touches. This calls for excellent timing.

The incoming swimmers should be encouraged to finish strong and to not glide into the touch. The backstroker in the medley relay has the most difficult assignment since he does not have good visual position. Relay men should start in the order in which they swim in the relay. Each swimmer will then know what to expect of the other. Practice conditions may differ in that the swimmers will be slower at the touch in full length races than they will be in practice where only widths or single lengths are being swum. Coaches should insure full distance relay practice from time to time.

Everyone, but the swimmer ready to take off and the takeoff judge, should be cleared from the immediate area so that the swimmer can use his own judgement in getting away to a fast and balanced start.

Faults to be Checked:

1. Failure to relax during preceding swimmer's race
2. Failure of incoming swimmer to finish strong instead of drifting in
3. Too much outside interference at the takeoff
4. Failure to take advantage of longer time for windup

TURNS

According to the rules governing turns in the free style events, the end of the pool or course must be touched by one or both hands before pushing off. Many style turns have been devised but there are three that are used commonly: the *Somersault Turn, Spin Turn* and the *Distance or Fall Away Turn*. The first two are sprint turns. The latter is a distance turn.

Somersault Turns are the fastest and the most difficult to master. They should not be attempted in a race until the sprinter has learned them well, for disastrous results can occur because of the complexity and speed of the maneuver. The strongest point in favor of this turn is that momentum is not lost in the approach. There must be no hesitation as the wall is neared. Just before the leading hand touches the wall the head and shoulders snapped down, the hips are raised slightly and the legs are tucked. The touch should be made with the back of the hand on a downward movement about 12 inches under the water. As the head is still going downward a quarter body twist is made to the side opposite the touching hand. The body continues to turn over as contact with the wall is made with both feet. On the pushoff the other quarter body turn is made leaving the body face down for the glide to the surface. The glide is upward. The body should be stretched with no arch in the back. This is a difficult maneuver for a beginner to master at full speed. It is best therefore, to first attempt it from a standing position about 3 feet from the wall. After several such tries he should try it from a swimming approach, then, through constant practice, build up his efficiency.

Faults to be Checked:

1. Slowing down for the approach.
2. Failure to draw the legs up fast and tight enough.
3. Raising the head as the wall is neared.
4. Touching too deep with the possibility of disqualification.
5. Failure to keep the head tucked on the twist causing turn to be too deep.

The Spin Turn can be used for sprinting and middle distance swimming. It is easier to learn but not as fast as the Somersault Turn. As the wall is approached the palm of the leading hand is turned outward and contact is made with the wall in front of the opposite shoulder, in a slight downward motion. As the hand touches, the head is snapped sharply in the direction of the opposite shoulder while the legs are drawn into a tuck position. The face is down and the body is kept as flat as possible throughout the turn. The free hand is used in a sculling motion to help spin the body. As soon as the body has spun in a half circle, the touching hand which is kept sliding around, is extended over the head with the other hand. Then the pushoff is made with a strong leg drive. The back will barely go under water throughout the turn. The direction of the pushoff will be straighter than that in the Somersault Turn.

Faults to be Checked:

1. Approaching too slowly and reaching for the turns.
2. Failure to draw the legs up and thereby slowing spin.
3. Failure to snap head in direction of turn.
4. Inability to spin in either direction.
5. Failure to reach across with the touching hand.
6. Failure to slide the touching hand on the spin.

The Distance Turns are excellent for distance swimming but are too slow for sprinting. They the often used in workouts and can be used in shorter races when the swimmer needs more air. As the leading hand touches the wall the fingers should be pointing upward with the body rolled to a position slightly on the side. The body should be driven in as close as possible with the elbow slightly bent. As soon as the hand touches the wall the legs are drawn up quickly under the body. The body reverses and the feet swing under the body and contact the wall. The arm is thrust in the direction of the pushoff and the head is snapped with it. The feet are in contact with the wall, the under arm is extended in the direction of the pushoff, the body is on its side and the face is turned back towards the wall in the act of getting the breath as the pushoff is ready to be made. As the legs are extending in the pushoff, the touching hand is carried over and slipped into the water with the other hand. The body rolls to a prone position on the pushoff, and into the usual glide.

Faults to be Checked:

1. Gliding in instead of kicking in close for the turns.
2. Attempting to get breath before the body has reversed.
3. Turning the body to a prone position before the pushoff.
4. Not snapping head in direction of pushoff fast enough.

Turns, Backstroke

The backstroke turns are covered in the rules with these following specifications:
1. The swimmer must be flat on his back when he contacts the wall on the approach.
2. He must be flat on his back when he pushes off from the wall.

This is the most difficult skill in competitive backstroking. It is difficult because the swimmer is on his back with little or no vision, and because there are specifications that must be followed if disqualification is to be avoided. The two turns that will be covered are the *Tumble Turn* and the *Spin Turn*. The former is the faster. Sprinters use it almost exclusively.

As the swimmer approaches the turn for the *Tumble Turn*, the leading hand contacts the wall about ten inches under water. The head and shoulders drop back with the hand as contact is made. At the time of contact the legs are drawn up in a tuck position and the body starts into a somersault. But, as the feet appear to be going over, the body spins to the opposite side. This is done under water. The head must be tucked slightly or the turn will be too deep. As the body spins, the free hand helps through reverse sculling and the feet are planted against the wall as in a backstroke start. The touching hand leaves the wall and meets the other hand overhead. At the instant of pushoff the arms are extended over the head. The head should be tucked slightly and the body should be stretched in the pushoff. The kick should start as the initial pushoff momentum is decreasing and just prior to the approach to the surface. The first arm pull is done as the body surfaces. The single arm pull or the double arm pull can be used although most prefer the single. If the single arm pull is used the other arm should be kept straight and under the water and not stricking out of the water. The pull with the first arm should be fast in order to bring the body out without losing the momentum built up by the pushoff.

Faults to be Checked:

1. Failure to snap head and shoulders back fast enough.
2. Failure to tuck legs.
3. Head is not kept in tuck position and turn is too deep.
4. Legs are spread.
5. Arching instead of stretching the back.
6. Inability to turn with either hand.

The Spin Turn is a great deal like the Front Crawl Spin Turn. As the hand contacts the wall at water level the head is tucked, hips are jacked, legs drawn up and the free hand reverse sculls as the turn is made to the side opposite the touching hand. The head and shoulders aid in the twist. The tighter the body jacks the faster the spin. As the body spins, the touching hand leaves the wall and is placed over the head with the other hand. The feet placed against the wall as in the start. The pushoff is made by extending the knees and stretching the arms overhead. The body is not under water as in the Tumble Turn. The breathing problem is not as acute. Too many Tumble Turns may aggravate a sinus condition. The Spin Turn can be used in workouts or in the longer races.

Faults to be Checked:

1. Inability to turn with either hand.
2. Failure to tuck tightly enough.
3. Failure to use head and shoulders as an aid in the spin.

Breaststroke Turn

Approach to the wall.—The swimmer should drive into the wall—coasting loses time. The swimmer should come into the wall with a good stretch, hands slightly apart, head in a lowered position to help streamline the body. Bend elbows on contact, hands to wall, then tuck legs up, turn sideward in any manner desired, but the prescribed form must be attained before the feet leave the wall in the push-off. Stretch hard and glide slightly, then go into under water (1) stroke as in the start.

Turns, Butterfly

The butterfly turns are covered in the Rules with the following specifications:

1. Both hands must contact the wall simultaneously and in the same place.
2. There can be no anticipation of the turn such as dropping the shoulder or turning the head.

Like the breaststroke turns, the butterfly turns are technical, and disqualifications do occur. Turning legally is a habit, and if the flyer habitually turns carelessly and illegally, he is very likely to do the same in a race.

As the hands contact the wall with the fingers pointed upward, the elbows should bend slightly in order that the body may get closer to the wall. At the instant of hand contact with the wall, the legs are drawn up under the body in a quick tuck. If the turn is to the left, the left arm is tucked quickly to the side as the body twists to the left. The head should snap in the direction of the turn, and the face should be turned upward and backward in the act of twisting so that a breath can be taken. The right arm and shoulder come out of the water and describe an arc to assist the body in the twisting movement. At the moment of pushoff, the right hand is plunged into the water joining the left hand for the pushoff and glide under water.

Care should be taken not to place the feet too high on the wall for the pushoff as this will force the "flyer" to pushoff too deeply. The push with the legs comes at the moment the right hand enters the water to join the left.

The approach to the wall is important as the "flyer" can get too close or he may glide too far. In either case, the turn will be difficult and much practice should be spent on this phase of the race. If the wall is too close for another arm stroke (which means recovering the arms over the water) the swimmer should keep the arms extended and kick forcefully the remaining distance. In no case should there be a letdown in speed for the faster the wall is approached, the quicker the turn will be.

It is advisable to practice the turns by placing the palms of the hands flat against the wall instead of grasping the scum gutters (where there are gutters) and pulling the body up to the wall. Pulling the body to the wall tires the swimmer needlessly, and when competition is in a pool without gutters, the swimmer has difficulty making the adjustment.

The pushoff and the sequence of kicks and pulls is the same for the turns as for the starts. The longer the race, the longer the swimmer may want to stay under and glide and kick.

Faults to be Checked

1. Poor timing of strokes on approach.
2. Raising head to breathe on approach and not waiting for turn to catch breath.
3. Failure to draw legs up fast enough.
4. Placing feet too high against wall on pushoff causing the swimmer to go too deep.
5. Pulling body to wall by grasping the scum gutters instead of placing hands against the wall with flat hands.

MISCELLANEOUS SUGGESTIONS

Plan the *SCHEDULE OF MEETS* carefully and arrange it as early as possible so the squad may get mentally set for the season. A green squad may be ruined by too many meets, especially if they are against superior teams. Mediocre competition on the other hand may make a superior team sluggish, or a potentially strong team dull and uninterested. Challenge the abilities of your particular squad.

TEAM MORALE is important and difficult to attain in an individual sport such as Swimming. At least some of the workouts should be conducted with every member of the squad present. The captain and key men should make it their business to develop and sustain the morale of other individuals who may need such encouragement. Do not mollycoddle the swimmers but try to make locker room and pool conditions as comfortable and conducive to spirited workouts as possible.

Encourage the men to participate in all forms of *WATER SKILLS* in the off-season. (Life Saving, Water Shows, Water Polo, Other Water Games, and summer meets if they are in condition.) Swimmers should be proficient in all strokes.

Post the *DAILY WORKOUT SHEETS* on the bulletin board and allow each swimmer to see what other swimmers are doing. Invariably the best swimmers are taking a tougher workout than the others. Keep these workout sheets for attendance purposes. If the *TIME TRIALS* are added they will serve as a *PROGRESS CHART*.

PLAN and CONDUCT MEETS carefully. See that they do not drag. Keep the spectators and participants posted on what is happening with a good announcer and announcing system. If good officials are not available, train some. If the team represents an educational institution, other faculty members should make good officials. Their interest and assistance may help in many ways toward promoting swimming.

A good *MANAGER* or a corps of managers is a necessity. Give every swimmer who tries out for the squad lots of help and encouragement, for whether they all make the squad or not, they are more apt to be boosters for the team.

In such a sport as swimming, where so much responsibility rests on the shoulders of each individual, many are certain to become high strung and nervous. These swimmers need to be treated accordingly. *INDIVIDUAL TALKS* are valuable when needed. Challenge the individual, build up his morale, and encourage him to do his best.

For clarity and intelligence regarding swimming regulations, etc., it is wise to order *SWIMMING GUIDES* early, and to get copies for the members of your squad. They will enjoy them for reference and the guides will make the swimmers cognizant of information they should be aware of in relation to statistics and other related material on competitive swimming.

CHAPTER X

Competitive Diving (Basic)

INTRODUCTION

From the primary stages where the pupil puts his head under the water to the performance of the most complex springboard dive, the art of diving requires highly specialized training of the diver with constant coaching and proper supervision. The instruction may require different methods. The instructor must use the facilities on hand and must endeavor to obtain other aids which will help the pupil learn the fundamental mechanics of the springboard.

Obviously each instructor must develop his own teaching approach. The methods in this book are already familiar to many instructors, but each year we have new men and women entering the swimming field who have not had the opportunity to formulate their own methods, and must, consequently, turn to some source of information to aid them in their teaching.

TEACHING A PUPIL TO DIVE

Instructor Approach

In most cases the personal approach of the instructor to any pupil is the determining factor in the successful teaching of diving. With youngsters, gaining familiarity with and having them trust the instructor, helps the teaching to progress more rapidly. With adults, it will be much better to explain thoroughly what the instructor intends to do, and then to go about the instruction very carefully. Seize upon any small accomplishment to compliment the individual so that the encouragement instills the desire to work and to learn.

Pupil Response

As the teacher begins the progression of instruction he must watch the response of the student very carefully. Many times the student will show fear. This must be guarded against. Often, rushing will make a student balk, and this will slow the progress and cause doubt in the mind of the student as to what the instructor is trying to do. It is always better to go back to the one simple accomplishment of the student, so that his confidence is regained and the progression can begin again.

Instructor Demonstration

It is obvious that the pupil must know what to do. Explain the procedure, and then go through the motions two or three times, showing him the different body

NOTE: Diving illustrations, this Chapter, by Coach Ben F. Grady, Coach of Swimming, and Diver Albert Cioccia, Jr., of the University of Pittsburgh.

movements until he gets the complete idea clearly in mind. Once the picture is in his mind, body coordination will come more rapidly.

PLATE 68. *Start of Dive*   PLATE 69. *Head Down—Entering Water*

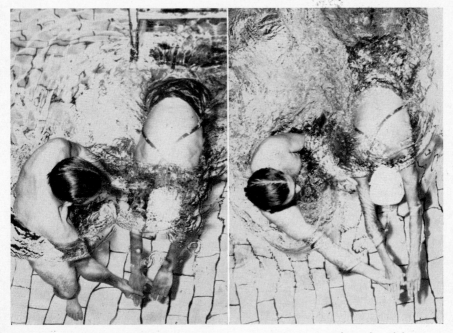

PLATE 70. *Head Under Water—Instructor*   PLATE 71. *Stretching the Glide*
Contact

"Security-Guidance" in Teaching Diving

One of the easiest ways to get a pupil started in diving is to get the individual on a ladder or step in the pool so that he is as close to the water as possible. The pupil is then ready to begin his first dive. Stand in the water beside the pupil and hold him by the hand. The instructor then can give the pupil the security and confidence that all will be well. As the pupil leans forward and begins to put his head in the water, the instructor should take a firm grip on his hand and guide the body forward. Have the individual let his head go under the water for only a fraction of a second. By doing this the pupil will feel secure in the dive. Then the possibility of a mouthful of water is lessened, and the fear of a new experience is eliminated by the presence of the instructor and his contact with the beginning diver. This is probably one of the most vital parts of teaching beginners to dive. It is here that the instructor must have a great deal of patience, must use tact, and must provide the individual with the necessary confidence and feeling of security.

PLATE 72. *Pupil Diving without Aid*

After this, the beginner can try the dive unaided, the instructor standing by and maintaining security-guidance. As the pupil performs the dive more often and becomes accustomed to being under the water, the instructor should have the beginner stretch the glide of the dive. All the while he must maintain contact with the individual.

Beginning of the Ankle and Knee Action

In all dives, the ankles and the knees play a paramount part in the proper diving mechanics. This start can be developed by having the pupil stand on the pool deck, rise on his toes and then drop back on the heels. Continued exercise will develop good ankle action and aid in the balance which is *so* necessary to good diving. The knees also have to be bent so that they work with the ankles in order to obtain the best leg spring. After this has been explained and the pupil has done it several times, the instructor should demonstrate the proper use of the ankles and the leg drive, by pushing off the ladder, extending the knees, and stretching the ankles. The pupil, then, should try to emulate the instructor and attempt to perform properly the leg, ankle, and arm action and push-off into the water. The instructor must realize that certain individuals will respond to diving much faster than others, and consequently, will progress more rapidly.

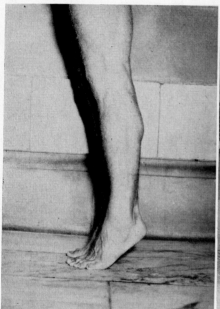
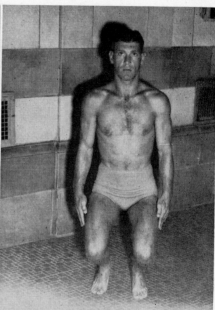

PLATE 73. *Stretching the Ankles*

PLATE 74. *Coordinating Knee and Ankle Action*

Increasing the Height of the Dive

Here, again, the instructor must use caution, tact, and encouragement in order to get the individual to take-off from a greater height. If the water is quite close to the edge of the pool the sit-dive can be used. That would be the same dive as described before, but from a higher level. The security-guidance method should be used whenever possible in order to maintain the student's confidence in the instructor. This security-guidance should always be part of the method used by the instructor and, as advanced methods and mechanics are initiated, there will always be a feeling of courage rather than fear in the individual.

Elementary Progressions

The Sitting Take-off—The sitting take-off is usually practiced from the side of the pool. The individual must keep the head down, lean forward, and try to learn the same process that was initiated in learning from the steps. Too often, at this

PLATE 75. *The Sitting Take-off*   PLATE 76. *The Foot and Knee Take-off*

stage, the beginner will bring the chin up which flattens out the chest and body on the water. The beginner must concentrate, The chin must be down on the chest. He may land flat on the water, stinging himself. Here again one should utilize the security guidance method in aiding the individual to dive properly into the water.

The Foot and Knee Take-off—Here is another progression for the pupil who has difficulty in diving from a height. By having the individual take a runner's starting position with the toes of one foot gripped on the end of the pool, and the opposite knee brought forward so that it is resting against the ankle of the opposite foot, the body will be in a good crouched position for a push-off. The arms are extended forward, and downward, so that the hands are as close to the water as possible, the chin resting on the chest. From here the instructor can guide the individual into the water with the greatest amount of confidence.

One Foot Take-off—Have the pupil stand on the end of the pool and raise one leg so that the leg is off the pool deck. The instructor should hold the knee of the up-raised leg firmly, and help the student fall over into the pool, holding or guiding the body so that the individual does not land on his chest or stomach. Use the leg as a body lever. The individual should concentrate on pressing the chin on the chest. In this way he should dive into the water without hurting himself. Every good beginning dive depends upon the ability of the pupil to raise the hips over the shoulders so that a head-first entry can be made. A good way of teaching this is to have the pupil attempt a semi-hand stand on the pool deck so that the feeling of raising the hips is acquired, and so that the up-side-down feeling becomes familiar.

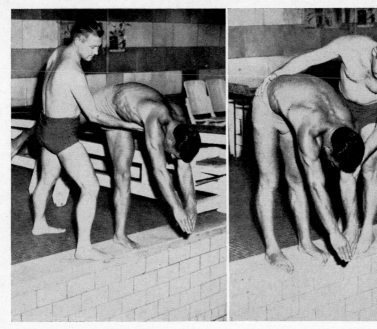

PLATE 77. *The One Foot Take-off*   PLATE 78. *Two Foot Take-off*

Two Foot Take-off—Have the student get a good toe-hold on the end of the pool. The student can now use the ankle and knee action so that he will be able to lift the legs and hips up over the shoulders simulating a hand stand when entering the water.

The Dive From the Board

Here again caution must be taken. Many times it is safe to have the pupil jump into the water for a few times to become accustomed to the height. The instructor should be in the water in front of the diving board in order to sustain the necessary confidence. Later the instructor may try a doubledive with the individual by standing beside him and taking a firm hold around his waist as they both drop into the water head first. This will enable the pupil to get the feel of the dive, and, as confidence increases the pupil can be permitted to try the dive alone. The element of security must always be kept in the pupil's mind as an aid to progress.

Faults to be Checked:

1. Forcing the pupil too much
2. Lack of security-guidance
3. Pupil not keeping the head down
4. Lack of ankle and knee action
5. Not getting the hips over the shoulders
6. Losing confidence in the instructor

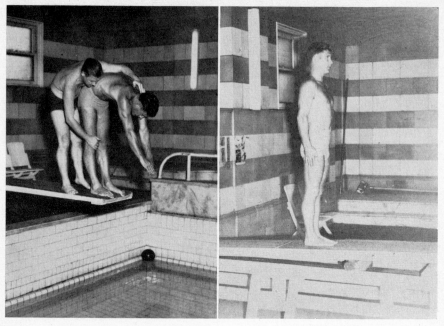

PLATE 79. *Dive from Board*   PLATE 80. *Body Posture on Board*

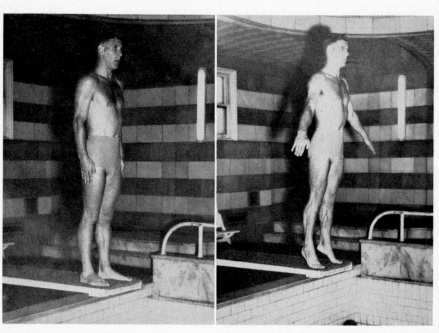

PLATE 81. *Starting Position for Board   PLATE 82. *Arm and Ankle Action on
Bouncing*   Spring Board*

FUNDAMENTAL BOARD WORK (FRONT TAKE-OFF)

Proper instruction here is most necessary for the successful advancement into the more difficult dives. Here, the instructor begins to train an individual in the highly coordinated exercise of using the head, arms, knees, and ankles.

Body Posture

To dive properly the body must be balanced throughout the run, hurdle, and take-off. The pupil should devote much time to learning how to walk out properly on the spring board. Each step should be the same length, the head is held erect, the shoulders are back in a comfortable position, the stomach is held in and there is no bending at the waist. The arms must always be lifted so that both are performing the upward motion evenly.

Ankle Action

Previously the importance of teaching the beginning diver to use the ankles and the knees when pushing off from a ladder or the side of the pool was mentioned. As is obvious to an instructor, any weight put on the end of the spring board will bend it. The pupil has to be taught, and has to learn to understand this point. As the pupil rises on the toes at the tip of the board, there is a slight vertical oscillation of the spring board. However, the board drops down again rapidly, so the pupil must begin by learning the action of the board. Standing flat-footed on the end of the board, rising on the balls of the feet, and then dropping down to the flat-footed position again, will develop in the individual a

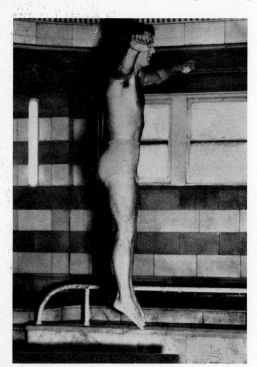

PLATE 83. *Arm Lift and Ankle Action*

PLATE 84. *Beginning Stance for Approach*   PLATE 85. *First Step of Approach*

sense of timing and rhythm with the oscillation of the spring board. The ease with which this is accomplished depends upon the coordinating ability of the individual pupil. Many individuals have stiff ankles which creates great difficulty in the timing of the board. The individual should practice rotating the ankles both inward and outward when in a sitting position. Thus the ankles will become more flexible, enabling the diver to get a better sense of timing and balance when bouncing the board.

Coordinating the Arm Lift with the Ankle Action

With the simple use of the ankles the diver must now coordinate the arm lift with the ankle action and in time with the oscillation of the board. The best way to start this action is to place the arms slightly behind the body when the feet are flat. The ankles, then begin to function. As the pupil rises on the balls of the feet, the arms move forward so that the ankles and the arms are lifting upward in a coordinated motion while the board is also coming up. This is only a fraction of a second, for as the board drops down again, the diver must follow the board in order to maintain body and board coordination. As the diver becomes more accustomed to the action of the board, he will be able to lift a little off the spring board. The student bounces so that the body rises approximately six inches off the board. This is high enough for the beginning diver. The body balance and the arm and leg coordination come slowly.

In practicing board bouncing it is best to spread the feet six or more inches apart on the board. If his board bouncing posture is poor, the diver can press the foot of the off-balanced side on the board to compensate for off-balance, and

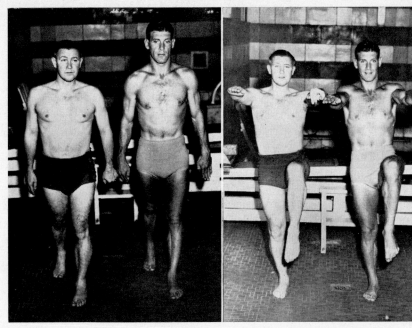

PLATE 86. *Second Step of Approach*   PLATE 87. *Third Step of Approach, Arms Up—Hurdle Leg Up*

regain body balance. If the board is warped or if there is a weak lamination in it which gives to one side, the body balance can then be recovered.

The Approach on the Pool Deck

Walking and pacing the steps—Having mastered the fundamental procedure of the arm lift, ankle action, knee action and body balance, the beginning diver is ready to learn the approach to the end of the board and take his hurdle. The rules of the Intercollegiate, A.A.U., and Olympic Diving require that there shall be three steps taken before the hurdle. More than three steps is acceptable, but two steps or less is not permissible, at least for competitive diving. With this in mind it is well for the instructor to walk through the three paces and hurdle on the pool deck, and then have the diver do the same thing. The steps should be checked for naturalness and even spacing. They must not be too crowded nor overstretched. Also, check the heel and the toe action so that the diver is not walking high on the toes.

Use of Arms—After this is properly checked, the arm action can be demonstrated. Coordinating the arms and the legs can be quite a tedious job for both the student and the instructor at the beginning. However, each step must be taken separately, yet not disconnectedly. The arms are placed in the most natural position for the diver. When the whole is put together some semblance of coordination will soon develop.

Instructor Guide—In order to teach this type of arm action the instructor should stand beside the pupil. They lock their little fingers together. From this position the instructor can walk through the approach and have the student follow his arm action. This will give the student a sense of arm timing coordinated with the leg action.

Combined Arm and Leg Action—The standard type of arm action as used today is as follows: the diver stands at a position of attention near the base of the board with the arms held down along the sides of the body, the palms of the hands facing inward toward the front of the thighs. As the first step is taken the arms are held in the starting position without any movement. On the second step the arms make a small outward circle so that they are slightly past the center line of the hips. On the third step the arms are lifted vertically along the sides of the body as the body weight is placed on the jumping foot, and the hurdle leg is carried up vigorously to raise the body to the peak of the hurdle.

The Hurdle

The development of a well balanced hurdle takes many hours of practice. The most elementary dives and the most complex dives, to be performed with the nearest amount of perfection, are dependent upon a good lift and the proper balance and timing in this movement. First have the student stand with one foot forward. The forward foot will be the one that the diver is going to place his weight on when beginning the jump. The arms are held in a position slightly to the rear of the body and will come forward as the weight of the body begins to rest solidly on the jumping foot. The back or hurdle leg comes forward and is brought up to a position even with the hips while the knee is bent and the toes are pointed downward. The toes should be slightly forward of the bend in the hurdle knee and never behind the knee or close to the jumping leg. By repeating the

PLATE 88. *Arm Lift and Hurdle Action*

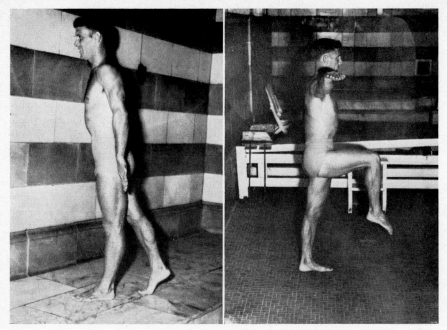

PLATE 89. *Start for Hurdle*   PLATE 90. *Hurdle Position*

action of bringing the weight forward, swinging the hurdle leg upward, the arms upward and outward, the diver will gradually get the rhythm and timing of the action. After this action is learned thoroughly the diver can do it with a spring, jumping up to the peak of the hurdle and bringing the two feet together at the top of the hurdle for the landing. Care should be taken to see that the diver, when performing the jump, keeps his back straight to eliminate forward bending at the waist. The forward bend will destroy the body balance.

The Approach on the Diving Board

After the student has become accustomed to taking the three steps and a hurdle with the proper body balance, arms, and leg action, he is ready to begin work on the spring board.

Method of Securing Starting Mark on Board—Finding a starting place on the board has often presented a problem. The best way to determine this is by having the diver stand at the end of the spring board with the heels even with the tip of the board and his back toward the water. Then the diver should take three steps and a hurdle inward on the board. From the spot where he lands he should execute an about face. He is on the proper starting mark, and this point ought to be marked by a small piece of tape visible on the side of the board. Now the diver is ready to take his three steps and hurdle out to the end of the board. When doing this he should go through the motions of his arm and leg and hurdle action, taking his jump and landing flatfooted on the end of the board. If everything is done properly he should land about an inch from the end of the board. The distance he lands away from the end of the board should be checked. Then have the diver come inward on the board. Check the tape mark, and, if necessary move it backward or forward the distance that he is short or over the end of the board.

Repeat this until the diver is consistent. He must land continuously at the same place on the end of the board.

Combining Approach with Spring—After the starting point for the approach and the hurdle has been determined, the diver can then go through the complete procedure, and take his spring with the board. Constant work will gradually develop the sense of rhythm, timing, and balance on the spring board.

Head Action on Approach—The head action here is very important in maintaining balance. From the starting point of the approach, the head should be held erect with the eyes focussed on the tip of the board. As the diver proceeds toward the tip of the board the eyes and the head are lowered slightly, so that in the hurdle the diver is able to maintain visual contact with the end of the board. When the feet make contact with the end of the board, the head is raised slightly, so that the diver maintains his best postural position.

Instructor checking body balance—The instructor must check the body balance of the diver, as he goes out on the board in his approach and hurdle. By standing at the base of the board the instructor will be able to see from behind if the diver is walking straight. The feet must be pointed straight ahead. Assuming an imaginary center line, the diver must pace out his approach so that the inner side of each foot lies parallel to this line. The diver must not step wide of this center line. Also he must not cross either foot in front of the other, walk pigeon-toed, or with the toes pointed outward. The instructor will be able to see whether both arms are performing simultaneously, whether one shoulder is higher than the other in the arm lift, whether the hurdle knee is going up straight or is crossing over in front of the body center line, whether the ankles and the toes are hanging straight and are not twisted sidewise as the board contact is made. If the diver's body is aligned correctly the take-off should be close to perfect, but when he loses sym-

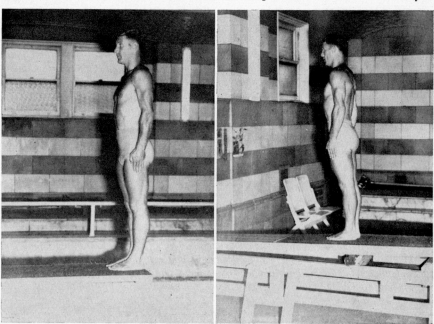

PLATE 91. *Position for Finding Hurdle Point*   PLATE 92. *Approach Position Determined*

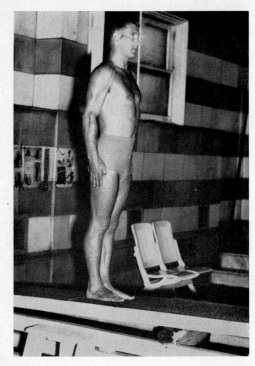

PLATE 93. *About Face and Starting Point Is Determined*

metrical balance the diver must compensate those positions to maintain this balance. He thus creates an insecure and inconsistant take-off. The entire dive then is out of balance, and the diver will be fighting for control throughout the approach, the dive, and the entry into the water.

AERIAL BODY MECHANICS

Proper Lift from the Board

In lifting from the tip of the board, the body is often leaned slightly forward in order to gain momentum for the upward pull of the arms and the springing action of the ankles and the knees.

This upward pull of the arms is actually a grasping of the air and a pulling of the rest of the body with it. The arms are brought rapidly but smoothly upward. Caution must be taken not to move the shoulders alone. The rest of the body can be drawn if the upper portion of the body is slightly tense. This tenseness of the muscles increases the pulling power of the shoulders.

Relation of Hurdle to Take-off

The take-off is wholly dependent on the hurdle itself. The angle of the hurdle, which is really board work, will determine to a great degree the projection of the body through the air.

Types of Hurdle

There are basically three types of hurdles. They are the Broad Jump Hurdle, which is done as a long, low arc on the board; the Spot Hurdle, which is a small, short hurdle that minimizes the return of the board action and power, thus necessitating overwork on the diver's part; the High Jump Hurdle, which is the most

PLATE 94. *Broad Jump Hurdle*

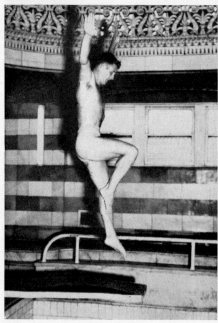

PLATE 95. *Spot Hurdle*   PLATE 96. *Desirable Hurdle*

desirable of all the variations of these types. With the High Jump Hurdle, the diver catches the board with its maximum power, and it throws him quite naturally into a high arc in the air which will enable him to perform the more complex aerial acrobatics with a minimum of hurried work.

Body Balance in the Air

In order to develop the maximum balance in the air, the pupil would do well to master the four primary acrobatic actions.

The Tuck Position—The diver must jump from the board after a high spring, fold the knees against the chest, grasp the shins with the fingers of the hands, then straighten the body, lower the arms to the sides, and drop vertically into the water. This is an elementary exercise.

The Pike Position—The elementary form is executed as the diver rises through the air. At the peak of his arc the diver tightens his stomach muscles, pulls his legs upward, toes pointed, ankles and knees together and straight. He touches his toes with his fingertips, and then drops his legs, straightens his body, and drops feet first, vertically into the water.

The Layout Position—In executing this action the diver jumps upward into the air with a straight body. Then the back is arched momentarily, straightened once again. The toes are pointed and the arms are extended above the head in a swan position. He then drops downward bringing the arms to the sides and entering the water feet first.

The Twist Action—The most difficult of all the elementary aerial actions is the twisting motion. Again, it should be noted, the ease with which this is learned is highly dependent on the inherent ability of the individual pupil. Some pupils execute the twisting action with ease, while others spend years attempting to coordinate the action properly. The most important element of the twist is the head action. The instructor would do well to work the fundamentals of this action with the pupil on the pool deck.

The pupil stands on the pool deck with his hands at his sides. The instructor has the pupil pick a point level with his eyes in front of him and then has him do an

PLATE 97. *Tuck Position*   PLATE 98. *Pike Position*

about face. Then the pupil must jump up into the air, raising the arms above his head, twisting his head in order to aid in turning the body. The chin should be high and away from the shoulder. Tilting the head from one side or to the other and not maintaining an even head rotation will cause the pupil to lose his body balance. When the pupil makes his jump and lands again he should be facing the point he picked directly behind him. This should be practiced several times on the pool deck. Then if the progress warrants, the pupil should pick a point in front of him and try a complete full twisting action returning to his starting point. He should repeat the identical procedure, the only change being that he makes a full revolution with his body for a full twist. These two exercises should then be attempted from the board. The diver on the board enters feet first exactly as he did on the pool deck, and performs the jumping half twist and the full twist.

The Running Front Dive

The most important preliminary dive is, quite obviously, the running front dive. As has been said, the body is leaned forward into the dive as the diver leaves the tip of the diving board. The arms are raised over the head, elbows straight, the hands locked together tightly. The head, again, is the controlling factor. The beginning diver must keep his chin on his chest in order to raise his hips to the proper height for a good head-first entry.

Learning To Use Legs—Gradually the diver will learn, with increased height of spring that his head need not not be so tight to his chest. The head must be adjusted to accord with the amount of spring the diver obtains, and also with the

PLATE 99. *Layout Position*   PLATE 100. *Twist Position*

speed and amount of leg rise behind him. This, only the diver can know as he becomes more familiar with the board and the diving process. As the diver nears the top point of his arc, he must not drop his shoulders. The pupil must realize that the legs do the dive, not the head. This is the one dive that is accomplished by the leg action and not by the head action. The chin is held off the chest until the fingers contact the water. Then the chin is tucked downward toward the chest in balance with the forward moving leg action. Practice alone can aid the diver in this dive.

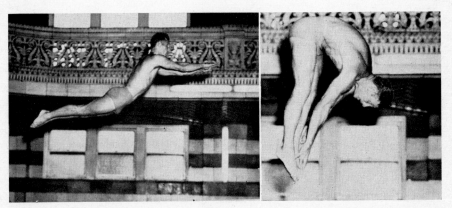

PLATE 101. *Running Plain Front Dive*   PLATE 102. *Front Jackknife*

The Running Front Jack-Knife—Most easily learned of all the dives is the front jack-knife dive or the pike dive. As the diver leaves the board on his lift he reaches for his height, pulls the stomach muscles inward in order to raise the hips, reaches down along the sides of the body, touching the toes or instep of the feet with the fingertips. The chin must be held high in order to maintain body balance. After touching the toes, the diver locks his hands together, and straightens the legs out behind and above him with his stomach muscles. During this recovery, he maintains body balance with a high head position. As his hands hit the water, he drops his chin on his chest and enters normally as he would in a plain front dive. The body should enter the water a little short of the vertical entry line.

FUNDAMENTAL BOARD WORK (BACK TAKE-OFF)

Back Bending Exercises

Particular importance should be placed on the beginning back dive. Very often in learning the back dive, a diver may progress more rapidly with the more complex back dives, at the same time acquiring an overall picture of diving.

The instructor should start again with the beginner on the pool deck. The fundamental process should be explained clearly to the diver. The instructor explains that he will place his hand in the middle of the back, that the beginner must lean over that hand arching his back. This must be done several times, first of all to acquaint the pupil with the feel of the back dive itself, and to gain confidence in the instructor. The instructor will find that often the pupil may be extremely supple. The process then is less complex. But if the diver cannot bend, the instructor might have the pupil relax as much as possible in his hands. The tenseness of the pupil is most frequently due to fear and lack of confidence in the instructor. Little progress is made until this is corrected.

Fall-off Back Dive—Security Guidance

The instructor then walks the beginning diver out on the board. At the end of the board, he turns the pupil around, has him place his feet wide apart, flat and full on the board, his heels against the tip of the board. The instructor then

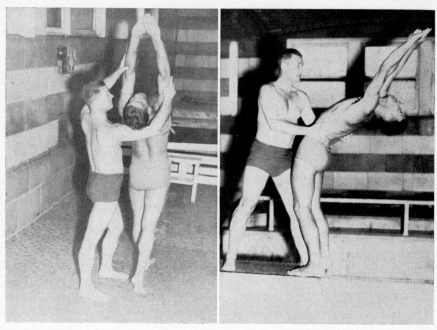

PLATE 103. *Checking Back Arch*   PLATE 104. *Security Guidance Fall-off Back Dive*

places his hands on the pupil's waist, just above the hips. The diver raises his hands above his head, locks the fingers, drops the head back on his shoulders. Then the instructor places one foot between the legs of the pupil in order to balance himself. Slowly he lets the diver drop back while holding him. The diver then arches his back and his arms drop back behind his head. The instructor must make sure that the diver does not bend the knees forward, that he does not stiffen and pull the chin onto the chest. If the diver is relaxed, the instructor lowers him, and feeling sure of the position lets go of the diver. If the head, arms, legs, and back are all in good position, the diver should enter the water nicely, avoiding water sting and the resulting fear. Above all, the instructor must not let go of the diver until he is sure of all these factors. Once the diver has become frightened, the progress is stopped, and it might be necessary to begin again. After repeated attempts the diver should gain confidence and absorb a familiarity with the back dive. He is then ready for the official approach.

The Approach to the End of the Board

The approach in the back dive is important in competitive scoring. The diver takes his stance at the point on the board at which he normally begins his pacing for the front dives. In an erect position, looking straight ahead, the diver walks through the normal approach without gaining momentum. At the point where he would normally take his hurdle, the diver extends one foot (depending with which foot he begins his pacing) across the other foot. For instance, a diver may cross

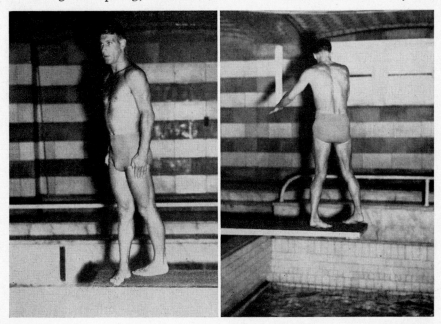

PLATE 105.   *Turning on End of Board for Backward Dive*   PLATE 106.

his left foot with his right foot so that the toes are close to the end of the board. Placing his weight on the right foot, the diver spins on the ball of that foot. At the completion of this spin both heels should be at the end of the board. The diver then is ready for the actual diving position. Keeping in contact with the board at all times, the diver slides one foot back in order to grip the end of the board with his toes. This position must be concrete to maintain balance for the diver while the other foot is slid in like manner to a similiar position.

Stance and Body Balance

Body balance is assured by assuming a triangular board position with the heels together, the toes slightly apart. Ankle and knee contact then is possible for utmost balance. At no time does the diver glance down at his feet. His eyes must be kept straight ahead, and after the turn at the end of the board, he must pick a spot in front of him at the opposite end of the board on which to focus. This should be at the

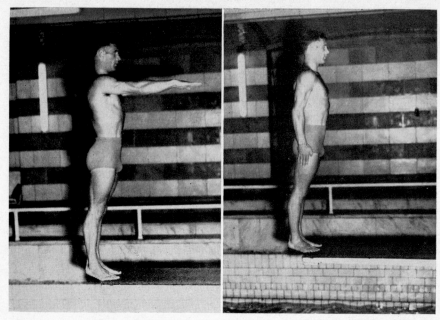

PLATE 107. *Using Arms to Complete Balance*   PLATE 108. *Arms are Lowered in Readiness*
on End of Board   *for Dive*

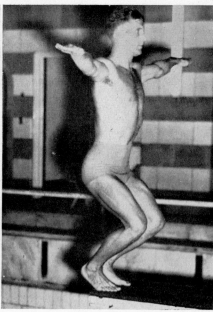

PLATE 109. *Arm and Ankle Action*   PLATE 110. *Arm, Knee and Ankle Action*
for Take-off

level of the eyes. It is a great aid in balancing. The arms of the diver then are brought slowly out in front of him, width of shoulders apart, palms down, fingers together, thumbs along the fingers: another assurance of complete body balance.

Coordination of Arm and Leg Action

After balancing, the arms are dropped slowly to the sides of the body. With his palms along his sides the diver then raises his arms sidewards, slowly and smoothly while rising on his toes at the same time. The arms are then brought forcefully down along the sides, as the diver bends his knees slightly forward and outward. The ankles are brought into play here. This downward motion depresses the board preparatory to springing upward and outward into the dive. As the diver drops, his back must remain straight in order to maintain the all-important balance.

Lift for the Take-off

It must be understood that all this is done in quick time. But, breaking down this action, we find that the diver's back must remain straight. Then, as his arms drop, the body weight is pushed into the board, and the arms begin the upward lift, which, in reality, is a complete body pull. Care must be taken that the diver does not merely lift his shoulder girdle, but that the arms have the power to assist the entire body in its take-off. At the very top of the spring the knees are stiffened and the thigh muscles are tightened to make them recover resiliently. As the spring returns from the depressed board and is transmitted to the diver, he lifts upward, leans his shoulders back, and arches his back slightly as he is driven into the air. As opposed to tumbling, where hip action is all important, diving depends largely on shoulder and head action. The hips of the diver must remain stiff with the straight back until he begins the actual aerial acrobatics. Otherwise, the hips bend the body awkwardly, which results in loss of balance, loss of manipulating control, and the diver may be thrown back into the board or out away from the board too far.

Faults to be Checked:

1. Stiff back
2. Pulling chin on chest
3. Dropping pupil when not in position
4. Poor posture on approach
5. Not picking spot on take-off position
6. Too vigorous arm lift (crow-hop)
7. Bending body forward at waist
8. Swinging hip action

ELEMENTARY COMPETITIVE DIVES

Required Dives

The five basic, required competitive dives are:
1. The Straight or Swan Dive
2. The Back or Back Pike Dive
3. The Gainer Dive, straight or piked
4. The Cutaway Dive, which is the Back Jack piked or straight
5. The Half Twist

Each of the required dives is chosen from one of the five groups of dives. However the year before the Olympic Games the F.I.N.A. recommends certain dives as the required dives for the Games. These are frequently changed. Our American A.A.U. and the National Collegiate Athletic Association conform to these requirements, and they change our standard competitive dives, so that the diver may have ample opportunity to master these dives.

Each of these competitive dives requires a different approach on the part of both instructor and diver. What is easily understood by one diver may be incomprehensible to another. Personality can never follow a code of rules set by any swimming or diving instructor. However, the basic mechanics of take-off and dive may aid greatly the less experienced diver. These five fundamental groups follow a pattern. The instructor may vary the progression to suit his own needs.

Forward Dive

This is the dive that most students like to learn first. But, outstanding coaches and highly rated divers will admit that it is actually the most difficult of the elementary dives to perform properly. The pupil must understand that the legs do all the work while the head and arms remain in a fixed position. A delicate sense of head balance must be maintained in order to control the up-swing of the legs. The head controls the entire body during the flight of the dive. Here are two useful exercises:

1. Have the student lie on the pool deck, raise the arms, and then arch the back and lift the legs off the deck. Repeat this exercise often. This will give an understanding of the use of back muscles and leg lifting.

2. Have the student jump from the board in a standing position, raising his arms upward, arching the back, legs pushed behind the center line of the body. He brings his legs down underneath his body in entering the water.

These exercises should teach proper use of the back in the swan dive. The head action is dependent on the sense of balance of the diver. The instructor may then have the student jump from the board using his approach and hurdle. He jumps, assumes the above mentioned position, and drops into the water feet first. This gives the student the feel of back-arching and the backward leg motion. Now to do

PLATE 111. *Forward Dive, Layout Position*

the dive itself. In the straight front dive, the student approaches the end of the board, takes his hurdle, brings his hands and arms up from the sides of his body and leaves the board. The hands are clasped together in front of the diver, arms straight, elbows stiff. As the legs rise the diver arches his back, pivots over his shoulders, drops his head, and prepares for a normal entry.

In the swan dive, instead of bringing the hands together, the arms are kept apart, the palms visible toward the outer periphery of the eyes, the chin is high, but not pushed forward. As the diver rises, the legs swing gradually up behind the diver, while the head itself controls this leg-swinging action. This might well be understood that the body is pivoting slowly on the shoulders. The thigh and back muscles snap the legs up behind the diver, and they continue to rise to the top of the dive. The diver should feel that he is falling flat on the dive. This is altogether proper.

While he drops, with his arms held apart and his head held high, the diver begins his preparation for the water entry. From the outstretched position, the arms are brought over the head, extended along the side of the ears, rather than dropped under the body and brought forward in front of the face. This is a frequent mistake among divers. From the arched position of the back, the head adjusts for the leg swing while the stomach muscles are tightened to straighten the back. The adjustment of the head compensates for the shortness of the dive or for the body over swing. At the entry, the diver should maintain his body line as he goes directly to the bottom of the pool. If this body line is broken, the over-arched back can injure the diver severely.

Faults to be Checked:

1. Arms back of the shoulders
2. Chin thrust too far forward
3. Carrying too much arch
4. Not using back muscles for leg-lift
5. Breaking body line in entry

The Back Dive

In beginning the Back Dive, it would be well if the pupil would practice bouncing the board and jumping forward on the board from a back take-off position. This will assure proper board mechanics in the back lift and take-off.

After mastering the drop-off back dive with the instructor, the diver is now ready to try the dive with the proper take-off. He must spring and swing the arms up to eye level, watching them ride above the head. Watching the hands, the head drops back, and the back arches. This is an excellent position for the dive. Knee and ankle action now come into play. As the body rises into the air, there should be a concentrated effort on the part of the diver to get the hips as high as possible above the shoulder level. At the top of the dive the body is stretched to its fullest extent, and the back is arched moderately under the shoulder blades. This not only adds to the beauty of the dive, but it aids as well in bringing the legs to the proper position. As the diver falls off in the arc of the dive, he must break the arch of the back by pulling in on the stomach muscles. The body then is straightened from the outstretched arms to the toes. He must follow the dive through without turning the head in the air or under the water. This fault is usually committed by the diver to get quickly and safely to the ladder at the side

PLATE 112. *Back Dive*

of the pool. This often causes the legs to be twisted at the finish of the dive.

In the back swan dive, the arms are placed in the same position as for the front swan dive. As the diver prepares for the entry he brings the arms close to the ears so that a straight body line will be assumed for the entry.

Faults to be Checked:

1. Dropping shoulders before completion of lift
2. Throwing head over too fast
3. Dropping the head to either shoulder
4. Not stretching on the entry

Reverse Dive

The Half Gainer Dive is similar in many respects to the back dive. The head shoulders, and arm action are the same. But, instead of the back approach to the board the diver takes the regular front approach.

One Foot Gainer Take-off—Using the one foot take-off the diver takes his four regular paces to reach the end of the board. One foot is at the end of the board as the other kicks high, somewhat as a football player kicks a ball. This enables the diver to lift the hips up higher than the shoulders as he leaves the board. His body moves away from the board, and he throws the arms over the head, watching them with his eyes and moving the head backward. He arches his back after dropping the shoulders toward the tip of the board. The recovery and entry into the water is exactly the same as the back dive which was mentioned above. This is referred to as the elementary one foot gainer take-off.

PLATE 113. *Reverse Dive. One Foot Take-off*   PLATE 114. *Reverse Dive. Two Foot Take-off*

Two Foot Take-off—Now for the half gainer itself as it is used in competition. This is the normal two feet take-off. The approach and hurdle here is identical to the running front dive. As the diver leaves the board and rises into the air, the arms are brought to a position similar to the position of the arms in the swan dive. The difference is that the body is inverted. The hips are lifted high so that the legs may rise above the shoulders. The shoulders then are dropped back, and the body is arched. The head continues through the arch, and the diver looks back toward the board. The toes are pointed and the arms are straight. After this momentary swan position, the hands are brought together above the head, with the arms straight and close to the ears for the entry.

The body must be straightened with the hip and stomach muscles. The entry is the same as the back dive and the swan dive entry.

Faults to be Checked:
1. Dropping shoulders back on hurdle
2. Looking up on end of board too soon
3. Keeping head down at end of board
4. Bending the hips, inhibiting hip lift
5. Turning the head to the side
6. Failing to force shoulders back continuously

Inward Dive
This dive can easily be worked up through a simple progression of the body manipulation exercises. The diver must jump off the board backward vertically, and enter the water feet first. Next jump back from the board, assume a tuck

PLATE 115. *Inward Dive, Pike Position*

position temporarily, drop it, straighten the body, and enter the water, vertically, feet first. The diver may then attempt the same exercise, but he remains tucked, drops the head forward toward the water and rolls from the air into the water. It cannot be stressed too greatly that the beginning diver must jump up and well away from the board. Injury often results if this is neglected. This will familiarize the diver with the high hip position and the head action. In this particular exercise, the entry is of less importance than the essential body mechanics. He must then jump back from the board, constricting the stomach muscles in order to raise the hips. He then places the hands on his shins, sliding them down toward the ankles. The diver, upon entry, is bent at the waist, arms and legs connected. He drops his head between his arms and drops the feet and arms together into the water. After practicing these, the diver is now ready for the dive itself. The jump should be made upward and outward, the chest up, and the legs slightly behind the vertical line of the body. As the body rises in the air, the hips are lifted up, the stomach sucked in. The arms cut down the side of the body to touch the toes. The touch should be only momentary. The stomach muscles aid in straightening the legs. Then the legs should flow smoothly into a straight upside-down body position for the proper entry into the water.

Faults to be Checked:

1. Feet high in front of the hips
2. Hips dropped on the take-off
3. Dropping head down at moment of lift
4. Lack of use of stomach muscles
5. Extreme forward reaching arms

PLATE 116. *Ground Instruction for Half Twist—First Position*   PLATE 117. *Ground Instruction for Half Twist—Second Position*

Twist Dives

This dive is begun exactly as in the front dive. As the body rises off the board, the legs are snapped up behind the diver. When the hips and the legs rise to a horizontal position with the shoulders, the head should be smoothly turned to the side. The arms are in a swan position and roll with the dive into the body inversion. The arm opposite the side toward which the diver rolls should be held high. The eyes should look along that high arm during the body roll. The chin is held high. Then, the other arm is also held high and dropped back so that the diver will have a good, inverted swan dive position. The head rolls simultaneously with the body. It is then dropped back onto the shoulders preparatory to the entry. Then, the diver is ready for the entry into the water exactly as he would be in the back dive. Tightening the stomach muscles, the arch should be taken out of the back, and the arms must be brought to an overhead position on the entry.

Faults to be Checked:

1. Beginning twist itself on the board
2. Dropping one shoulder on take-off
3. Twisting, before head, shoulders, and legs are horizontal
4. Twisting hips, independent of body
5. Losing swan position of arms
6. Incorrect head position for back dive entry

SPINNING ACTIONS

Forward Spinning Action

The spinning actions are essential to the more complex competitive dives.

PLATE 118. *Half Twist in Air*

These spinning dives are either done in a tuck or a pike position. To perform these dives there are certain fundamental mechanics that must be mastered in order to progress to the more difficult competitive dives.

Tuck Spin—The forward front somersault in tuck position is the foundation upon which every forward spinning dive is built, from the single somersault through the 3½ somersault. In learning the proper technique for the front somersault, the diver must begin in the most elementary stage and gradually add to the technique. In presenting the front somersault to the beginning diver, the instructor first must give the diver a good picture of the proper action in order that the diver understands exactly what makes his body spin. It is not very helpful to a beginning diver to have an instructor tell him to push his head down and grab his knees. He may get around and he may not. But if the diver is shown that to spin properly he must push his head and shoulders down, lift his hips and try to go under the body to grasp the shins, he should spin properly. The usual fault in a spin is that the knees are brought up to the chest instead of being pulled away from the chest. The head and the shoulders should be forced *down* toward the knees. A simple exercise for the spin is to have the diver, while standing on the pool deck, raise one leg back of him and then roll the shoulders and the head downward trying to grasp the leg that is back of him. After trying this a few times the diver will begin to feel the proper action in the forward spins. The next step is to have the diver stand on the edge of the pool and then assume a tuck position. From this position he should roll forward, at the same time forcing the head and shoulders down. After this has been done several times he will become familiar with the turning motion. The diver is now ready to attempt the second step. This step is similar to the dive and the front roll on the gym mat. It gives the diver a chance to get his hips up in order to go into his tuck position as he enters the water. This gives the beginner a chance to get his spring and lift first, and then to complete the action afterward. After this is mastered the diver is ready to attempt to spring upward, perform his tuck action, and then to turn over, so that he lands feet first in the water. When the diver is able to get around and enter the water with a straight body he can be sure that his mechanics are being performed properly. Having mastered this simple action, the diver is now ready to repeat the same thing from the board. The diver should be observed closely in order to see that his head and shoulder action is right, that the legs are in back of him, and that he is not bringing his knees up to meet his hands for the tuck. The diver should have the feeling that he is pulling his knees away from him, and that he has to force his head and shoulders down to stay in as close to his knees as possible.

Since the head and the shoulders are forcing the forward spin they have the control over the spin. To check the spin the head is raised and the pressure is released from the shoulders. This stops the forward action while the legs are stretched out to put the body in balance for the entry.

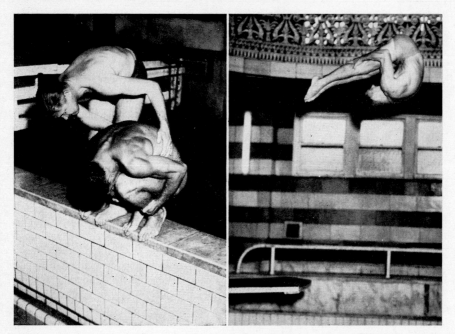

PLATE 119. *Beginning for Front Somersault*   PLATE 120. *Front Somersault in Pike Position*

The Pike Action—The action for the pike somersault is the same as for the tuck. Head and shoulders start the action. The legs and hips are lifted upward and backward so that the head and shoulders are forced under for good spinning action. The hands grasp the back of the legs at the knees. As the spin progresses, the arms bend at the elbows and draw the head and shoulders down toward the legs. The spin is checked just the same as in the tuck somersault.

Backward Spinning Action

The action of the back somersault is essential in the performance of every backward spinning dive; it is the basis for every dive from the back somersault through the back 2½ somersault and in the gainer spinner dives.

The diver should begin it just as though he were beginning a simple back dive. The lift from the board should be upward and outward as usual. The arms are carried just above the shoulders. Then, after the head is dropped back, onto the

PLATE 121. *Back Somersault—Tuck Position*   PLATE 122. *Back Somersault—Pike Position*

shoulders, the arms continue in the arc downward to gather up the legs as they are bent and brought into the tuck position. The diver should grasp his shins just below the knees, sliding them slightly upward as he squeezes his knees in for the pull into the position itself.

During this pulling action, the shoulders are stretched back with the head movement. When the diver is three-fourths of the way through the dive, he must push the legs away from the body, straightening the knees. Then the head is brought forward to a normal position in order to check the body spin. The arms should be brought to the sides of the body, fingers pointed downward, arms stretched. The diver must take care to keep his body straight for the entry, with no bending at the hips. This is the correct entry position.

Faults to be Checked:

     1. Hurrying the take-off
     2. Dropping the shoulders before lift
     3. Chin too high on take-off
     4. Bending forward and down from the knees
     5. Not lifting hips on the take-off
     6. Loss of body and hip alignment on take-off

CONCLUSION

The dives described in this chapter are basic and are considered essentially for the beginning diver. The advanced diver will go beyond many of these elementary procedures. In order to advance through the pyramid of skills—no diver, no matter how accomplished he is, can neglect the basic mechanics of diving. Often, divers acquire faults which are rooted in the most fundamental actions. The diver, as well as the instructor, must watch for these faults. No instructor is right—no instructor is wrong. But, the value of that instructor can be determined only by the accomplishment of his divers.

This has been an outline for teaching and learning. From this, the instructor and the diver must use their own initiative, must formulate deviations peculiar to the diver, must reorganize the process according to the individual.

Beside the instructor, the diver can learn most from the divers against whom he competes. The success of the method can be determined only when effort is intense and, above all, constant.

Exercise, supplementary equipment (trampoline, sand board, etc.), diet, daily schedules, are all helpful aids if obtainable. But for lack of them, perseverance, and plain "guts" can push the individual through the skills to a knowing, well-coordinated plane where the art itself becomes amazingly simple and completely unforgettable.

PLATE 123. *Back Somersault—Layout Position*

CHAPTER XI

Competitive Diving (Advanced)

Arrangements for all photography and its usage in this Chapter were made through the courtesy and permission of The National Collegiate Athletic Association and the Department of Athletics and Physical Education, The Ohio State University.

The revisors are deeply appreciative of the cooperative effort of Mr. Mike Peppe, Coach of Swimming, The Ohio State University as well as that of the various divers presented and identified on each plate.

Photography by Vernon Scott Gilmore.

This Chapter is supplementary to the preceding Chapter XV. It is designed for comparative visual usage by advanced divers and diving coaches.

Illustrations of the following recognized competitive dives are presented in the order listed:

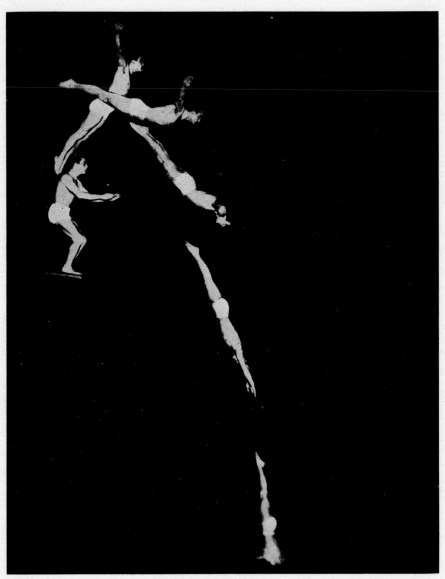

PLATE 124. *Front Dive (Swan)*
Diver: Marino of The Ohio State University

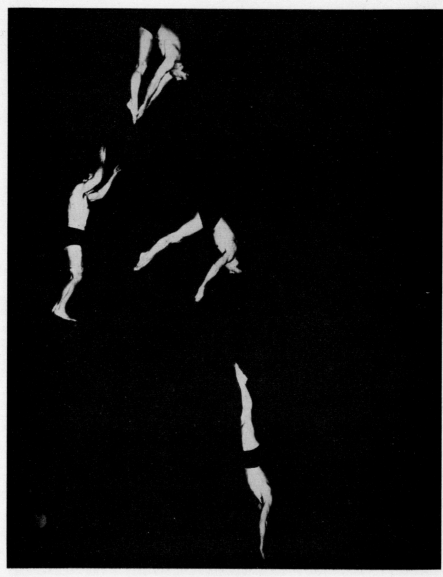

PLATE 125. *Pike Dive*
Diver: Calhoun of The Ohio State University

PLATE 126. *Back Dive, Straight*
Diver: Neuner of The University of Oklahoma

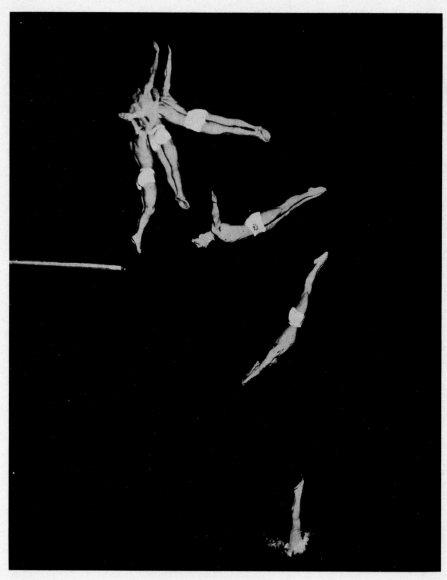

PLATE 127. *Reverse Dive, ½ Twist*
Diver: Marino of The Ohio State University

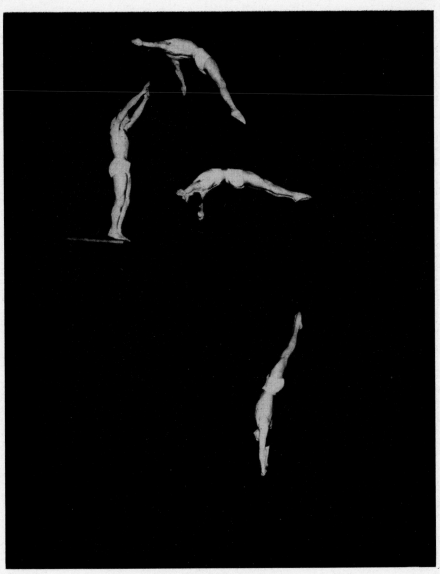

PLATE 128. *Reverse Dive, Straight*
Diver: Marino of The Ohio State University

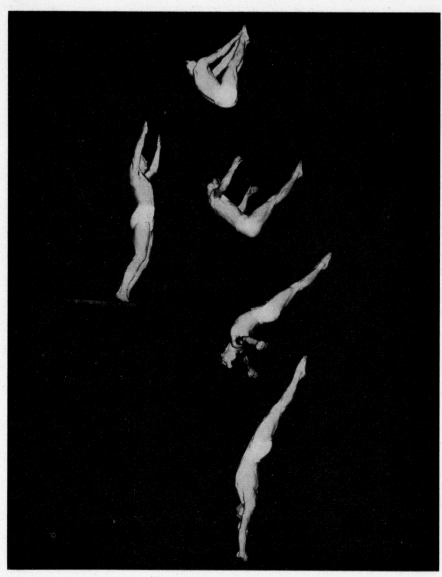

PLATE 129. *Reverse Dive, Pike*
Diver: Harlan of The Ohio State University

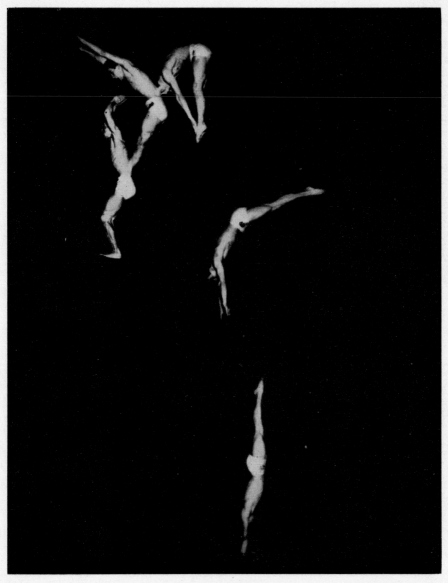

PLATE 130. *Inward Dive, Pike*
Diver: Marino of The Ohio State University

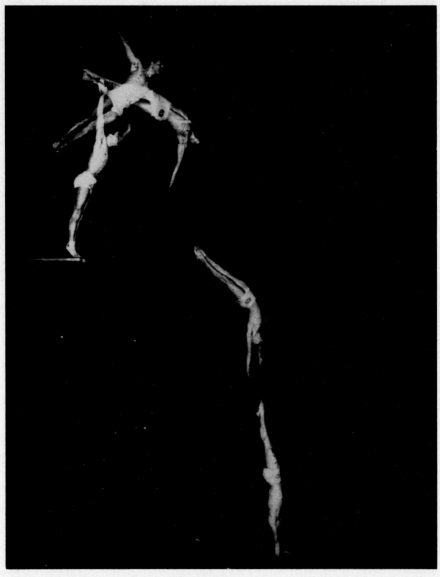

PLATE 131. *Front Dive with ½ Twist*
Diver: Marino of The Ohio State University

PLATE 132. *Flying Forward 1½ Somersault, Tuck*
Diver: Billingsley of The Ohio State University

PLATE 133. *Forward 1½ Somersault, Tuck*
Diver: Coffee of The Ohio State University

PLATE 134. *Forward 2½ Somersault, Pike*
Diver: Calhoun of The Ohio State University

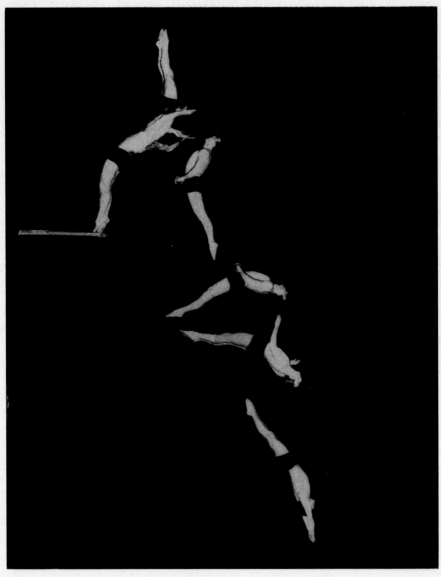

PLATE 135. *Backward 1½ Somersault, Straight*
Diver: Calhoun of The Ohio State University

PLATE 136. *Reverse Somersault, Straight*
Diver: Marino of The Ohio State University

PLATE 137. *Reverse 1½ Somersault, Straight*
Diver: Marino of The Ohio State University

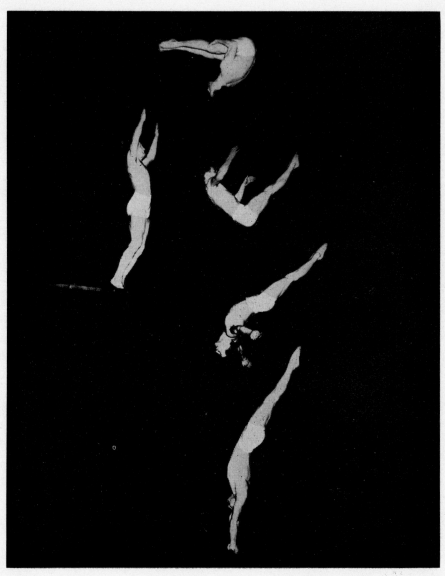

PLATE 138. *Reverse 1½ Somersault, Pike*
Diver: Harlan of The Ohio State University

PLATE 139. *Inward 1½ Somersault, Tuck*
Diver: Coffee of the Ohio State University

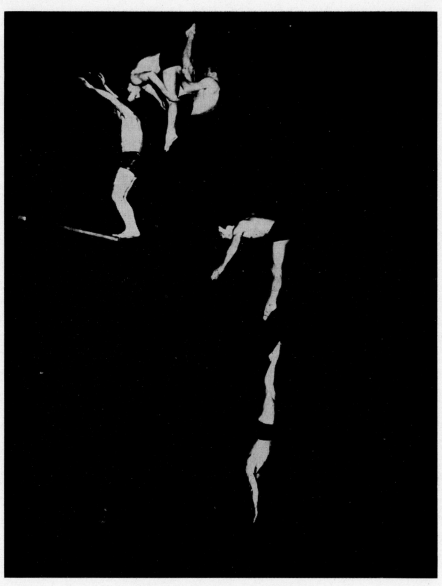

PLATE 140. *Inward 1½ Somersault, Pike*
Diver: Calhoun of The Ohio State University

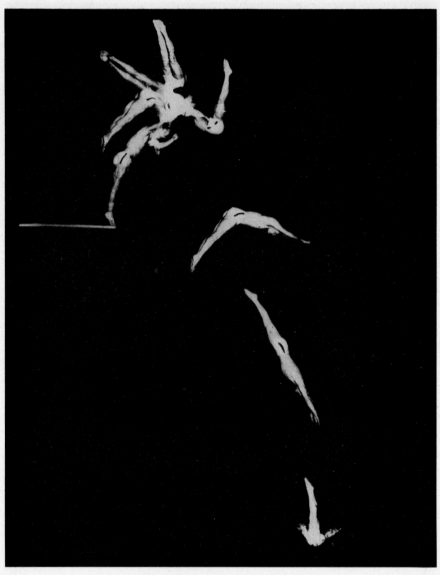

PLATE 141. *Full Twisting Forward 1½ Somersault*
Diver: Anderson of The Ohio State University

PLATE 142. *Back 1½ Somersault, 1½ Twist*
Diver: Calhoun of The Ohio State University

PLATE 143. *Reverse ½ Twist Straight, with 1½ Somersault, Tuck*
Diver: Calhoun of The Ohio State University

CHAPTER XII

Life Saving

Life saving skills are an essential part of military training. Prompt application of such skills have saved many men from plane crashes, sinking ships, and other disasters. This, again, is a skill which should be known to all persons, military or civilian. Disaster may strike as suddenly at any yacht club landing or community swimming pool as it may in the middle of the ocean, and only through prompt action will lives be saved. Any person who can swim should be trained and ready to help those who, through inability or panic, can not.

METHODS OF TEACHING LIFE SAVING SKILLS

The techniques for the performance of life saving skills have been so well standardized that detailed analyses and descriptions beyond those presented in the following methods outlined are not in order in this manual.

(1) Dive Approach

Form the men in single rank along both sides of the swimming pool. Direct them that the technique will be to dive out, not up, falling on the stomach. The back is to be arched, the head held up, the arms at full extension forward and as the body strikes the water the arms are brought sharply downward and backward. Have the Number One's dive and swim toward the center. Then have the Number Two's dive. For individual checking, the Number One's may be directed to peel off from the head of the line. Then the Number Two's.

(2) Jump Approach

Form the men along both sides of the swimming pool. Direct them to count off by two's. Instruct them that the technique will be to jump for distance, not for height. Body inclined forward, arms extended forward, in front of the chest, legs in position for frog or scissor kick. As the body sinks in the water to the hips, the legs deliver a sharp kick. Entry of the body will be partially broken by the forward angle of the body. Next, the hands are brought sharply downward to prevent further immersion of the body. Have the Number One's jump, level off, and swim toward pool center. Repeat with Number Two's.

(3) Rear Approach

Form the men in single rank on the deck. Direct them to count off by Two's. Number One's take two steps forward. Have Number Two's line up behind Number

PLATE 144. *Level Off, Preliminary to carry*

One's. Instruct them that the technique will be to walk (swim) up behind the victim, reach their right hand over victim's right shoulder (or left hand over victim's left shoulder), grasp the victim's chin with the hand, with third finger above the point of the chin and the fourth finger below, press forearm against victim's shoulder and pry. Direct the Number One's to perform the approach on the Number Two's. To drill the Numer Two's have both ranks about face.

Repeat in shallow water. Instruct them to make the approach while leaning forward, then reverse by leaning backward. Finally grasp the chin and walk (swim) away with victim.

Repeat in deep water. Direct the Number One's to form a rank in center of pool, backs to bulkhead. Number Two's leave bulkhead, make approach, level and tow victim to bulkhead.

An optional drill is to have victim hold on to the gutter or bulkhead until the rescuer has obtained a proper hold. Then Command, "Push-Off" after hold of each rescuer has been checked.

(4) Front Approach

Form swimmers in a single rank on the deck. Direct them to count off by two's. Number One's take two steps forward. Number One's, on command, about face, line up facing Number Two's. Instruct the men that they will perform the drill according to whistle and verbal command. They will hold each position until the whistle blows again. Between signals, the instructor checks for individual error, step by step.

Whistle—"Swim In" Number Two's take a step toward Number One's.

Whistle—"Reverse" Change from forward lean to backward lean.

Whistle—"Take Wrist" Reach across with right hand and grasp victim's right wrist (or reach with left for left wrist)

Whistle—"Swim" Start swimming away to draw victim into horizontal position on surface.

Whistle—"Turn" Rotate own wrist, turning thumb toward water, to turn victim on his back.

Whistle—"Come to Chin" Retain grip on wrist but draw victim to you by bending own elbow. Reach with the swimming hand to the chin.

Whistle—"Swim" Release grip on wrist, turn to other side and swim, towing victim by chin.

PLATE 145. *Fireman's Carry*

(5) Underwater Approach

Form and instruct the swimmers as for front surface approach.

Whistle—"Dive"	Number Two's bend knees and walk in crouch to Number One's. Put hands on Number One's knees.
Whistle—"Turn"	Push on one knee, pull the other. Keep contact with victim, "walking with the hands up the body."
Whistle—"Take Chin"	Reach with one hand as in rear approach. Use other hand to press upward against small of victim's back.
Whistle—"Swim"	Release hand at back, retain grip on chin. Tow.

(6) Fireman's Carry

Form swimmers in two ranks. Direct them to take standing position with partner in the shallow water area.

Whistle—"Support"	Float partner on his back supporting him with hands or by placing one knee under hips.
Whistle—"Reach"	Place your nearest hand between his thighs, from above. Support by placing that hand under his hips. Grasp victim's near wrist with your free hand, as if shaking hands with that wrist.
Whistle—"Duck and Roll"	Duck head in space between victim's near arm and side, roll him over your shoulder. Before emerging, shift your grasp on victim's wrist from your one hand to the hand which was placed through victim's legs.

(7) Saddleback Carry

Assemble swimmers in shallow water in manner prescribed in drill #6.

Whistle—"Support"	Float victim on his back, supporting him with hands or knees. Stand at his side, facing his head.
Whistle—"Reach"	Throw the victim's far arm over your near shoulder and around the back of your neck. Reach with your near arm, under victim's far arm around his back and to the back of the victim's head.
Whistle—"Turn and Reach to Carry"	Turn *away* from the victim, bring your free arm around in an arc, and with your back to victim, reach with free arm backward and wrap around victim's legs at the knees, from above. Lift and carry.

(8) Tired Swimmer Carry

Form the men in two ranks in the manner described in drill #4. Direct the Number Two's to approach and carry Number One's. Direct the rescuer to give the following instructions to the tired swimmer:

(1) Put your hands on my shoulders.	(5) Keep your chest up.
(2) Keep your elbows straight.	(6) Put your head back.
(3) Lie on your back.	(7) Keep your eyes on me.
(4) Spread your legs apart.	

(a) Body Position

(b) Victim's Chest High

PLATE 146. *Tired Swimmer Carry*

PLATE 147. *Group Instruction in Cross Chest Carry*

PLATE 148. *Cross Chest Carry Wearing Clothing*

(9) Cross Chest Carry

Direct swimmers to repeat drill #3, but with the addition of the following instructions:

Whistle—"Come to Chest"	Retain grip on chin. Bring other arm over top of victim's opposite shoulder. Extend hand across victim's chest and under his far arm. Clamp elbow down on victim's chest. Place your upper hip under small of victim's back. Press upward.
Whistle—"Release Chin and Swim"	Release the grip on the victim's chin. Turn onto that side and swim. Carry victim on your hip, using side stroke. Press your elbow tightly down on victim's chest.

(10) Hair Carry

Direct swimmers to repeat drill #3, but with the addition of the following instructions:

Whistle—"Bring Hand to Hair"	Retain grip on chin. Bring free hand in, palm to back of victim's head, fingers extended upward. Curve fingers to contour of victim's head to forehead with fingers leading. Double up the fist, knuckles uppermost. Victim's hair should be held in palm and between fingers. For *hair carry*, the cadets may be directed to employ the following substitute method: Victim raises one arm and cups hand on top of fore part of head. Rescuer slips his finger tips in this cupped hand from above.
Whistle—"Release Chin and Swim"	Release the grip on victim's chin. Turn onto that side, straighten the elbow of the carrying arm and swim using the side stroke.

(11) Head Carry

Direct swimmers to repeat drill #3, but with the addition of the following instructions:

Whistle—"Bring Free Hand to Face"	Retain grip on chin. Bring free hand in and place along side of victim's face, palm over ear, middle finger extending along victim's jaw line, thumb pressed down over eyebrow.
Whistle—"Bring Chin Hand to Face"	Release the grip on chin and place that hand along other side of victim's face, middle finger down jaw line, thumb over eyebrow.
Whistle—"Carry"	Lean body into backward position, carry the victim, using frog, vertical scissor or horizontal scissor kick.

(12) Two-Man Carry

Form the men in a single rank on the deck. Count off by 3's. Direct the Number One's and Three's to take one step forward. Have Number One's and Number Three's about face. Instruct them to perform the following command:

Whistle—"Take Position"	Step (swim) to victim's side, one rescuer on each side of victim. Grasp victim's near upper arm with your near hand.
Whistle—"Swim"	Turn on side, facing victim, and tow him as he floats on his back, each rescuer using the side stroke.

(13) Clothing Carry (A)

Direct swimmers to repeat drill #3, but with the addition of the following instructions:

Whistle—"Bring Free Hand to Collar"	Retain grip on chin. Bring free hand in and grasp collar of jacket, coat or shirt. In case of T-shirt, grasp all of shirt from tail to neck by drawing it up in a roll. Unbutton shirt collar of victim.
Whistle—"Release Chin Hand and Tow"	Bring the hand from the chin into swimming position. Use frog kick on the back or turn on the side and use side stroke.

(14) Clothing Carry (B)

Form the men in a single rank on the deck. Count off by Two's. Have Number One's take two steps forward. Have Number Two's line up behind Number One's. Instruct them to proceed as follows, equipped with shirt or pair of trousers.

Whistle—"Approach"	Swim up to the victim, and reverse by doubling knees and leaning backward; place crotch of trousers in armpit.
Whistle—"Fix Trousers"	With crotch of trousers under shoulder of victim, draw far leg of trousers over his other shoulder. Grasp ends of both trouser legs with one hand.
Whistle—"Tow"	Use frog kick on back, or scissor kick on side.

(15) Clothing Carry (C)

Form swimmers as described in drill #14. Instruct them to proceed as follows, equipped with shirt or pair of trousers:

Whistle—"Approach"	Swim up to victim and reverse.
Whistle—"Fix Trousers"	Place crotch of trousers against back of victim's neck; draw each trouser leg forward over the shoulder nearest to it; loop downward and backward under that same shoulder. Grasp the ends of both trouser legs with one hand.
Whistle—"Tow"	Use frog kick on back or scissor kick on side.

(16) Board and Rope Tows

Count off by Two's and have Two's form in a line down the center of the pool facing the One's each of whom is equipped with a kickboard, towel, article of clothing or line.

Whistle—"Shove Off"	Each Number One swims with kickboard or line to within two or three feet of the Number Two. Extend board or line to the victim, retain own grip on it, reverse, and tow.
Whistle—"Tow"	Use frog kick or vertical scissor on back or horizontal scissor on side.

(17) Miscellaneous Tows

(a) Count off by Two's. Have Number Two's enter water five feet from bulkhead. Number One rescues Number Two with the following methods:
    1—Retain one hand grip on bulkhead, reach with other hand.
    2—Retain two hand grip on bulkhead, extend foot.
    3—Grip bulkhead with one hand, extend pole, towel, board or article of clothing.
(b) Count off by Three's. Have Number Three's enter water ten feet from bulk head. Three's are rescued by:
    1—Number One grips bulkhead with one hand, and grips wrist of Number Two with other hand; Number Two reaches free hand to Number Three.
    2—Number One grips bulkhead with one hand and grasps one ankle of Number Two with other hand. Number Two lies in prone float and extends hands to Number Three.
    3—Number One grips bulkhead with one hand and grips wrist of Number Two with other hand; Number Two extends one or both of his legs out to Number Three.
(c) In single rank, in water, along the bulkhead men count off by two's. Number One's face bulkhead, Number Two's face outward. Last man in line goes to far side of pool. Remaining men form chain by clasping hands. One end man of chain grips the bulkhead with free hand. The rest of the chain extends out to victim on far side. Then all men in chain flex elbows, bringing victim to safety.

(18) Retrieving a Person from Bottom

Pair off (count off by two's). When Number One's are ready to shove off for rescue, the Number Two's swim to bottom and lie there. Number One is instructed to stop swimming before he is over the victim, perform a surface dive, approach the victim while descending at an angle, grasp victim by chin, wrist, hair or clothing (See DRILLS 3, 4, 10 and 13) return to surface at an angle, level and tow.

(19) Supporting Another Man in the Water

Pair off (count off by two's). Perform the following in accordance with instrucitons:
(a) Support partner by holding one or both hands under his hips. Assume vertical float position. Tread water using frog or scissor kick. If only one hand is used to support partner, use free hand in sculling motion.
(b) Support partner by placing one hand under his feet.
(c) Support partner by using one hand and arm in chin level. (See DRILL #3). Tow slowly ahead or in circles, swimming gently.
(d) Support partner by grasping one arm of victim between elbow and shoulder. Tread water or swim slowly in circles, using frog, vertical scissor or horizontal scissor.

(20) Release from Front Strangle (A)

Form the men in a single rank on the deck. Count off by Two's. Have Number One's take one step forward; about face, and line up facing Number Two's. In-

PLATE 149. *Land Drill for Front Strangle Hold*

struct the men that they will perform the drill according to whistle and accompanying verbal command. They will hold each position until the whistle blows again.

Whistle—"Strangle"	Number One's apply strangle hold to Number Two's, with head over left shoulder of the Number Two's.
Whistle—"Prepare to Break"	Number Two's place *left* palm against *left* side of partner's face, and grip partner's left elbow with right hand.
Whistle—"Duck and Turn"	Push to the *left* with the *left* hand, duck head and turn own face to the *left;* push upward and over back of own head with right hand. Turn partner into an about face position.
Whistle—"Bring Hand to Chin"	Retain grip on partner's elbow. Bring other hand from position against partner's face, under his arm, over the top of the shoulder of that arm, take chin level position. (See DRILL #3)
Whistle—"Release and Tow"	Release grip on the elbow; retain grip on the chin; Tow, using frog, vertical scissor or horizontal scissor kick.

Repeat the drill, with Number One placing his head over the right shoulder of Number Two.

Repeat in deep water. Form the men so that the Number Two's have their back to the bulkhead, gripping the bulkhead; Number One's in line in the water, facing

Number Two's two feet away. When Number One applies the hold, the Number Two's let go of the bulkhead, sink under water and perform the break.

(21) Release from Front Strangle (B)

Form the men as in DRILL #20 (A). Have them perform according to command and instruction:

Whistle—"Strangle"   Number One's apply strangle hold to Number Two's.

Whistle—"Prepare to Break"   Number Two's bend knees, place hands against hips of partner, draw forehead down chest of partner.

Whistle—"Break and Turn"   Complete ducking action, continue pressure against hips; spin partner around by pushing with one hand and pulling with the other. Shift hands from front of hips to back of hips. (Partner now has back to you.)

Whistle—"Level and Tow"   Assume rear approach position described in DRILL #3, level and tow.

(22) Release from Back Strangle

Form the men in a single rank on the deck. Count off by Two's. Have Number One's take one step forward; Number Two's line up behind Number One's.

Whistle—"Strangle"   Number Two's apply strangle hold around neck of Number One's from behind, with *left* hand uppermost.

PLATE 150. *Land Drill for Back Strangle Hold*

Whistle—"Prepare to Break"	Reach upward with left hand and grasp partner's left elbow. Reach upward with right hand and grasp partner's left wrist as though shaking hands with it.
Whistle—"Duck and Turn"	Pull downward with the right hand; push upward with the left hand; duck and turn head to the *right*. Pull partner's left hand around behind his back; press downward and against partner's back to push partner's feet away. Retain grips on both elbow and wrist.
Whistle—"Bring Hand to Chin"	Release the grip on partner's elbow and take hold of his chin with that hand. Retain grip on partner's wrist.
Whistle—"Release and Tow"	Release the grip on the wrist, level partner and tow.

Repeat in deep water. Form the men in the water, with Number One's facing and gripping the bulkhead with both hands. Number Two's apply rear strangles. Number One's let go of bulkhead, submerge and perform the release.

(23) Release from Double Grip on Wrist

Form the men as prescribed in DRILL #20.

Whistle—"Take Grip"	Number Two extends his left wrist and Number One grasps it with both hands.
Whistle—"Prepare to Break"	Number Two extends his *right* arm across to shake hands with the *right* wrist of partner. Pressing down, he forces partner to knees. He places his *right* foot against partner's *left* shoulder.
Whistle—"Break and Turn"	Pull with the right hand, press (not kick) strongly against partner's shoulder with the foot; retain grip on wrist.
Whistle—"Level and Tow"	This is now the position of the front surface approach and the same techniques are employed (See DRILL #4).

(24) Separating Two People

Form swimmers in groups of three. Indicate which will be clasped in a double front strangle hold, and which one will be the rescuer. Instruct the men that the technique to be followed is:

(a) Swim up to the two persons in strangle grip.
(b) Select the person to be rescued; do a handstand on his shoulders, to force both persons under water.
(c) Spread legs as for a frog kick, swing one leg around and forward, and place the foot on the shoulder of the person not to be rescued.
(d) Shift hands from the shoulders to the chin of the person to be rescued.
(e) Straighten the legs, pushing with the feet against the shoulders of the person not to be rescued.
   Retain grip on chin of other person.
(f) When the two persons have been separated, begin the carry. If the person left behind is a swimmer, he will be able to reach safety by himself.

Drill by sending two men into deep water and require the third man to perform the rescue. Each of the three has a chance to act as rescuer.

PLATE 151. *Group Instruction: Obtain Hold Before "Victim" Lets Go of Scupper*

ARTIFICIAL RESPIRATION

The purpose of the respiratory system of man is to supply oxygen to the body tissues and to remove the products resulting from the combustion of that oxygen. The rate of respiration is determined by the respiratory center of the brain which increases or decreases the frequency of inspiration according to the degree to which carbon dioxide is present in the blood. Cessation of the process for an extended time makes death inevitable.

The lungs themselves have no contractile power. It is the respiratory muscles which cause inspiration and expiration. The heart of a person submerged under water will continue to beat, the blood will circulate, but the respiratory muscles will become paralyzed because of the continued accumulation of waste products. Hence, when the submerged person is brought from the water, the muscles cannot resume their normal function. It only remains, therefore, for some artificial means to be employed to remove some of the waste products and to stimulate the respiratory muscles to involuntary action. Such a method must simulate normal breathing as nearly as is possible; must be in the same manner and tempo and must bring about the same systemic effects.

Mouth-to-Mouth Method of Resuscitation

Mouth-to-mouth rescuscitation has been proved to be far more effective than manual methods of artificial respiration. It moves a larger amount of air in and out of the lungs. It is easily learned. It has saved many lives in actual emergency. This method should be used in reviving all unconscious and non-breathing victims of drowning, electric shock, smoke or gas inhalation, drug or chemical poisoning, injuries to chest, head, neck, and abdomen. It helps prevent asphyxia by maintaining an open air passageway in victims who are unconscious but still breathing.

Step 1. Clean the throat if necessary. Place victim on his back (face up). If foreign matter is in mouth, turn head to one side, force mouth open and wipe throat clean with fingers or piece of cloth. Make certain tongue is not pushed back into throat.

Step 2. Start breathing process immediately. Insert thumb between victim's teeth, hold jaw upward so head is tilted backwards. Close his nostrils with other hand. Take a deep breath and place your mouth tightly over victim's mouth and your own thumb, blow hard enough to make his chest expand. When the chest moves, take your mouth off to let him exhale passively. Repeat about every 4 seconds.

This process must be continued until the victim breathes naturally or until a physician pronounces him dead. Rescuer must remain at victim's head during transportation in order to keep the air passageway open, and to start mouth-to-mouth breathing at once if natural breathing stops.

Back Pressure—Arm Lift Method of Artificial Respiration

1. Position of the subject

Place the subject in the face down, prone position. Bend his elbows and place the hands one upon the other. Turn his face to one side, placing the cheek upon his hands.

2. Position of the operator

Kneel on either the right or left knee at the head of the subject facing him. Place the knee at the side of the subject's head close to the forearm. Place the opposite foot near the elbow. If it is more comfortable, kneel on both knees, one on either side of the subject's head. Place your hands upon the flat of the subjects back in such a way that the heels lie just below a line running between the armpits. With the tips of the thumbs just touching, spread the fingers downward and outward.

3. *Compression phase*

Rock forward until the arms are approximately vertical and allow the weight of the upper part of your body to exert slow, steady, even pressure downward upon the hands. This forces air out of the lungs. Your elbows should be kept straight and the pressure exerted almost directly downward on the back.

4. *Position for expansion phase*

Release the pressure, avoiding a final thrust, and commence to rock slowly backward. Place your hands upon the subject's arms just above his elbows.

5. *Expansion phase*

Draw his arms upward and toward you. Apply just enough lift to feel resistance and tension at the subject's shoulders. Do not bend your elbows, and as you rock backward the subject's arms will be drawn toward you. Then lower the arms to the ground. This completes the full cycle. The arm lift expands the chest by pulling on the chest muscles, arching the back, and relieving the weight on the chest.

The cycle should be repeated 12 times per minute at a steady, uniform rate. The compression and expansion phases should occupy about equal time; the release periods being of minimum duration.

6. *Additional related directions:*

It is all important that artificial respiration, when needed, be started quickly. There should be a slight inclination of the body in such a way that fluid drains better from the respiratory passage. The head of the subject should be extended, not flexed forward, and the chin should not sag lest obstruction of the respiratory passages occur. A check should be made to ascertain that the tongue or foreign objects are not obstructing the passages. These aspects can be cared for when placing the subject into position or shortly thereafter, between cycles. A smooth rhythm in performing artificial respiration is desirable, but split-second timing is not essential. Shock should receive adequate attention, and the subject should remain recumbent after resuscitation until seen by a physician or until recovery seems assured.

CHAPTER XIII

Survival at Sea

Men who go to war at sea, whether in submarines, ships, or aircraft, must be trained in survival at sea. Their knowledge of what to do must be complete, and their training must be so thorough that their reactions in time of emergency are instantaneous, for disaster at sea seldom allows its victims a second chance. When a plane ditches, a destroyer blows up, or a transport burns, those who survive will be those who know what to do and do it. Danger, at sea, comes not only from the enemy. The sea itself is dangerous, as is, in fact, all water when men must enter it in times of emergency or stress. The skill of learning how to survive at sea is not limited to crews of Navy, Coast Guard, or Merchant Marine ships which have been bombed, torpedoed, or set on fire by enemy attack. Navy, Air Force and commercial flyers may be forced down, or shot down at sea, and once in the water they face the same problems as shipwrecked sailors. Army and Marine troops, hitting an invasion beach in an amphibious landing, crossing a river in enemy territory, or scouting through a treacherous swamp, may also face the same problems. Those men who have learned how to swim, and keep their heads in an emergency, will have the best chance of survival.

ABANDONING SHIP

The deck of a transport will probably be crowded but in days of quiet sailing following embarkation, a man may devote some of his time to an unofficial examination of the life-boats. He should know that they are seaworthy, that the davits are not corroded and are well greased, that the tackle is in good condition and that extreme cold has not frozen the grease around movable parts. The lifeboats should be fully equipped with oars, oarlocks, steering oar, sail, edible emergency rations, fresh water, medical supplies, waterproof flashlights with good batteries, a flare pistol, fish lines, fish hooks, a knife and a means of catching rainwater. If all is not as it should be, the facts should be made known to the proper person so that necessary repairs and replacements may be made immediately.

The life rafts and rubber boats may also be checked but due to the fact that the equipment is so compactly stowed, thorough examination should be performed only by the person whose duty it is to do so. Life rafts are now equipped with dehydrated bait, assorted hook and line rigs, a collapsible fish net, a fish spear, a corrosion-resistant knife which will float, gloves, radio, and sail. Every man assigned to a life-boat should memorize the location of it, should be able to reach

PLATE 152. *Proper Training Saves Lives*

it in smoke or pitch darkness and should ascertain how many of the others also assigned to the boat are skilled in the handling of it. Whenever a life raft is lowered it should have a line attached to it to prevent it from striking men in the water and to keep it from being carried beyond reach.

Every officer and man aboard a transport or warship should have learned the plan of the ship. He must know an exit from every spot where he may be.

He should make a mental tabulation of all of the possible means to escape. He should note life boats, life rafts, rubber boats, timbers lashed to the rails or freeboard, knotted lines and cargo nets. He should be prepared with an alternate course of action for every emergency. Warships under battle conditions will, of course, be stripped, therefore life-boats are not to be considered as the only means of escape. His choice may lie between line, cargo net and jumping.

He should next begin to assemble items to be taken with him in case of an emergency. A jacknife may be used to cut twine, to section fish so that the liquid may be wrung out of the pieces, and to assist in the removal of clothing. A pair of gloves will protect his hands if he must go down a line into the water, a precaution many times more important if his hands should chance to be burned by fire or powder. A white hat will help to attract the attention of rescue planes and ships. A piece of cotton or lambs' wool in the ears may prevent the rupture of eardrums

(a) "Mae West"

(b) Inflated Belt

(c) Kapok Jacket

PLATE 153. *Life Jackets Which Bring Them Back Alive*

by the concussion of gunfire. A whistle will attract the attention of rescue ships at night and in fog, and will help men to gather in groups.

Clothing will be important to him for several reasons. It provides vitally needed warmth when adrift in a boat in cold air temperatures and when shore is reached. It will hold in his body heat while he is immersed in the water and will give protection against burning oil or gasoline on the surface of the water. It affords a shield from the burning rays of the sun. It provides a means of support in the water. It will make him less visible to sharks. Some experienced seamen recommend that heavy woolen underwear be constantly worn by men who will leave a ship by life boat or equipped with life jacket. Think carefully before discarding shoes. They may be needed later to protect against coral cuts and "immersion foot."

The life jacket cannot be considered a flawless article of equipment. There is extreme possibility of injury to any officer or man who is equipped and forced to jump from any appreciable height. Jackets not provided with a crotch strap may turn inside out and cover the face and head of the jumper. If the collar or top strings have been tied, they may become tightened and choke the jumper as he submerges. The waist type jacket tends to form in a roll high on the chest and to numb the arms. Cork jackets must not be worn if a jump from a height is necessary, for upon impact with the water the jacket will strike the chin with a force sufficient to break the neck or both arms. Cork preservers may cause a non-swimmer or an unconscious person to float in the water feet uppermost; incidents in which this has happened have been recorded. The kapok jacket, unless especially treated, is inflammable and to wear it in burning oil or gasoline would be dangerous. The newest equipment has been made flame-proof. The officer or man wearing a life jacket will find it difficult to board a rubber boat or to climb a line to the deck of a rescue ship.

It is important that the jacket be inspected for the presence of holes and worn spots. It may have been partially burned, punctured by bullets or ripped by shrapnel or splinters or long exposure to weather may have rotted the fabric. The zippers may become rusted.

Despite these disadvantages and despite the precautions which must be taken, the life jacket is a valuable aid. It is protection against shrapnel, it greatly lessens the concussion effect of underwater explosions, it helps to conserve body heat and it is a means of support in the water. Insofar as the unconscious person or the non-swimmer is concerned, it may be the only means of support.

When the ship has been hit, there are a number of definite steps that should be taken by any officer or man. The exit route should be followed according to plan and when he is topside he should quickly take the best inventory he can of existing conditions. He should note the state of the sea, the presence of oil or flame, the motion of the ship, the location of debris in the water, the direction of the nearest raft or rescue ship, and the location of powder cans and similar available floats.

He should hasten to his assigned station and await orders. Above all, he must not abandon ship until the order to do so has been given or until it is obvious that communications have been disrupted and this step must be taken. One Pharmacist's Mate had time to evacuate the wounded between the time that the U.S.S. *Vincennes* received a direct hit and the time he was ordered to abandon ship. Only two were lost of more than 4,000 aboard the *President Coolidge*. Many sup-

PLATE 154. *Disembarking with Full Equipment*

posedly stricken craft have stayed afloat for hours and even for days. No one can say for just how long a vessel will stay afloat. This will depend upon the nature of the damage. The U.S.S. *Juneau* sank in seven and one-half seconds and the six or seven men who were blown into the water by the explosion were the only ones who survived.

There is a second reason why the ship should not be abandoned prematurely. Before that order is given, planes and debris and guns are jettisoned over the sides. When it is apparent that all hands must take to the water, a crew of men to whom the task has been assigned will throw overboard all timbers, boards and floats of any kind, which might kill men already in the water.

When the order to abandon ship is given, the officers and men will leave in boats, or by means of lines and cargo nets. **Jump only if absolutely necessary.** Diving is a rash procedure, for if a man strikes his head upon a piece of floating debris his chances of survival are slim. If the height is great and the nets and lines are short, he must go down the knotted line to its end and then drop. The poor swimmer should abandon ship by line and be equipped with a life jacket.

Remember these rules:

1—The Master of the ship and his officers have spent years at sea. They are best able to issue orders to crews of lifeboats. Keep your head. Keep quiet. Obey their orders at once.

2—Always dress warmly. Sleep in your clothes. Exposure to sun and cold are some of the greatest dangers faced by men who have been forced to spend long periods in small boats.

3—At all time of the day or night keep your life preserver and a full canteen of water with you. Crushing a kapok life preserver together makes it lose buoyancy but this can be regained by fluffing it up as you would a pillow.

4—The order to "Abandon Ship" does not mean that you should leave the ship. It means you should go to your "Abandon Ship" station to which you are assigned when you come on board.

5—**Jumping overboard is one of the most dangerous things you can do.** If you are wearing a cork or balsa wood life preserver it can break your neck when you hit the water, or you may be caught in the ship's turning propellers.

6—Nets, ladders and lines hang over the sides of ships at all "Abandon

PLATE 155. *Use Hands and Feet; Never Slide*

Ship" stations. Use them to board lifeboats or rafts or to get into the water. Get away from the ship fast.

7—You should act on your own only after the order "every man for himself" has been given, even in extreme emergency. If you must jump, go feet first, clinch your life preserver tight to your body with your arms. Put your hands under your chin to hold the preserver down to lessen the shock when you hit the water.

8—Keep clear of the ship's side. Lifeboats and rafts are unsinkable but both may turn over if not handled properly. Don't get caught between the ship and lifeboat or you may be crushed.

9—When getting into a lifeboat or raft be sure your feet are on the bottom boards. Sit down at once and keep the greatest weight in the center of the boat to keep it from tipping.

10—Set a good example. You know that your actions will influence others, so keep cool and use common sense. Follow the directions of the person whose job it is to get you through in safety.

Use of Lines

1. Wear gloves if possible. Take care not to burn the hands. Salt water will increase the pain, and the blood will attract sharks. 350 men from the *Wasp* burned their hands so badly coming down the lines that hospital care was necessary. A fire hose is another means of descent.

PLATE 156. *Grip Tightly*

PLATE 157. *Cargo Net Drill*

2. Use both hands and feet in ascending and descending. Develop the strength and the skill to enable you to progress rapidly in both directions.
3. Judge the pace of the man below you. Do not crowd him. Make sure the line is knotted at regular intervals. This will make the descent more orderly.
4. Look for men in the water below you before you let go of the line.
5. When in the water after descending, leave the area below the line immediately unless you have a life saving task to perform.
6. When waiting to climb to the deck of a rescue ship, men should not crowd and congregate at the line in numbers. They should take positions to climb in an orderly manner.
7. A loop may be tied in the bottom of a line lowered from the side of a rescue ship. If you are injured, stand in the loop and be drawn aboard.

PLATE 158. *Listen to Your Instructor*

Jumping

1. *IF YOU MUST JUMP,* give thought to all the hazards, methods and cautions.
2. The height may vary between the 87-foot leap some men made from an aircraft carrier, to the two foot step-down necessary to abandon a sinking cruiser.
3. The greater the height, the greater the need for caution. If you jump wearing a chin-strap helmet, your neck will probably be broken.
4. If the jump is a long one and you are able to swim, throw your jacket into the water instead of wearing it. Your gas mask may also be thrown.
5. If there is oil on the water and only a light breeze is blowing, jump to the windward. Do not jump to leeward.
6. Men who jump from the side of a ship that is still in motion may be drawn into the propellers.
7. Don't start the jump by sliding down the side of the ship. Rivets and barnacles are likely to begin a work of mutilation that the sharks will finish. Jump from the lowest deck possible.
8. Make full allowance for the list of the ship. Men on the *Oklahoma* in Pearl Harbor poorly judged the list of the ship and fell onto the deck. Similar accounts are given in the sinking of the *Repulse* and *Prince of Wales*.
9. If it is necessary to jump from the side, jump away from the list. The ship may capsize after you are in the water and pin you beneath it. Moreover, any loose materials will slide off of the sloping deck and may fall upon you.
10. Always consider that portion of the ship that is under water. When jumping

PLATE 159. *Jump Only as a Last Resort*

from the side toward the list or from the side away from the list, it is always possible that you may strike this submerged portion.

11. Before you jump, look into the water below and see that other men are not below you. When once in the water, get away quickly lest some other person jump on you.

12. Jump with good balance. Hit the water feet first. If you strike the water stomach first, you will possibly suffer fatal internal injuries.

PLATE 160. *Jumping Into Burning Oil*

13. Unless other reasons strongly forbid it, you should plan to abandon ship on the side away from the enemy.

14. If you are wearing a waist type jacket and are jumping from a height not exceeding 30 feet, hold the collar and have your elbows against your sides to hold the jacket down.

15. Review in your mind: helmet, jacket, gas mask, oil, fire, wind, waves, tide, screws, barnacles, list, swimmers in the water, other jumpers, balance, the enemy, debris, and closest rescue.

16. Debris may be foe as well as friend. You must realize that swells will so move debris as to deceive you as to its position. White caps may throw debris into an area that was clear an instant before.

17. When jumping from heights greater than 10 feet, keep legs together.

18. When jumping from heights in excess of 10 feet, never hold the arms at right angles to the body. The shoulder bones are broken by the impact and swimming with two broken shoulders is difficult to say the least.

19. The legs should be extended. The feet may be pressed against each other or crossed at the ankles. The latter method will prevent the legs being drawn apart as the open trouser legs catch the water on entry.

20. The hands may be held at the sides, or may grip jacket or clothing at the shoulders, or may be folded across the chest and gripping the jacket.
21. If you must jump into oil or flame, first draw your socks up around the outside of your trouser legs.
22. Keep covered. Avoid sunburn.

After Jumping

1. To regain the surface of the water following a jump entry, various methods may be employed. The dog paddle, side stroke, elementary back stroke or breast stroke may be used.
2. If there is oil or flame present on the surface, first swim underwater, clear the surface by a splashing action with the hands, emerge, breathe, submerge and swim underwater again.
3. Avoid reappearing at the point of entry, come to the surface at some distance away. Others may be jumping to the same spot.
4. Emerge carefully, to avoid debris or some other solid object.
5. Try to emerge in an area not crowded with other men. Some weakend swimmer may grab you before you can take a much needed breath.

PLATE 161. *Know How to Swim Through Fire*

PLATE 162. *Release of One Hook Lowers Raft Ready for Use*

IN THE WATER

While the ship is being abandoned, strong swimmers should stand by to render assistance to the poorer swimmers and to receive the stretcher cases which will be lowered over the side. The wounded must be placed aboard rafts, they must be transported by means of life saving carries to a safe distance, or clothing must be inflated to support them.

All must leave the immediate vicinity of the ship with dispatch. There are eight particular reasons why it is important for one to do so:

1. Suction

PLATE 163. *Side Stroke for Stretcher Carrying*

PLATE 164. *Carrying Patient in Stretcher*

2. Timbers tossed beneath the surface
3. Fumes
4. Enemy shellfire
5. Underwater explosions
6. Oil and flame
7. Jumping men
8. Falling debris

The degree of suction created by a sinking ship is highly variable, and will depend upon the size of the ship, the rapidity with which the sinking takes place, the buoyancy of the cargo and the degree to which the ship has been flooded. One seaman who jumped 15 feet from a battleship by day felt no suction. Another, who abandoned ship by way of a porthole one-half an inch above the water, did feel a definite drawing force as his ship went down. Still another seaman reported that he was on a destroyer that sank in seven minutes. He felt the suction from a distance of 100 feet even though the ship was well flooded. In most cases a distance of 150 feet will suffice for safety but this must not be regarded as a satisfactory minimum.

The second danger lies in the return to the surface of boats, timbers and other buoyant objects that have broken loose from the submerged ship. Occasionally these pieces will fly 30 or 40 feet into the air, becoming a deadly missile as they ascend through the surface and as they fall.

Fumes are the third danger to be avoided. They may be created by exploding torpedoes and bombs, by the shellfire of the enemy or by burning paint. Poison gas is always a possibility.

The enemy shellfire itself, with the accompanying shrapnel bursts, constitutes a fourth danger from which to escape. The ship is a target and to remain with it is to remain in the line of fire.

The fifth danger is termed "immersion blast injury." This refers to the crushing power of an underwater concussion caused by an exploding depth charge, torpedo or bomb. Continued bombing of the *Hornet* is known to have killed several men

PLATE 165. *Hoisting Stretcher Aboard Ship*

in the water. Depth charges are a constant hazard, because, if set, they will explode as a ship sinks. Some men have been affected only by a temporary paralysis of the legs, others have died immediately, and some have been rescued only to collapse several minutes later.

From immersion blast injury studies, the following tentative conclusions have been drawn: the best swimming position is that of the elementary back stroke with feet at right angles to the source of explosion. To tread water with the back to the blast is less dangerous than it is to tread water while facing the concussion center. The side stroke swimmer experiences greater injury to that side which is immersed. Tension of the stomach muscles and buttocks at the moment of the explosion will result in less injury than if the muscles are relaxed. The kapok life jacket provides definite protection against the blast.

Oil and flame present a sixth hazard. Fuel oil is poisonous if swallowed.

Fire is to be avoided if possible, for men have not only been severely burned but have suffocated for lack of oxygen or have seared their lungs by inhaling the flames.

The seventh danger arises from the ever present possibility that those who remain close to the ship may be seriously or fatally injured by other men who jump upon them.

The final reasons that dictate that open water should be reached as quickly as possible are these: Loose debris will slide and fall overboard as the list becomes more pronounced and later the ship itself may capsize. Moreover, explosions aboard the craft may blow heavy materials into the air, some of which will fall into the water.

First Dangers After Abandoning Ship

1. Your first concern is to avoid debris and suction.
2. Your second concern is to avoid objects that may break loose from the ship after it submerges.
3. Keep swimming until you have reached a point where no injury is possible.
4. Get away from fumes of explosives and fire.
5. If there is danger of underwater explosion, swim on your back with feet at right angles to source of explosion.
6. If there is a thin layer of oil on the water, swim through it using a sweeping breast stroke, with feet low and head high. Form a line with five or more men. If the layer of oil is thick, deflate your life jacket and swim underwater, surge perpendicularly from the water, take a breath and submerge again.
7. If there is flame on the surface, do as follows. If the flames are no more than two or three feet high, you may swim through the fire using a sweeping breast stroke. Form single or double columns of five or more men if possible. If the flames are high, you must discard your life jacket and swim underwater, splash the flames away before emerging, surge as high as possible into the air, breathe, submerge and swim underwater again. Judgment must be exercised while swimming underwater in order that the best spot be chosen for emersion. By day, the clear and lighter areas can be seen. At night the darkest spots will be chosen for emersion. A hat and other clothing will afford protection. Remember to swim into wind.
8. Get quickly away from the ship to avoid other men who will be jumping. There is a possibility that the craft may capsize, loose objects may slide from the decks and debris be blown into the air by explosions. Get out of the line of enemy fire.

Awaiting Rescue

The man who has managed to get clear of a sinking ship must prepare himself for a long siege in the water. He should remain in the vicinity because rescue ships or planes will come to this spot if the sinking is known. He should assemble with others to form groups in order that morale may be sustained and rescue made more probable. He must steel himself to face the possibility that help may not come for many hours.

In the meantime he will be confronted with difficulties. Cold is a factor which must be considered. The temperatures of Alaskan and North Atlantic waters definitely limit the time in which a person may remain immersed. The cold water of the Aleutians has caused several men to contract pneumonia. One seaman reported that although the water of the South Pacific at first felt warm, after six hours he felt the cold more than he did the pain of his wounds.

An immediate attempt should be made to reach articles of debris which will provide support, preferably those which are not only buoyant at the moment of discovery but promise to remain so for some time. A large object is more desirable than a small one, but it is not necessary for the piece to be large enough to permit a person to climb upon it.

The secret lies in the manner in which the debris is used. Only a minimum of pressure must be put upon it. The water will perform the major part of the task of keeping a man on the surface. He needs only to place his hands on the debris and press down just enough to maintain his floating position.

The possibility of the handicap of wounds or cramps always exists. If this is the case, the swimmer must select the stroke which is least painful and will permit the greatest rest and relaxation. A man with cramps will need to assume a floating or back stroke position that will enable him to breathe freely and to massage the affected muscles.

Knowledge of the techniques of clothing inflation not only will substitute for the use of debris for support but also will be an invaluable aid to the individual afflicted with cramps or wounds. Almost every article of clothing can be utilized, and because these articles have so many advantages, it is also important to be able to swim while wearing them.

The ability to swim with limited equipment is desirable. It may be necessary to retain possession of these articles. The person who employs the wrong methods may find the task an impossible one. The most essential fact to learn is that most of these articles need not be a burden for their buoyant properties can be used to provide support to the swimmer.

There is another danger which may be faced: strafing by enemy airmen.

Each man in the water must select the strokes he will use in accordance with his abilities and needs. The elementary back stroke is preferable if the water is smooth. In rough water the breast stroke is a good choice. Some men have found that the spray in choppy seas has made breathing difficult and have employed a side stroke with the face turned to leeward. An overhand stroke should be used when the swimmer must get away from a sinking ship or when he must use speed to escape other dangers.

Use of Debris for Support

1. Before you leave the ship, look for the location of debris that may provide support or be dangerous in collision.
2. If there is a wind, go after debris to the windward. Debris to the leeward may be blown away faster than you can swim.
3. When the debris is captured, tie your jacket to it so that you will be able to submerge if strafed. Remove your shoes and tie them to the debris also. You will need them if you reach shore.
4. The debris need not be large in size to support you. Do not try to climb up on it. Let the water hold you up.

Relief of Wounds or Cramps

1. Select the stroke that permits greatest immobilization of the injured or cramped part.
2. Elementary back stroke will be the best selection if the water is smooth. The arms alone may be used in breast stroke, sculling, finning, elementary backstroke or treading. The side stroke position will permit one arm to be trailed by the side.

PLATE 166. *Floating Debris Gives Welcome Support*

3. Relief from cramps may be obtained by a position permitting relaxation and massage.
4. Cramps in the extremities may be caused by cold or fatigue. Massage stimulates circulation.

Clothing as a Life Preserver

1. Almost any article of clothing can be used for a homemade life preserver.
2. Every man should be able to swim on the surface or underwater while clothed.
3. Pillow slips, mattress covers, night shirts, pith helmets, sea bags and bed sheets may be used in a similar manner. These should be kept wet.
4. Apply the least pressure necessary and the article will hold air for a longer time. Do not attempt to climb up on this improvised support.
5. Mattresses, covered powder cans, inverted pails, hot water bottles, canteens or similar objects also may be used to provide artificial support. One swimmer, with one inflated knapsack held under each arm, can support two or three other persons.
6. When an air pocket or bubble is to be captured with a sheet, shirt or similar open cloth, the article must be gently dropped on the water and the ends must be drawn together without the application of any downward pull until all edges have been secured.

PLATE 167. *Nine on a Mattress Cover*

Ways a Man Uses Clothing to Survive

1. He jumps into the water, catching an air bubble in his shirt.
2. He inflates his garrison cap by placing his thumbs on the inside of the cap at the ends, holding the cap by pressure of the thumbs from inside and the fingers from outside. He draws the cap down on the water, catches a bubble inside of the cap, and lies in a back float position.
3. He inflates his own shirt by tucking the outside of his collar inside. He buttons all buttons, tucks shirt tails into the trousers leaving room for air pocket. He creates an air pocket at the shoulders by taking a breath, bending forward into a tuck or turtle float, and blowing into the opening between two front buttons. He must bend forward until his face is below the opening.
4. He inflates the shirt of a shipmate by taking a breath, grasping the shirt sleeve of his shipmate with thumbs and forefingers, submerging, and blowing up through the open end of the sleeve.
5. He removes his shirt by lying in a back float position to unfasten the buttons and to shake the shirt down the lowered arms.
6. He inflates his removed shirt by dropping it gently on the water, catching an air pocket. He carefully gathers all edges together. When all edges are secured, he uses this captured bubble for support.
7. He may remove his shirt and inflate it by tying the sleeve ends together and looping them over the neck so that the shirt buttons are against his chest. He then draws the rear tail under the shirt and up toward the front buttons. The side tails are drawn around his body and tied in apron fashion at his back. He inflates this improvised lifejacket by blowing through the collar.
8. He inflates the sleeves of his shirt by the following method: A knot is tied in the end of each shirt sleeve and the sleeves are then inflated by drawing the shirt down on the water or by blowing into the sleeve at the shoulder.

(a) Garrison Caps Have Flotation Value

(b) Lie on Back to Remove Clothing

(c) Inflate Shirt and Trousers

(d) Wait for Help

PLATE 168. *Clothing for Support*

9. The shirt can be removed and put on backwards. Both hands grasp the tail of the shirt, lift it above water and quickly draw it down. Lean back into a float position to prevent the air from leaking out by way of the collar.
10. He removes both of his shoes by taking a breath, assuming a tuck or turtle float position, and reaching to the feet with the hands.
11. He unbuttons his trousers and removes them slowly. He will gently shake his legs to cause the trousers to slip off. He must be sure that the trousers are not in a tangle after removal.
12. He inflates his trousers in the following manner: secure all buttons; tie a single knot in the end of each trouser leg. Insert hands inside the waist with palms turned inward. Trap an air pocket by drawing the trouser waist down on the water surface.
13. He may inflate his removed trousers by blowing in through the open waist. He will find this easier to do if he submerges first.
14. He may inflate his trousers by untying one leg, and blowing through this opening to inflate both legs, being careful to re-tie the open leg.
15. He may inflate his trousers in this way: Hold the trouser by the waist in the left hand. Plunge the right hand underwater and under the held waist. This action will force air bubbles underwater, which rise to the surface and are trapped in the waist. This procedure is commonly called "fanning."
16. He may inflate his trousers by holding one side of the trouser waist against his forehead as he jumps from the gunnel.
17. He captures an air bubble with pillow slip, inverted metal waste basket, or a sheet.
18. Men are arranged in groups of four. One is the victim, the others his rescuers. They will help the victim in two ways:
    a. The three rescuers will inflate the clothing of the victim by blowing into his shirt sleeves and up his trouser legs.
    b. Each rescuer will remove his trousers, tie knots in the ends of the legs and inflate them. Each will place the float he has created under the victim; one at the neck, one under the hips and one under the ankles. The three rescuers will then transport the victim for a specified distance.

Swimming with Equipment

1. If the equipment can be carried underwater, consideration should be given to the possibility that its buoyant qualities may be utilized to advantage.
2. After three or four hours in the water, equipment will probably lose its buoyant properties unless permitted to remain floating on the water surface.

Dangers from Strafing

1. Men in groups must scatter when an enemy plane approaches. Men swimming alone are difficult targets.
2. If you must swim on the surface, swim at a right angle to the flight of the strafing plane. Get out of the line of fire.
3. To avoid discovery, hold a cushion, pail or piece of driftwood over your head.
4. The best defense is to surface dive to a depth of three or four feet. When you emerge, be ready to go down again immediately, if necessary.

5. Men clinging to a life raft or rubber boat may attract an enemy flier. Submerge under the boat but be sure that you retain a grip on a line attached
to the boat.

ABANDONING PLANE OR DITCHING

Certain types of planes sink more rapidly than others. Some aircraft are so constructed that escape is difficult.

Practice in ditching routine must be taken many times before the plane leaves
the ground.

Proper preparation for ditching requirer:
1. That ground crews should inspect the rescue gear furnished with planes.
2. That pilots and air crews inspect their gear as a check on the above.
3. That pilots and airmen learn and practice dunking drill.

No equipment, however efficient, and no instructions, however thorough, guarantee success. Drill and inspection are the master keys to safety.

DITCHING CHECK-OFF LIST

1. Is raft in good condition?
2. Is charger bottle full?
3. Does raft contain:
   Whistle.
   Metal reflector.
   25 feet of 75-pound test line.
   Jacknife.
   Combination compass and waterproof match container—are matches in it?
   Fishing kit.
   Smoke grenade holding clamp.
   Patching material.
   Rubber cement.
   Roughing tool.
   Pliers.
   Scissors.
   Six leak plugs.
   Hand pump for keeping up air pressure.
   Jointed oars.
   Sail fabric.
   First aid kit.
   One package emergency rations per man.
   Two 12-ounce cans of emergency water per man.
   Two H-C smoke grenades.
   One can fluorescein dye.
4. Check for unauthorized gear that might prevent raft from inflating properly
5. Are life lines clear so they will not foul when raft inflates?
6. Are automatic and manual releases in proper condition?
7. DO YOU KNOW YOUR DRILL?

Abandoning Parachute

Each aviator will probably have a life jacket or a pack type of small raft that
must also be made buoyant.

PLATE 169. *Water Landing. At Contact with Water, Straighten Body Arms Overhead, Slide Out of Harness*

This raft will be in a container, which in turn is attached to the "D ring" of the life jacket by a light, 1-inch webbing. This is done so that when he gets out of the harness as soon as he touches the water, he won't find the 'chute is being blown surely and steadily away from him, carrying the raft with it!

Also attached to the life jacket will be a dye sea-marking device, consisting of three ounces of fluorescein dye powder packed in a waterproof fabric container. This supplements the marker now provided for life rafts, and colors the water a yellow green, visible for eight miles at 5,000 feet altitude. Ripping off the tape on the bottom of the package, after the flier is in the water with the jacket inflated, releases the dye—which is visible for about two hours. Consequently, if a water landing takes place at night or under adverse weather conditions, don't release dye at once—wait until the dye will be of the most value to any searching crew.

Abandoning Plane, Ditching or Dunking Skills

1. Plan. Practice. Drill. These are essential to perfection and to safety. There is no time to do your planning after the landing. Practice and drill not only will perfect your movements and procedures but also will acquaint you with the fact that the actual differs from the theoretical.

2. Check all ditching equipment before taking off. You may have to abandon your plane in fog, snow, rain or darkness.

3. Know every article that you may or will need and where it is stowed aboard the plane. Be sure that you can reach all items quickly.

4. Follow the directions given by your flight instructor relative to safety belt and position to be taken when crash is imminent.
5. Get clear of the plane. The tail will usually be the last part to sink. Get out of the cockpit, so that you are not in the plane if it suddenly plunges beneath the surface.
6. Do not inflate your life jacket until clear of the plane.
7. Take with you water, food, navigating instruments, signal devices and valuable papers and charts.

Boat and Raft Skills

1. Inflate the rubber boat as judgment directs. Do not inflate it if strafing is imminent, or if fire is present.
2. Know where rubber boat is stowed, if it can be reached from the outside, and if the boat is attached to the plane by a painter.
3. Secure the raft to you by a light line before launching it. Use the charged cylinders to inflate the boat. Be prepared to inflate it by hand if necessary.
4. Launch the boat to the windward side unless there are sharp edges on the plane that may puncture the rubber. If the lee side is glassy smooth, use the same procedure.
5. If the raft has become fouled, only one man should get into the water to free it. The line between the man and the raft must be tied.
6. Be cautious about inflating the boat if the plane is sinking rapidly. The boat may become fouled with the plane. Loose pieces of debris released underwater as the plane sinks may puncture the boat from below.
7. Don't discard your other gear. Keep your life jacket, clothing and 'chute. The 'chute may be utilized as an effective sea anchor and a means by which rain may be caught, or as a sun shade and a sail.
8. Lash all loose equipment. Most of it is so made that it will float but it still may be blown away if the boat capsizes.
9. Step lightly into the rubber boat. Distribute the weight in the boat. Take special care that your shoes do not tear the fabric.
10. Make an appraisal of the situation and determine upon a course of action. If it appears probable that the plane is going to stay afloat, secure the boat to it with a light line that will break if the plane suddenly sinks.
11. If there is more than one man aboard the boat, each should stand watch. It will be his task to keep up a search for ships, planes, submarines, or land, to note tides and currents, to anticipate changes in the weather and to note and repair leaks.
12. Gear usually is provided to enable you to fish. The catch, cut into small squares, may be put in a piece of cloth and squeezed to provide water.
13. If only your rubber jacket is available do not inflate it until you are in the water. If strafing is likely, do not inflate until the hostile planes have left.
14. The rubber pads from the parachute and the mattress and canteens from the plane will make good artificial float supports.
15. If any enemy plane approaches, cover the boat with the dark side of the sail.
16. Take precautions against sunburn. Keep on your clothes, rig a shade with parachute or sail.

(a) *Inflation of Life Raft. Pull Locking Pen—Turn Handle of CO₂ Bottle Counter Clockwise*

(b) *Boarding Raft. Grasp Hand Grips; Kick, an Pull Body Over Small End of Raft*

PLATE 170. *Rubber Life Boat*

(c) *Retrieve Raft Container. Procure Emergency Equipment at Once*

(d) *All Buttoned Up. Wear Jacket Inflated at All Times. Sea Marker Pack Is Worn Ready for Instant Use*

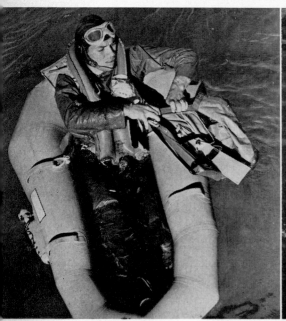

17. If a rubber boat has been capsized it can be righted in the following ways:
    a. Push down on the lee life line, reach over and grasp the weather life line. Lean backward and pull the boat toward you.
    b. Tie a line or piece of clothing to the life line on one side of the boat. Turn the boat around in the water, drawing the attached line across the width of the exposed surface of the boat. Lean backward and pull on the attached line, while the toes press against the near side of the boat.
18. To enter a boat properly you will assume a prone floating position on the water, kick your legs and wiggle aboard snake fashion, and roll in.
19. Boarding may also be performed in this way: Tie your wet flying suit or your parachute to the bow. This will help to keep that end from tipping as you enter at the stern.

PLATE 171. *Rubber Boats Are Easily Capsized*

20. To help another flier or a wounded man aboard, get into the water on the windward side, reach across the boat and grasp the hands of the person to be assisted, brace yourself against the boat and draw him aboard, or, get into the boat and draw him aboard in the manner prescribed for drawing a life saving victim onto a pool deck.
21. You must be aware of the possibility of strafing attack. Be ready to submerge to a safe depth and with a line tied to you and the boat. Be ready to capsize the boat, turning the dark side up, as you submerge holding to the life line or to a line attached to the life line.
22. Always keep the raft tied to you whenever you are adrift in heavy seas.
23. Avoid debris or wreckage with sharp edges that will puncture fabric.
24. Be careful in the use of knives or any sharp edged tool.
25. If you must land through surf with a rubber boat, the proper preparation will permit you to take this step with some discomfort but with little danger. If you must remain in the boat, drag all available sea anchor you can devise. If you are able to take to the water, tie a line to yourself and to the boat.

Don't tie a slip knot and don't tie the line to your limbs or around your neck. Do your best to hold a high and level position on the surface. The breakers will cast the boat in and you will be drawn behind. If you must cling to the boat, hold the stern end down and the bow high.

26. If you must get out of the boat don't dive. Be sure you have a line attached to the boat, place hands on sides and drop into the water feet first.

FINAL RESCUE

Considerations Relative to Final Rescue

1. If you are being rescued by plane, make no efforts to reach the plane or to board it until the pilot has maneuvered into position. Men in the water have been killed by the propellers.

2. If you are being rescued by crash boat, hold your position until the boat is maneuvered to you.

3. If you are a member of a group awaiting rescue, neither you nor the others should crowd into a small boat. Someone may be forced 'into the screw and the boat may be capsized. The weak, the wounded, the poor swimmers, and those without life jackets should be taken aboard first. The last to board must be the strongest swimmers. All those in the group should keep away from the boat and move in to board when ordered to do so by the officer in charge.

4. If it is a ship that has come to your rescue, there again will be danger of drifting into or being drawn into the screws. Be prepared to sprint away if it suddenly becomes necessary for the ship to get under way before it rescues you.

SURF, TIDES AND CURRENTS

To every man adrift at sea may come the sight of land. That shore should bring safety and security, but even a friendly beach may cause the death of him who had the battle nearly won. The crushing power of wave against rock is tremendous, the pounding surf may stifle breathing, and currents and tides may fatigue muscles already weary. Grass, kelp and coral will present their individual barriers to keep men from land.

There are ways in which the swimmer may overcome each of the difficulties he may encounter as he nears the shore. Some dangers may become friendly forces if he acquires pertinent skills and knowledge. That acquisition should take place under controlled and favorable circumstances. It should not be delayed until the moment of emergency is at hand.

Considerations Relative to Surf, Tides and Currents

1. Grass may cling to the arms and legs. Don't struggle against it. Gently shake the limbs until the grass floats free.

2. When you are still some distance from shore but in seas sufficiently heavy to cause the waves to break in combers, breast stroke and side stroke will prove to be the best to use. Swim with these waves or follow a diagonal course with the face turned to leeward for breathing. Don't try to resist the waves. The power they possess is often underestimated.

PLATE 172. *Coming in Through Surf, Distribute
Weight Properly*

3. Whenever you must swim into high waves, lower your head and plunge through each comber. Don't try to swim over it.
4. There are three major methods by which you may reach shore through surf:
   a. Swim toward shore while in the trough between waves. Turn and face outward as the next wave reaches you, lower your head and pierce it as it rolls past you. Turn immediately, swim toward shore again.
   b. Swim toward shore while in the trough between waves. Let the next wave pick you up and carry you briefly but as it begins to break you will perform a surface dive and submerge beneath it. If the bottom is smooth, you will set your feet and shove upward and forward in a bobbing action. Repeat until shore is reached.
   c. Utilize a method called "body surfing." Riding high and in a prone float position with feet together and arms at full extension, you will be lifted and cast forward by the breaking crest. You must take note of what lies ahead before starting this run, for you may travel fifty or more yards at a high speed. Experienced body surfers have learned to approximate the moment when they must surface dive to break the ride.
5. The contour of the beach is the factor that determines the nature of the surf, the backwash, the presence or absence of riptides and currents. Gently sloping beaches will cause the heavy surface to be far from shore, and an abruptly sloping beach will cause the breakers to be formed close in and to fall on top of themselves. The farther out the breakers are formed, the greater will be the lift and carry they will provide.
6. Tide must be noted too. The point at which the breakers form will be different for low and high tide. When the tide is coming in, or flowing, the waves may be used to greater advantage. When the tide is ebbing, the backwash slows the force of the incoming waters.
7. The tide may run diagonally to the beach and a current may be formed by

this action. It is unwise to swim against this or any other current. The best procedure is to swim with the current along the beach until it eddies inward, or to swim diagonally with it and across it.

8. Riptides are like rivers in the ocean and are caused by the contour of the bottom. They are bound on both sides by eddies that swing back toward shore. A swimmer should never attempt to fight a riptide. He should swim diagonally with it and to its edge, then swing into the eddy and be carried in toward shore.

9. There will probably be currents where there are rivers, inlets or lagoons. Here you may be required to make a choice. If there are coral reefs present, the opening may be out directly from the valley from which a stream is flowing. You will not want to be in surf breaking over coral reefs, nor will you want to swim against the current. You may be forced to either come through the opening next to the reef rather than through the center, or wait until the tide is running in to carry you against the current. The possible openings in reefs may also be discovered by the action of the breakers; those waves that continue their run toward shore when all others are breaking betray the presence of an area clear of coral.

10. Backwash or "undertow" is simply the receding of the major portion of the water that has been carried in as a breaker. It may be disconcerting because it is moving in the direction that the swimmer does not want to go. Fortunately the water travels in two directions at two levels, and the direction of the flow of the water on the upper level is toward the shore. Therefore, the swimmer who finds himself in the force of the backwash has only to push off bottom, emerge at the surface and go with the breakers in toward shore.

CHAPTER XIV

Pool Facilities and Equipment

Increased interest in swimming in recent years has already resulted in the construction of many fine swimming pools, and many more will be built. In fair weather or foul, day or night, these pools are in use daily as a part in the greatest mass swimming instruction program ever operated. This is a long step from the early days when programs were, of necessity, conducted from a pier, lake front, or ocean beach.

PLATE 173. *Naval Aviation Standard Enclosed Pool (164 4" x 75')*

In conjunction with a swimming pool some additional equipment always adds greatly to the all-round development of swimmers as well as making teaching easier and surroundings more healthful.

A classification which describes an item of equipment as "essential," "semi-essential" or "desirable," has limited application. The degree of necessity for its provision is determined by each individual head coach. He must take into consideration the magnitude of the entire program, the particular skills which must

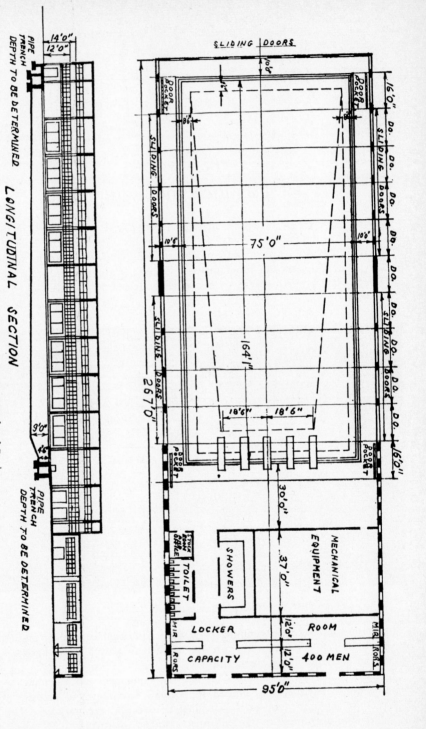

LONGITUDINAL SECTION

FIG. 17. Naval Aviation Standard Enclosed Pool

be taught, type of existing or otherwise available facilities, and the numbers, needs and previous experience of those under instruction.

When a head coach is ordered to take over any swimming program, one of his first actions should be to take a detailed inventory of facilities and equipment, in order that he may adjust schedules, methods and materials of instruction to fit those facilities, in order that he may immediately request any needed items found lacking, and in order that he may have constantly at hand a complete listing in the event that either information or report should be requested of him.

It is for this reason that the following information is presented in a form which may serve as a check list. In taking inventory, the head coach may add his own supplementary comment relative to number, original quality and present condition.

A CHECK LIST FOR FACILITIES AND EQUIPMENT

NOTE: The degree of necessity of various pieces of equipment is shown by the numbers in the column at the right. 1—Essential; 2—Semi-essential; 3—Desirable; 4—Optional. . . . Where the degree of necessity differs between Naval and Civilian use, the Civilian choice will be marked by a bracketed number as [2].

Permanent

Pool (Length dimensions must be accurate to a fraction of an inch)

Size—75′ x 42′ 1
    100′ x 35′ 1
    150′ x 75′ or 164′ x 75′ 2
    2 pools (164′ x 75′) (60′ x 30′) 3
    2 pool (75′ x 42′) and a diving pool (25′ x 42′) .... [2]

Depth—Shallow end: 4-6 feet 1
                   2½-4 feet 1
    Deep end: 10 feet 1
                   12 feet 2
                   14 feet (diving pool) .... [3]

(Civilian pool sizes and depths will differ greatly depending on the age group and the organizations that are being served.)

Shape—Rectangular .... [1] 3
Contour—Spoon or hopper design. 1 ft. drop each 15 ft. 3

Structure—
Concrete tank 1
    Designed to withstand pressure
    Walls plumb and true
    Drainage pipes set
    Consisting of: Reinforced concrete
                 5-ply membrane water-proofing of felt and asphalt
                 Tile lining
Steel tank and Gunite 3
    Welded steel frame
    ¼″ lap welded plates
    2″ lining of gunite cement with reinforced mesh spot-welded to plates

PLATE 174. *Harvard University Pool*

PLATE 175. *A Naval Air Station Outdoor Pool*

Lining—

Gutters level at lip 1
Mortar to be half lime and half cement with water-proofing 2
Cement grout to fill all pockets and joints 1
Face with glazed tile on sides and on ends with the exception of non-slip
    band for facing turns ....[1] 3
Bottom, deck and end of lane to be unglazed tiling 3
Deep gutters around all four sides of the pool 1
Drains connecting with the sewer at 10 ft. intervals 2
Drains equipped with common shut-off valve ....[1] 3
Spit trough on pool deck near gunnel, gutters used only to break waves [1] 3
Recessed with lip protruding beyond gunnel edge 1
Sloped slightly toward drains 1
Designed so no sudden wave will wash contents into pool 1
Impossible for swimmer to catch arm or foot in it 1
Sturdy enough to withstand weight and pull of temporary equipment (lane
    markers, goals, etc.) 1
Rounding, not flat, at lip ....[1] 2
Narrow enough to permit gripping the lip with the hands in water drills
    and racing turns 1
Deep enough so swimmers' fingers cannot reach bottom 1
Depth and contour such that when water is raised over level of gutter, waves
    will break and die ....[1] 2
Wide enough to facilitate cleaning 1
Drains sufficient in size to permit immediate drainage 1

Coping

Width of from 12-16 inches ....[1] 3
Maximum raise of from 2-3 inches above the deck ....[1] 2
Slope of ⅛ inch away from pool 1
Constructed of non-slip tiling ....[1] 3

Decks—

Width along side of pool: 8 feet 1
                     10 feet ....[1] 2
                     15 feet ....[2] 3
Width at ends of pool: 8 feet 1
               10 feet ....[1] 2
               15 feet ....[2] 3
If deck is over 5 feet wide, drain is placed in center (unless spit trough
    alongside of coping) 1
If deck is less than 5 feet wide, slope away from the wall to drain at inside
    edge of coping 1
To be of non-slippery material 1

Ladders—

Recessed into bulkhead. No protruding part 1
Built of tile ....[1] 2

Openings in each step for drainage ....[1] 3
If rungs, reinforce by bars set in concrete 1
Use the scum gutter as one step or rung 1
Hand-rail set in coping. Noncorrosive material 1, 3
Number to be installed:
    Two at shallow end, one at deep end 1
    Two shallow, two deep, two center 3

Outlets—

Located in deepest portion of pool 1
If only one, to be 4 times size of drain pipe 1
Outlets sufficient in size and number to permit pool to be drained in 4 hrs. [1] 2
Outlet openings covered with dark, rust-proof gratings 1
Pipe connections to permit water to be drained to sewer as well as to re-
    circulation system 1

Inlets—

Located to produce uniform circulation of water 1
Located not more than 1 ft. below water line 1
Whether located at 4 corners of the pool, at both ends of the pool, or all
    around the pool 1
Cover with removable grating at least twice the area of the opening 2
Proportioned to supply volume of water required at that point for best
    circulation 1
Inlet opening designed to spread the flow of water in shower or fan rather
    than narrow stream 1

Distance and depth markings—

Depth should be marked at both ends at 5 foot depth and at point of
    greatest depth 1
    With durable paint 1
    With colored inset tile ....[1] 3
Length of pool to be marked at 5 ft. intervals, beginning at shallow end.
    Each foot is marked by a vertical line 1
Finish points for competitive races to be marked. Accompanied by engineer's
    certificate of measurement. Meters and yards. Pin strip ....[1] 2
Mark playing area divisions for water polo ....[1] 2
Mark lanes with 12 inch line down the center of the lane to within 3 feet
    of each end. End line in a T. Continue line on end of bulkhead. Seven
    feet from center of line to center of adjacent lines ....[1] 2

Non-slip band for racing—

Non-slip tile, if tiling is used in rest of pool. May be a strip across end of
    pool, or a patch at end of each lane ....[1] 3

Drinking fountain—

Recessed, or so no possibility of accident 1

Spit receptacles or spittoons—

Recessed. Constant flush 1

Vacuum connections (for suction cleaner)

Non-corrosive material 1
Easily accessible and easily serviced 1

Tunnel around pool—

Five feet minimum head clearance all around the pool. All pool plumbing
accessible. Lighted 1

Underwater portholes—

At sides of deep end 3

Pool enclosure—

An outdoor pool with concrete bulkheads to break the wind, if weather permits
year-round outdoor swimming 3
An indoor or convertible enclosure, if weather does not permit use year-
round 1
Strongly constructed. No draughts 1
Abundance of portholes. Double to prevent condensation of moisture 1, 3
Partially of glass brick (prevent sweating ports) 3
Exits adequate in dimensions and number. (Large enough to bring in portable
equipment) 1

Roof of pool enclosure—

Contour to minimize echo 1
With skylight if adequate illumination not otherwise possible. Double to
prevent sweating 1
Supported by girders and braces to which may be attached ropes, nets, etc. [4] 2
High enough to give 12 foot clearance over 3 meter board 1

Office for coaches—

With large plate glass windows overlooking the pool 1
Vision also over shower and locker rooms 2
Of adequate size for personnel and fixtures 2

Shower rooms—

Adequate in size for peak load 1
Non-slip floor 1
Walls and ceiling waterproofed 2
Impervious surfaced ceiling or similar material 3

Drying room—

Floor space adequate 1
Non-slip 1
Walls and ceiling waterproofed 2

Locker rooms—

Adequate floor space 1
Non-slip 1
If locker arrangement is permanent, lockers to rest on concrete copings. Make
cleaning and disinfecting of floor easier ....[1] 3
Adequate portholes and artificial lighting 1

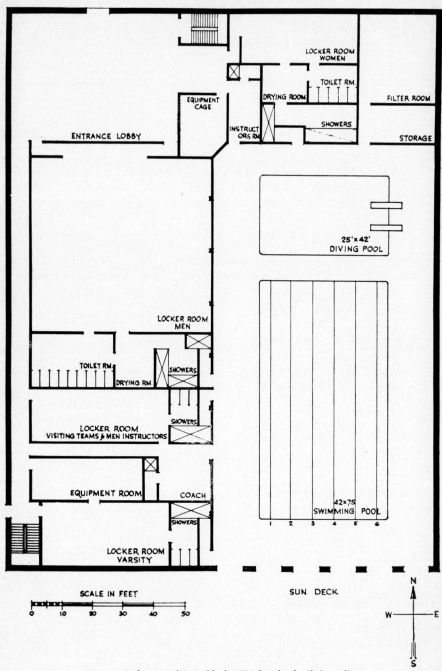

FIG. 18. *Indoor Pool Suitable for High School, Club, College*
(Permanent Bleachers on North and West Sides)

Room for equipment issue and checking—

Adequate in size 1
Located to give vision of shower room, pool, and entrance from outside . . . . [1] 3

Heads—

Adequate in size and in number of fixtures 1
One accessible from locker room and shower 1
Good drainage 1

Bleachers—

Adequate bleachers for one side, or one side and one end, arranged so all may
    see the swimmer in the adjacent lane . . . . [1] 4
Same as above plus available space on opposite side for temporary bleachers [2] 4
Same as above with individual chairs in permanent bleacher section . . . . [3] 4
Of depth and dimensions to prevent any person wearing street shoes to enter
    pool by this route 1

Entrances to pool deck—

Through pool office 1
Via shower and footbath 1
No direct entry from outside or from balcony 1

General over-all plan—

Outside entrances lead to balcony or locker rooms only 1
Double doors at outside entrance 3
Arrangement such that men in bare feet do not walk in same area where
    street shoes have been worn 2

Classroom—

Ventilated, lighted, heated . . . . [4] 1
Equipped with bulletin board, blackboard and motion picture screen . . . . [4] 1
Storage space for charts, etc. . . . . [4] 3

Storerooms—

For janitorial equipment 1
For suction cleaner, wall brush, etc. 1

Underwater portholes 4

Safety—

Depth markings clearly defined 1
Deck and coping non-slip 1
Coping raise is not high enough to cause swimmer to trip 1
Pool contour such that slope is gentle. Not abrupt drop 1
Gutter contour such as to prevent an arm or leg to become caught in it 1
Ladders, drinking fountains, etc., recessed 1
Drainage, gutter contour and over-all plan contributes to best sanitation 1
Shower, locker and drying rooms have non-slip floors 1
Diving boards and jumping towers not set where injury against bulkhead is
    possible 1

Pool depth sufficient for high jumps and dives (fancy) 1
All equipment durable and strong 1
Outlets, drains, etc., of non-corrosive material 1

Miscellaneous—

Sun deck. Enclosed by bulkheads (If pool not outdoor) 3

Semi-permanent

Recirculation and sanitation system—

One centrifugal pump with pressure gauges 1
Sufficient to circulate entire pool volume every 12 hours 1
                            every 8 hours .... [1] 2
Auxiliary pump 3
Hair and lint catcher with pressure gauges. Non-corrosive. Slotted. Possible
   to take down and clean quickly. With by-pass 1
Soda ash dispenser 2
Alum pot 2
Automatic chlorinator .... [1] 2
Filters with pressure gauges 1
Water heater. With inlet and outlet thermometers. Automatic thermal control . 1

Fixtures for floating lane markers—

Recessed into gutters .... [1] 3
Sturdily set in concrete of bulkhead 3
Removable for replacement 3
Of metal or material which will not crystallize 3

Diving fixtures—

Attachments through pool deck to which the diving standards are bolted .. [1] 2
Three meter and one meter .... [1] 2
With adjustable fulcrums .... [1] 3

Jumping tower—

Sturdily built. Solidly fixed .... [4] 1

Bulletin board, blackboard, scoreboard— 2

*Clock—*Electric 1

*Record boards—*Sports program and varsity .... [1] 2

Pool enclosure—

Abundant artificial lighting on bulkheads 2
Plugs and outlets. Numerous. 110 and 220. Serve all areas. For lights, spots,
   phonograph, public address system, etc. .... [1] 2
Seating. Adequate for needs. Semi-permanent or temporary 3

Ceiling—

Acoustical material to deaden sound 2
Attachments for block and tackle, lines, nets 2

Lighting fixtures. Abundant in quantity 1
    Indirect 3

Office for coaches—

Telephone, attachments, light plugs 1
Automatic sanitation alarm 3
Master control switch. All lights 2
Wall hooks for clip boards 1

Shower rooms—

Shower fixtures. Adequate in number and flow 1
Soap holders or dispensers 1

Drying room—

Hooks for towels. Neatly attached to wall 2

Locker rooms—

Lockers. Adequate in number. Some full size 1
Wash basin. Porcelain. Soap tray. Hot and cold water 2
Drinking fountain. Angled stream. Not in gangway 2
Mirrors over wash basin. Also auxiliary mirrors 1

PLATE 176. *Shower Room Interior*

Clock 2
Bulletin board 4' x 8' 1

Equipment and check room—

Bins for stowage of equipment 1
Bin with mesh bottom and drain, for wet suits 1
Shelving for stowage of equipment **2**

Heads—

Head fixtures 1

General over-all plan—

Adequate artificial lighting everywhere 1
    Indirect lighting. No dark spots 3
Adequate ventilation 1
    Air conditioning 3
Adequate heating everywhere 1
    Hot air, in at floor level 3
Public address hookup to entire building 3
Intercommunication system 3
Paint. Bright, durable. The lighter the color the brighter the pool 1

Instruction aids—

Diving pit and tumbling belt .... [3] 4
Blackboards, bulletin boards 2
Rope and cargo net attachments .... [4] 1

Safety—

Hot water radiators to be covered 1
Receptacles to keep soap off of the floor 1
Lighting adequate to prevent accident 1
Sanitation equipment to insure pure water. (Heads, showers, recirculation
    system) 1
Water heated to prevent contraction of colds 1
Solid foundation fixtures for diving and jumping equipment. 1
Electric circuit breaker 3
Sanitation system automatic alarm 3

Temporary or Movable Equipment
Pool—

Colormeter and indicators for alkalinity and chlorine tests 1
Thermometers, to record water and air temperatures 1
Sanitation equipment. Suction cleaner, wall brush, mesh net, mops (swabs),
    pails, hose, etc. 1
Guard seat or tower 3
Racks, with hangers, for clothing and life jackets .... [4] 1

Coaches' office—

First aid kit 1
Desks, files, bookcase, chairs, lamps, etc. 1
Administrative forms, testing, operational record, permanent forms, attendance, inventory, equipment issue, etc. 1
Typewriter and office supplies 1
Bulletin board 1

Shower rooms—

Soap 1

Drying room—

One or more benches 3

Locker room—

Combination locks or fixed locks with keys .... [4] 3
Scales 2
Benches or stools 1

Equipment room—

Cotton shorts or swimming straps 1
Towels 1
Hand trucks or carts. To move wet towels and suits 2
Overshoes or clacks for issue to officials or visitors 2
Swimming suit sterilizer .... [3] 1

Instruction and competition—

For instructional use:
    Flutter or kick boards 2
    Rubber jackets 4
    Swim cans .... [1] 2
    Life jackets 4
    Wooden guns 4
    Clothing (white work or cadet khaki) 4
    Packs 4
    Paddle board or surf board 4
    Ropes suspended for climbing and descending 4
    Cargo nets, suspended 4
    Mirrors: 3
        Small, portable, on stand with swivel 3
        Full length on stand or affixed to wall 3
    Platform 12-22 feet high. Accommodate 4-6 men 4
    Camera and projector .... [3] 2
    Diving pucks and bricks 4
    Benches or low tables. For land drills 4
    Rubber boat or raft 4
    Model cockpit 4

Essentially for both instruction and competition—

Hand rope. To mark finish lines for races. To serve as a rescue device. To
    section off areas of the pool. 1
Stop watches. For instruction, testing and races 1
Portable blackboard on stand 2
Spring boards and mats ....[1] 4
    Extra spring boards and mats. Use interchangeably ....[3] 4
Recording desk on deck 2
Portable bulletin board 3
Water basketball goals ....[2] 1
Water polo goals ....[2] 1
Water polo balls ....[2] 1
Block and tackle ....[4] 3
Floats for game boundaries. As markers or to support boundary lines ... 3
Microphone and amplifier 3
Megaphones 2
Whistles 1
Clipboards 1
Polo caps. Cotton twill 1

Essentially for competition—

Floating lane markers ....[1] 2
Removable starting platforms ....[1] 3
Markers to hold name plate at end of lane 3
Devices for scoring diving 3
Back stroke hand grips. Removable ....[3] 4
Starting gun and blank shells ....[2] 4

Safety—

Bamboo poles 1
Hand line 1
Flutter boards 2
Can floats ....[2] 4
Ring buoys 4
Posters bearing printed regulations ....[1] 4

Miscellaneous—

Index file 3
Clothes wringer 3
Face plates (pearl diving masks) 4
Show or special equipment
    Colored lights, props, spots, screens, etc. 4

At Beach, Ocean, Lake or River
Safety

Boat fully equipped 1
Life rings 1
Underwater view plate 1
Hand line 1

First aid kit 1
Torpedo buoys 1
Surf or paddle board 2
Blankets 1
Heat pads 1
Whistles or horns or siren 1
Guard tower 1

SANITATION AND MECHANICAL EQUIPMENT

Although the administrator or the head of the swimming department may delegate these duties to an officer on his staff, it must never be forgotten that it is the administrator himself who must assume all responsibility.

He is obligated to keep himself informed of the condition of the water, to be familiar with the type and condition of the items of mechanical equipment, to be aware of the degree to which janitors and engineer are capably performing their duties, and to be able to suggest remedial procedures if difficulties develop.

These duties may be facilitated and clarified in two ways. A form, on which it is required that every action pertaining to sanitation of the pool be recorded, will provide the administrator with the information which will enable him to discover any neglect of duty and to anticipate or prevent any possible sanitation dangers. A second aid will be the preparation of a check list of all tasks and duties related to sanitation.

Such forms or lists may present the items in their order of performance throughout the day, according to the person who will be assigned to perform them, or according to the classification of the task itself.

Typical Pool Regulations, Navy

SUBJECT: Swimming pool, Regulations concerning.

    1.   The management and operation of the station swimming pool shall be under the supervision of an officer to be known as "Officer in Charge Swimming Pool". He will be assigned in writing by the Commanding Officer. The Officer in Charge shall be responsible for the following:
        (a) Temperature of the water.
        (b) Cleanliness and sanitary conditions of pool, building, and
            facilities, in accordance with standards established by the Medical
            Officer.
        (c) Supervision of life guards and other personnel assigned.

    2.   The Public Works Officer shall be responsible for the general maintenance of the pool, building, and the mechanical installations. He shall make regular weekly inspections to determine the condition of equipment and the necessity for repairs.

    3.   The Medical Officer shall establish sanitary standards to be observed in the operation and use of the bathing facilities and shall provide pertinent rules and regulations whenever necessary or advisable. The Medical Officer or a duly qualified officer of the Medical Department, designated by him, shall make regular and frequent inspections of the pool and the premises to see that the established standards are complied with.

    4.   The swimming pool shall be operated on a daily routine schedule. The schedule shall be published by the Officer in Charge, subject to approval by the Commanding Officer. It shall establish the hours at which the pool will be available for use by officers, cadets, and enlisted personnel.

Dist: All Heads of Depts.
      All Official Bulletin Boards.

Temperatures of the water and air should be taken and recorded three times daily. The water temperature should never be above 80° and never below 75°, which is the best average range for instruction periods of more than one hour in length. The air temperature in an indoor pool should be approximately the same as that of the water.

Residual chlorine in the pool water should be tested *3 times* daily by colormeter and orthotolidine. The residual chlorine concentration should not be less than .4 parts per million nor more than .6 parts per million when chlorine is used. When chloramine is used not less than .7 parts per million and not more than 1.0 parts per million should be used.

Alkalinity.—The water must be slightly alkaline in order for the alum to form a protective floc on the top of each filter. A neutral reading is one of 7.0. Best reading is from 7.4 to 8.0. This reading is to be taken and recorded three times daily.

An attendance record is necessary because the number of swimmers is related to bacteria count and amount of residual chlorine. This record is usually the total for the day, but may be listed according to periods.

Hours of Operation.—The number of hours the pool was in use will be recorded. The number of hours the filters and pumps were operating will be filled in by the engineer.

MAINTAINING CLEANLINESS

1. Arrange the routing of swimmers so that they do not walk in bare feet where others who were wearing shoes have walked.
2. Require that the decks be washed daily with an antiseptic solution. A phenol compound in proper solution will kill fungi. A 2% solution of chlorine in hypochlorite, when diluted with 10 parts of water, will keep the tile bleached.

Specific

All screens and drain gratings should be examined frequently.

Clearness or cloudiness of the pool water should be recorded daily. Cloudiness probably means that the chemicals are not in correct proportion or that the filters are not functioning properly.

Bacteriological tests should be made at least twice a week. It should be possible to keep the water as free from soil and vegetable bacteria as is drinking water. If the quantitative test shows presence of more than 100 colonies of bacteria per cubic centimeter, the cause should be immediately investigated and remedied. If the qualitative tests shows presence of bacillus coli, there is cause for alarm.

The springboards must be washed and the mats removed, cleaned and aired, at least once a month.

Draining of the pool should take place at least once every 12 months, depending on attendance. At this time, the bulkheads and bottom are thoroughly scrubbed with acid, the grouting between any tiles is examined and is replaced if loose or missing, the surface may be repainted, and the gratings and other underwater fixtures are examined, and repaired or replaced.

Pressure readings for hair strainer, and filters will also be filled in by the engineer.

Backwashing of filters, cleaning of hair strainer and overflow into the gutters are

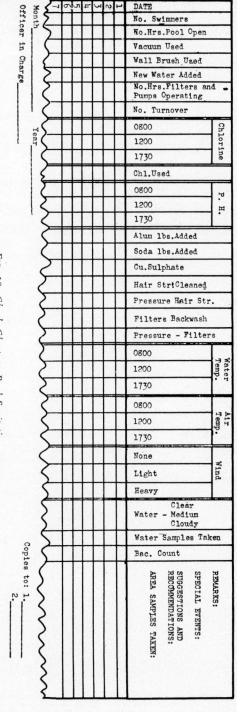

FIG. 19. *Check Chart on Pool Sanitation*

actions that must be recorded. *The number of* gallons of fresh water and *the amounts of chemicals* added must be noted. Notation will call for the number of pounds of soda ash put into the dispenser, the rate of the chlorinator pulsations and the pounds used, and the amount of copper sulphate added.

The use of the suction cleaner and the length of time it was in use must not be omitted from the record. The same applies to the wall brush.

Cleaning

The decks of the pool, locker rooms, shower rooms and heads must be hosed down each day. This should be followed by a cleansing with an antiseptic solution. The pool bulkheads, between the water level and the gutter, should be carefully cleaned each day. The water level is first lowered two or three inches, then the bulkhead is cleaned with a damp cloth and cleanser in such a manner that none of the cleanser drops into the pool, the surface is rinsed with a wet cloth, and then the pool is flooded to flush the water surface. Before the pool is flushed, the scum gutters should be scrubbed. Cloths, brushes and mops used at the swimming pool must not be used in any other work. The deck must be mopped and cleaned in a manner to prevent any run-over or slopping into the pool.

CHAPTER XV

Pool Administration

No formulae apply alike to all situations and the presentation of pertinent problems which follow has general application to all types of programs.

Some phases of the organized plan demand strict standardization from which any departure is not permitted without pressing reason. Nevertheless, in the final analysis, the true measure of an instructor's worth may be found in his ability to adjust himself smoothly and quickly to the particular needs, facilities and problems which the situation presents. The teacher who accepts and applies without adaptation the recommended procedures of another fails to obtain full value. The same principles apply to administration.

All that can be given is a general over-all pattern. The suggested plans and forms offered in this chapter are meant to be just that and nothing more; there is no intent to convey an impression that these procedures are to be applied universally and without alteration.

The same caution will hold true for the enumeration of administrative duties which follow. Each administrator must rely upon his own judgment to select the essential and ignore that which has no application to him.

PLATE 177. *Group Instruction Outdoors*

OBJECTIVES

There are four major administrative functions: adequate equipment, competent personnel, time allotment, and achievement of standards. The first three of these are closely related to the satisfaction of the fourth.

Facilities and Equipment

These are the tools with which the work may be accomplished. If they are inadequate, immediate steps must be taken to insure the provision of that which is needed. In the meantime, temporary adjustments must be made in the program.

Personnel

Instructional personnel should be of sufficient number and with qualifications to guarantee that all hands receive thorough training.

Time

Skills are mastered because the swimmers are given ample time to attain them in the water. No moment may be wasted and if more time is needed, the administrator must find it.

Achievement of Standards

Every man must reach a given standard of achievement. The administrator must provide that all efforts culminate in the earliest possible mastery of those minimum requirements. The administrator must so employ time and facility and personnel as to hasten the realization of this objective. He has no choice but to perform his task implicitly.

ADMINISTRATIVE DUTIES AND RESPONSIBILITIES

1. Make a detailed analysis of the situation.
    a. How many periods are available for aquatics?
    b. What is the length of each period?
    c. What facilities and equipment are available?
    d. How many men will come to each period?
       What is their previous experience?
    e. What personnel have been assigned to assist?
    f. What are the requirements for the program?
    g. What difficulties have been encountered in the past?
    h. What are the standards and regulations now in effect?
2. Work out a plan of class organization and routine.
3. Work out schedules and procedures for testing.
4. Work out a plan for keeping individual swimming achievement records.
5. Work out a plan of teaching procedure in accordance with syllabus requirements.
6. Work out an assignment of specific responsibilities for the officers in the Swimming Department.
7. Provide for the organization of the swimming sports program.
8. Work out a program of sub-squad practice periods.
9. Organize the varsity swimming and varsity water polo programs.
10. Work out all necessary schedules.

11. Provide for periodic inspection of equipment and request replacement, repair and new equipment.
12. Plan procedures for initial testing.
13. Plan the nature of the procedures which are to precede teaching.
14. Hold staff meetings in order to establish policy and to settle controversial questions of procedure.
15. Keep tabulations of facts and figures pertaining to the work of the department. Supplement these with graphs.
16. Incorporate into the program any meritorious suggestions received from members of the staff. Give credit where credit is due.
17. See that the sanitation of the swimming pool is maintained at the highest possible standard.
18. Make the quickest and best possible adjustment to a situation lacking in facilities, time and personnel.
19. See that pertinent information and pictures are posted on the bulletin board.
20. Plan the procedure for mustering and keeping attendance records.
21. Work out any necessary watch bills for the swimming pool watch.
22. Work out a list of rules and regulations and provide for enforcement of them.
23. Be familiar with the parts of the mechanical water circulation, purification and heating system.
24. Supervise the taking of water samples for bacteriological tests.
25. Specifically instruct the engineer and janitors in the performance of duties pertaining to upkeep of the swimming facilities.
26. Work out the details applying to other than instructional periods, such as sub-squad practice and recreation periods.
27. Provide for special entertainments, including special demonstrations, shows, aquacade stunts or acts.
28. Work out a program for presentation of a demonstration of skills. Be prepared to speak to Red Cross, Y.M.C.A., physical education and other organizations.
29. Learn what is being done in similar programs elsewhere.
30. Make further study of the purposes for which the swimming program is being carried on. Provide for adequate instruction.
31. Establish certain objectives, in terms of both quantity and quality, for the swimming department to achieve.
32. Make a study of the methods and requirements necessary to do this.
33. Keep a record of all oral and written communications pertaining to requests, policies and responsibilities.
34. Be responsible to acquaint superiors with any problems and facts they may consider important.
35. Obtain a release of responsibility for duties performed about the swimming pool by personnel over whom the administrator has no control.
36. Make the necessary arrangements, to work closely with the Medical Department.
37. Be prepared to make recommendations pertaining to swimming pool cleaning, repairing and painting.

38. Devise a grading scale for marking all students.
39. Provide that every safety precaution is taken.

Swimming Schedules

The schedule of periods during which swimming instruction is to be given should be precise and definite. The following schedules, designed originally for use in the Naval Aviation Training Program, are typical of those used in activities where swimming must be considered of secondary importance. In the final phases of flight instruction, the acquisition of the specific skills essential to flying are of paramount importance, but even here provision will be made for aquatics.

Flight Preparatory School swimming schedules have been set up in different ways. The most common practice has been to proceed on a wing arrangement, with one wing reporting in the morning and the other in the afternoon, alternating each week. Each period is approximately only one hour and thirty minutes in duration with the first 45 minutes devoted to instruction and the second to Sports Program.

Another procedure has been to schedule instruction for three days a week and Sports Program for two days. One school assigns the entire time of alternate weeks to instruction and Sports Program. A sample Flight Preparatory School schedule appears below:

Day	First 45 Minute Period	Second 45 Minute Period
Monday	Instruction	Subsquad
Tuesday	Instruction	Sports Program
Wednesday	Instruction	Subsquad
Thursday	Instruction	Sports Program
Friday	Instruction	Sports Program
Saturday	Instruction	Self-Testing and Subsquad

Three different procedures for scheduling are found in the Pre-Flight Schools. There may be 10 or 12 periods of one hour and thirty minutes' duration per week. The periods may be 45 minutes in length but 20 or 24 in number. In each case, there is a five-week lapse between the first week of instruction and the second. Finally, the schedule may be so arranged that each incoming battalion takes up swimming as its first athletic activity. Normally, three athletic instruction periods are scheduled daily and two platoons are assigned to each period for an entire week.

In order to obtain the swimmers for a period of two weeks without interruption, the new or incoming battalion is placed with the battalion which has been aboard for nine weeks. This gives one battalion three weeks of swimming at the time when the schedule is initiated. Example:

Battalions 6 & 11 Swimming ⎫
Battalions 7 & 9 Military   ⎬ 1st Period
Battalions 8 & 10 Academics ⎭

Battalions 7 & 9 Swimming ⎫
Battalions 6 & 11 Academies ⎬ 2nd Period
Battalions 6 & 11 Academies ⎭

Battalions 8 & 10 Swimming ⎫
Battalions 6 & 11 Military   ⎬ 3rd Period
Battalions 7 & 9 Academics ⎭

Note: The advantage of this system is that the cadets receive instruction in the swimming program the first two weeks, thus giving the weak swimmers more time to perfect their swimming.

At later stages of training the cadets will be undergoing specialized ground school and flight instruction. They must transfer from the main field to outlying fields. They fly for long hours, and represent all stages and phases of training. This means that while the periods of instruction may be made definite, it will not be possible to proceed on the basis that the same men will report regularly to the same pool for the same number of lessons and without interruption. The following is a sample Operational Base schedule:

0750   —Cadet class
1045   —Inspection
1050   —Life Guard Training Period
1130 to
1330   —Officers' Swimming Period (recreation)
1330 to
1430   —Physical Training Instruction Period
1450   —Cadet class
1630   —Cadet class
1800 to
2100   —Recreational Swimming Period

Assigning Duties and Responsibilities

Two tasks which must be performed have to do with the staff personnel. First, the abilities and particular aptitudes of the members of the department must be carefully analyzed and individual responsibilities so assigned that the greatest efficiency will result. The officer who possesses a background of experience in organization may be put in charge of the sports program; the man who is careful in detail may be entrusted with keeping individual swimming achievement records.

Second, a rotating schedule of teaching assignments must be drawn up. In this plan, it will be wise for the officer in charge to include his own name, even though it be only for an occasional period. The plague of an administrative position is that the administrator becomes affixed to his desk chair and becomes divorced from the arena in which challenge and interest abound. There is, in addition, a morale value which will accrue when the head man "takes his hitch."

The officer in charge of the department must allocate responsibilities to his assistants. The mark of a good administrator is to be found in his ability to obtain and utilize the help of his staff. This may be accomplished by planning and by the specific assignment of responsibility. The poor administrator will either attempt to do everything himself, or will plan nothing and will expect his aides to keep the department in order. Most assistants are capable of using their own initiative, but this quality is most efficiently utilized when it is directed to the performance of a specific major duty.

Precisely what those duties will be and to whom and how the assignments will be made must be decided by the administrator. He should list the important tasks to be done and post a form indicating each instructor's duties.

Life Guards

Every provision must be taken to insure safety. The importance of the use of life guards is universally recognized. Rules for life guards will not apply equally well in all cases. The tests devised for the qualifying of guards will differ according to the duties to be performed. For example: the guard at an ocean beach must be able to swim in surf and to launch a boat; the guard in a pool must know the rules of safety and sanitation and must be adept in the performance of carries in water that is not rough.

One of the most important features of any guard examination is to ascertain if that person knows every detail of the procedure he is to follow if an accident occurs.

The following requirements for guard qualifications are those which have been chosen to be in effect at all naval schools, stations, and centers:

1. Pool—Pass the "B," "A," and "AA" tests.
2. Beach—Pass the "B," "A," and "AA" tests in surf.

Some procedure to be followed in case of accident should be outlined for guards, such as:

PLATE 178. *A Protected Beach*

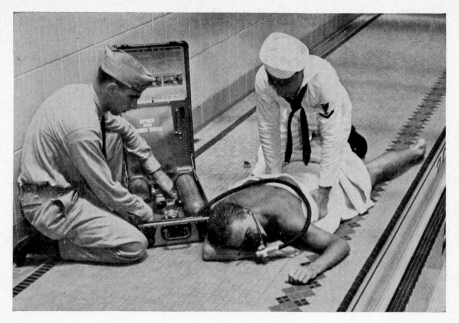

PLATE 179. *Inhalator in Use*

Treatment in Drowning Accidents

1. Send for a doctor at once.
2. Administer artificial respiration immediately.
3. Call for ambulance.
4. Clear swimmers from area where the victim is being treated.
5. Provide blankets, towels, chemical heat pads, and inhalator apparatus.
6. Notify proper officials immediately and submit report of the accident as soon as possible.

Instructions to Guards.—Guards will be given instructions relative to the enforcement of rules, conduct while on duty, care of equipment, and tasks to be performed when coming on duty and before going off duty.

Guards may be required to construct a chart in accordance with the following instructions:

Pool Guard Danger Chart.—The guard must make his own decision as to where the prime danger points in his pool are located and remember that circumstances alter the situation; act accordingly. What may be the most important point in one pool is not necessarily the most important at another. Study the pool layout, acquaint yourself with the different problems which each pool presents. Type of patrons, attendance, congestion, and water visibility are all factors which should contribute to the procedure to be taken by guards.

Here is the guard's danger chart—study it and know it:

1. Area in front of the diving board—Swimmers should be cautioned against the danger of being dived upon while swimming in this area. Divers should determine that they will not strike those swimming near the diving board.

2. Deck—Space around the water area. Enforce the "no running rule." Many injuries have resulted from indiscreet running. The runner not only endangers himself but others whom he might bump or skid into.

3. Semi-Deep Water—The danger here is limited to non-swimmers, who, not being able to touch bottom, travel hand over hand on the trough or railing. If accidentally pushed, they are over their depth and consequently are in danger.

4. Shallow Diving—This is especially dangerous to inexperienced swimmers who dive into water at such an angle that they are very apt to hit bottom, causing injury.

5. Deep Water—Non-swimmers are cautioned not to use this area unless properly supervised. Many swimmers also use this area for underwater swimming and danger exists in their losing consciousness while doing so. It is imperative that the water at all times be clear enough to see the bottom. When the water is exceptionally clear, it may appear shallower than it actually is and mislead patrons who are not familiar with the pool.

6. Ladders—Do not permit any play around the ladders. They should be used only for climbing in and out of the pool, and the user should always face the ladder. No diving should be permitted from the ladders.

7. Diving Boards—The danger here is in the improper use of the diving board. Encourage the use of the step instead of "sidemounting." Permit only one person on the board at a time. "Double bouncing" should be prohibited. Allow no horseplay on the board.

8. General Pool Area—The entire pool layout must be watched for rough play, ducking, pushing, "cutting corners," etc. Allow no equipment in the pool, such as water wings, balls, inner tubes, sticks, rocks or other objects to be retrieved by diving. Exception to this rule may be made only upon permission of the swimming instructor to a supervised group.

9. Swimmers' Entrance—A desire to get into the water as quickly as possible leads patrons to run from the entrances to the pool. This should be prohibited.

10. Guard Stand—The guard stands are for the exclusive use of the life guards. Do not permit anyone else to use them or climb upon them. Determine that the tower is securely anchored to permit the guard to dive without tipping the tower.

Grading

Grading is an established phase of the Naval Aviation Physical Training Program and it therefore becomes necessary for the administrator to devise a grading scale to apply to swimming. A problem arises from the fact that there are three major objectives to be taken into consideration. These are: proficiency in aquatic skills and mastery of the knowledge taught as part of the instruction; attendance; and the development or maintenance of physical condition. Each is important, but it is very difficult to decide just what shall be the relative value assigned to each of them.

It is possible to reduce these factors to two by assuming that physical condition is reflected to a great extent in the ability to pass the swimming tests and in all other activities of the program.

The problem of attendance may be partially disposed of in one of two ways. First, it may be determined that each absence is to reduce the earned grade by 10%. Second, the full earned grade may be allowed but will be considered to be incomplete until every absence is made up.

GRADE SCALES FOR CADETS (SAMPLE)

U. S. NAVY FLIGHT PREPARATORY SCHOOLS

Grade   *Determined by these standards*

0.00........Has not passed the "D" test.

1.00........Has not passed the "D" test, but effort is obvious and cadet has shown improvement.

2.00........Has passed the "D" test.

2.50........Has passed the "C" test.

2.75........Has jumped from 3 foot height into deep water.

3.00........Has swam 20 feet under water.

3.20........Has unofficially passed the tired swimmer carry of the "B" test. (Cadets do not officially pass the "B" test at this school.)

3.40........Has demonstrated ability to scull 60 feet and fin 60 feet.

3.60........Has demonstrated the ability to tread water for 15 minutes, using any style.

3.80........Has unofficially passed the "B" 200-yard test. Four strokes in 5 min. 30 sec.

3.90........Has been in active attendance 83% of the time (10 out of 12 instructional periods), and has passed all requirements.

4.00........Has been in attendance 91% of the time (11 out of 12 periods), and has passed all requirements.

WAR TRAINING SERVICE SCHOOLS

Due to lack of swimming facilities at some War Training Service Schools, it is not possible for all schools to give a swimming test. Therefore no grade is required.

U. S. NAVY PRE-FLIGHT TRAINING SCHOOL

0.00........Has passed no part of the "B" test.

0.25........Has passed one part of the "B" test.

0.50........Has passed two parts of the "B" test.

1.00........Has passed all parts of the "B" test.

1.30........Has passed the "B" and one part of the "A" test.

1.60........Has passed the "B" test and two parts of the "A" test.

1.90........Has passed the "B" test and three parts of the "A" test.

2.20........Has passed the "B" test and four parts of the "A" test.

2.50........Has passed the "B" test and five parts of the "A" test.

2.60........Has passed Checkout test No. 1.

2.70........Has passed Checkout test No. 2.

2.80........Has passed Checkout test No. 3.

3:00........Has passed Checkout test No. 4.

3.20........Has swum 440 yards clothed.

3.40........

2.60........Has passed Checkout Test No. 1.

2.70........Has passed Checkout Test No. 2.

2.80........Has passed Checkout Test No. 3.

3.00........Has passed Checkout Test No. 4.

3.20........Has passed 440 yard swim clothed.

3.40........Has passed 45 minute tread or swim in place.

3.60........Has passed 50 yard carry.
3.80........Has passed one mile swim.
4.00........Has passed 440 yard maintenance test.

The mile and maintenance swims are for grading only, do not go on cadet's permanent athletic record.

Make-Ups.—Some cadets will absent themselves from swimming instruction periods for legitimate reasons; others will, for reasons not clearly discernible, plead to be excused. In order to insure that every cadet will receive an acceptable minimum number of hours of instruction, it is recommended that the cadet be required to make up the periods that he has missed.

Public Relations

There are several methods by which the water safety program may be publicized. It must be remembered that public demonstrations, speeches and articles must be cleared by someone in authority. In the Navy this will be done by the Commanding Officer or Public Information Officer. With approval of the proper superior, any or all of these ideas may be developed.

Radio talks and special broadcasts
Speeches and addresses
Newspaper articles or swimming column in the activity paper
Photographs and posters
Emphasis upon *water safety* in the training program
Open house presentations, cross-section exhibition should be ready for any visiting group
Magazine articles by free lance writers and reporters
The publication of a weekly swimming schedule
The circulation of memoranda relative to swimming requirements, hours, etc., each week
The selection of appropriate and conspicuous places for posters.
The provision, if possible, for swimming time and instruction for faculty members or officers and their families
The inclusion of films on swimming, life saving and water safety as a part of the regular theater programs.
The organization and presentation of a swimming jamboree, with competition.
The adoption of a policy of "visitors welcome at the pool at all times," sub-squad instruction period excepted.
An exhibition group to demonstrate the strokes and skills taught in the swimming training program.

The program for a demonstration will vary according to the audience. No two should be exactly the same. A general pattern may be followed, however, with variations to fit any given situation. Here is a typical sample:

DEMONSTRATION OF NAVAL AVIATION WARTIME SWIMMING

1. Introduction
   A. Why swimming is important to the Naval Aviator
   B. Changed emphasis due to wartime needs

C. These skills are taught to all Naval Aviation cadets
2. Deck drills in basic strokes and life-saving breaks
3. Preliminary skills
4. Staying afloat for 5 minutes or more
5. Water demonstration of basic strokes
   A. Elementary back and inverted breast strokes
   B. Orthodox, high and sweeping breast strokes
   C. Side stroke
   D. Overhand strokes
6. Bobbing—to escape strafing and flame
7. Forced breathing and underwater swimming
8. Submerging to escape strafing—direction, depth and timing
9. Correct and incorrect way to board a rubber boat
10. Inflation and use of life jackets
11. Clothing demonstration
    A. Jump from height, clothed
    B. Form line, swim through imaginary flame
    C. Inflation of clothing
       (1) Blow in space between buttons
       (2) Blow in sleeve of shipmate
       (3) Remove shirt, capture air bubble
       (4) Make life jacket of shirt, inflate
       (5) Use garrison cap for support
       (6) Remove trousers, tie legs, inflate
       (7) Submerge and blow in trousers
       (8) Untie one trouser leg, inflate and re-tie
       (9) Inflate trousers by fanning

PLATE 180. *Time Out for Laughs. Comedy Diving and Swimming Show.*

(10) Perform clothing carries

(11) Place inflated trousers under injured man, transport to the bulkhead

Such public demonstrations have a dual purpose:

1. To impress upon every adult and youth the vital importance of swimming
2. To impress upon the public a realization and appreciation of what the Navy is doing to train every Naval Aviation cadet.

APPENDICES

The Naval Aviation Swimming Program

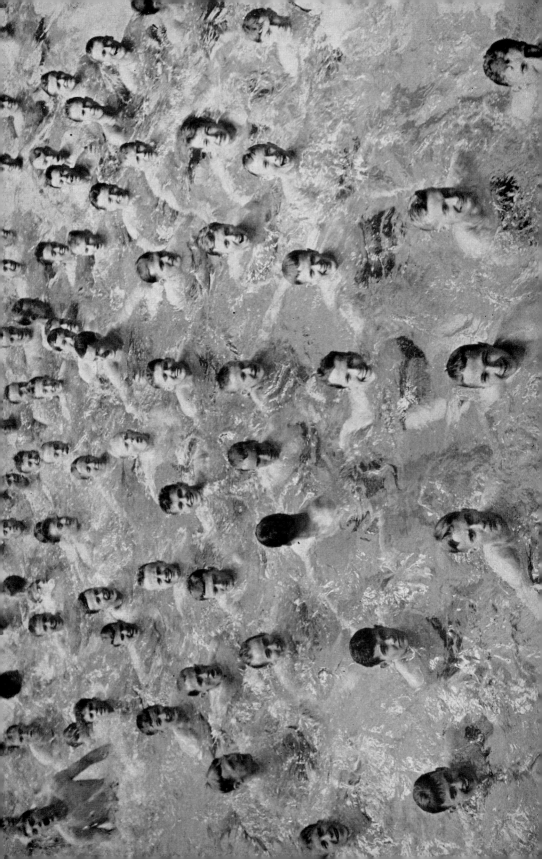

The Naval Aviation Swimming Program

The following material is presented for the use of cadet and officer personnel in the various levels of the Naval Aviation Physical Training Program. Provision is also made for enlisted men. The intent is to illustrate in sequence the over-all continuity of the aquatic program. The responsibilities regarding each phase of the program are defined and are to be followed. Lesson Plans, Drills, Tests and their administration for all stages are described and the specific reference to the text is listed. Included with the description of the drills will be found progressive stick figure illustrations of the more essential skills. These should be studied carefully and used together with basic swimming instruction. It is important that both instructors and pupils not only comprehend the precise movements to be performed but also to visualize the stroke as a complete series of movements to produce the finished stroke. These illustrations are excellent visual aids and it is suggested that similar portrayals be made for bulletin board use.

APPENDIX I

ONE HUNDRED SWIMMING DRILLS

These points are important to the best interpretation of the drills that follow:

1. All of the drills have been presented in the form that the instructor will use in giving them to the cadets.
2. Suggestions as to procedures to be followed may be obtained from Chapter VIII, section on Testing, and from Chapter II, section on Specific Organization Procedures for Drills.
3. Every drill must be clearly explained.
4. The selection of the procedures and the organization of the group for the drill must be planned. Every pool will require that the instructor make his own adaptations.
5. The instructor must avoid the use of the pronoun "I." Say, "The drill is," not, "I want you to do this."
6. The instructor must place the emphasis in command upon the movement and not upon the body part. He will not say, "ARMS up." He will say, "Arms pulling through *TOGETHER.*"
7. There are two drill positions which have not been adequately explained elsewhere.
   a. Kicking while in prone position and grasping the bulkhead.
      Grasp the gutter or top of gunnel with one hand. Extend the other arm underwater with palm against the bulkhead and the fingers pointing toward bottom. Press away with lower hand, pull with upper arm.
   b. Kicking while in back float position and grasping the bulkhead.
      Stand with back to bulkhead. Reach with each arm over the nearest shoulder and grasp the gutter. Pull with arms to raise feet to the surface.

Drills for Preliminary Skills

1. Standing in shallow water, submerge and:
   a. Hold breath for five seconds.
   b. Hold breath for 30 seconds.
   c. Open eyes.
   d. Exhale.
   e. Walk across the pool with face in water and arms outstretched.
   f. Successive exhalations and inhalations.
2. Standing in shallow water:
   a. Relax every muscle and slump into the water.
   b. Perform a tuck float.
3. From a push-off in shallow water, practice:
   a. Prone glide to partner.
   b. A prone glide and come to a standing position.
   c. A back glide with support.
   d. A back glide and come to a standing position.
   e. A prone glide with arm pull.
   f. A prone kick glide.
   g. A back kick glide.
   h. A turn from back down to prone position.
   i. A turn from prone to back down position.
   j. Changing direction.
   k. To the rear.
   l. Underwater swimming.
4. In water 5-7 feet deep, practice:
   a. Regaining the surface (by two methods).
   b. Leveling to horizontal prone position.

Drills for the Horizontal (5-min.) Float

5. While in shallow water, face away from the bulkhead, grasp the gutter and practice the leg action.
6. Push off in a back glide and practice the arm and leg actions.
7. Practice the arm action, leg action and breathing while your partner throws water in your face.
8. From a push off, practice.
   a. The arm action of the elementary back stroke.
   b. The arm action of the dog paddle or overhand strokes.
9. Jump into the deep water while attended by expert swimmers.

Drills for the Vertical Float

10. While standing on the deck.
    a. Assume the floating position.
    b. Assume the floating position and add hand sculling action and breathing.
11. In deep water, assume the position of the vertical float. Start with one hand grasping the gutter. Release and float.

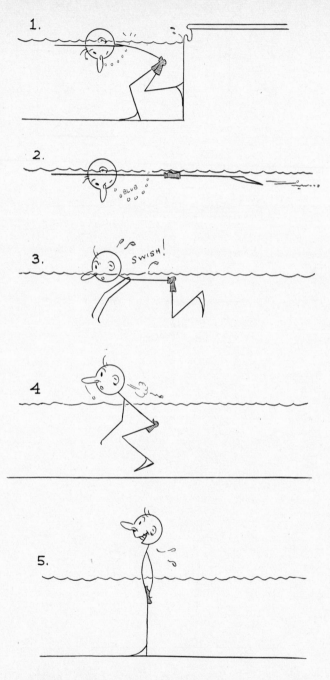

PRONE SHOVE-OFF, GLIDE AND STAND

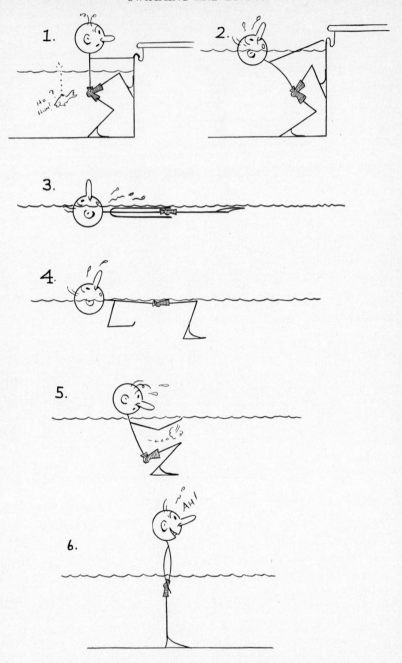

BACK SHOVE-OFF, GLIDE AND STAND

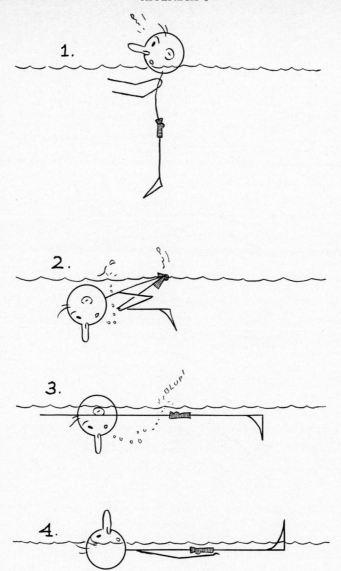

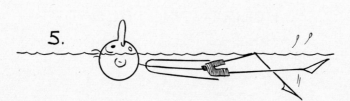

LEVELING WITH TUCK AND EXTENSION

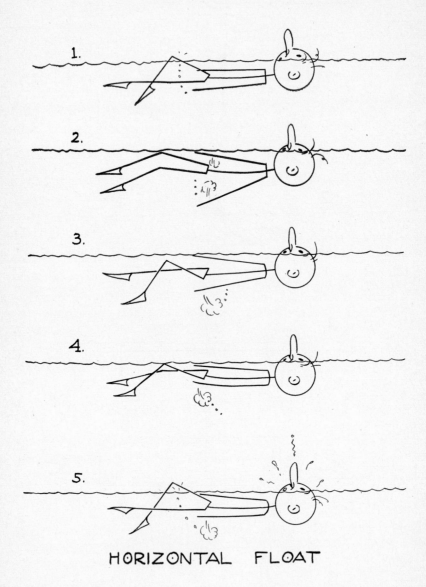

HORIZONTAL FLOAT

Drills for Finning

12. Learn the movements that correspond to each word command:
    a. "UP."
       The fingers are drawn along the body sides.
    b. "OUT."
       The hands extend outward, palms turned aft.
    c. "TOGETHER."
       The hands are pulled through to the thighs.
13. While standing on the deck or in shallow water, practice the hand and arm movement to command.
14. From a push-off into back float position, practice:
    a. Finning.
    b. Finning in combination with frog or scissor kick.

Drills for Sculling

15. Learn the movements that correspond to each word command:
    a. "OUT."
       Both wrists are rotated, and hands moved outward.
    b. "TOGETHER."
       Wrists are rotated and hands are drawn in to thighs.
16. While sitting on bottom in shallow end or with partner support, practice the sculling movements to command.
17. From a push-off into a back float position, practice:
    a. The sculling action.
    b. Sculling in combination with flutter kick.

Drills for Treading

18. While grasping the gutter or gunnel with one hand, practice treading:
    a. With single scissor kick.
    b. With frog kick.
19. In deep water, practice treading:
    a. With kick alone.
    b. With hands alone.
    c. By swimming the breast stroke while in upright position.
    d. With the arms and legs in combination.
    e. With the arms held above water.
    f. For a specified length of time.
20. In groups of six or more, tread water while receiving a stretcher bearing a victim.

Drills for Dog Paddle

21. Learn the movements that correspond to each word command:
    a. "ONE-TWO-THREE"—
       Pull with one arm, recover with the other.
       Perform three leg kicks.
    b. "FOUR-FIVE-SIX."
       Complete the cycle of arm pull and recovery.
       Perform three leg kicks.
    c. "ONE-TWO-*IN*-FOUR-FIVE-*OUT*."
       Coordinate breathing with the actions of arms and legs.

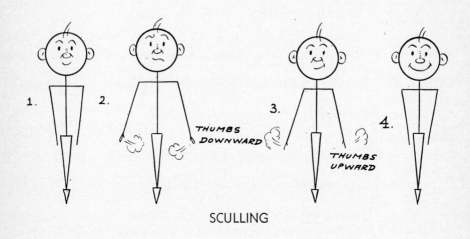

SCULLING

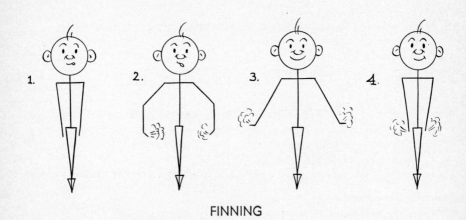

FINNING

22. Lying on a bench or table, practice:
 a. The arm action.
 b. The arms and legs in combination.
 c. The arms and legs in combination with breathing.
23. Standing on the deck or in shallow water, practice to commands:
 a. The arm action.
 b. The arm action and breathing in combination.
24. From a push-off, swim:
 a. Lengths for form.
 b. Sprint lengths for speed.
 c. Distance.

Drills for the Elementary Back Stroke

25. Learn the movements that correspond to each word command:
 a. "UP."
 The hands are drawn along the sides to the top-most ribs, and begin to be drawn to the shoulder tops.
 The knees are flexed and angled outward. Heels are drawn up.
 Inhalation is performed through the mouth.
 b. "OUT."
 Hands are extended from the shoulder into position for the pull. Each arm bisects the angle between the shoulder and the head.
 The heels swing downward and outward to extend the legs sideward.
 c. "TOGETHER."
 The arms pull steadily through to the thighs.
 The legs complete the whip together.
 Exhalation is begun through mouth or nose or both.
 d. "HOLD" or "GLIDE."
 The glide position is held without movement.
26. Standing on the deck or in shallow water, practice:
 a. The arm stroke.
 b. The kick of one leg and then the other.
 c. The arms and one leg in combination.
 d. The arms, one leg and breathing in combination.
27. Lying on the deck, practice:
 a. The separate parts of the stroke.
 b. The complete stroke.
28. From a push-off, and with or without partner support, practice:
 a. The glide position.
 b. The arm stroke.
 c. The leg kick.
 d. The arm stroke and leg kick in combination.
 e. The arm stroke, leg kick and breathing in combination.
29. While grasping the gutter, practice:
 a. The leg kick.
 b. The leg kick in combination with breathing.
30. Following either a circle or wave pattern, swim:
 a. Lengths for form.
 b. Sprint lengths for speed.
 c. Distance.

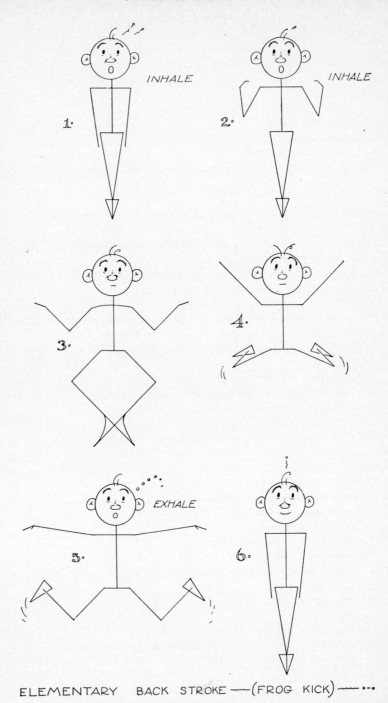

ELEMENTARY BACK STROKE —(FROG KICK)——•••

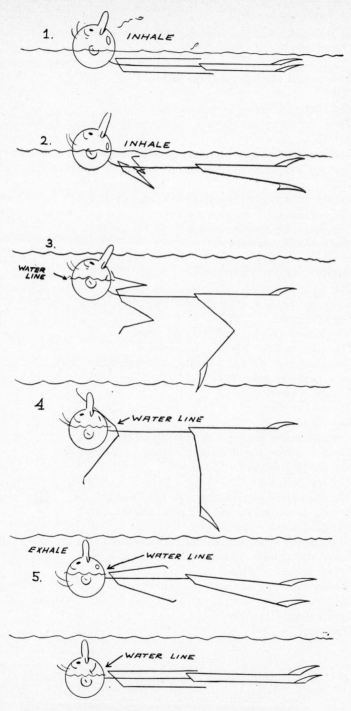

ELEMENTARY BACK STROKE
WITH VERTICAL SCISSORS KICK

Drills for the Breast Stroke

31. Learn the movements that correspond to each word command:
    a. "AROUND."
       The arms pull outward and backward to a point even with the shoulders.
       Inhalation is made through the mouth.
    b. "UP."
       The hands are drawn in to the chest.
       The knees are spread outward and the heels are drawn up toward the body.
    c. "OUT."
       The hands are extended into the glide position.
       The legs are extended outward and begin the whipping action of the leg kick.
       Exhalation is begun through mouth, nose or both.
    d. "TOGETHER."
       The palms are turned outward ready for the pull.
       The legs complete the kick.
       Exhalation is completed.
    e. "HOLD" or "GLIDE."
       The glide position is held without movement.
32. Standing on the deck or in shallow water, practice:
    a. The arm stroke.
    b. The kick of one leg, and then the other.
    c. The arms and one leg in combination.
    d. The arms, one leg and breathing in combination.
33. From a push-off, practice:
    a. The glide position.
    b. The arm stroke.
    c. The leg kick.
    d. The arm stroke and leg kick in combination.
    e. The arm stroke, leg kick and breathing in combination.
34. While grasping the gutter, practice:
    a. The leg kick.
    b. The leg kick in combination with breathing.
35. Swimming either lengths or cross pool, practice:
    a. Sweeping breast stroke.
    b. Breast stroke with body in near vertical position.
    c. Breast stroke with vertical or horizontal scissor kick.
    d. Breast stroke underwater.
36. Following either a circle or wave pattern, swim:
    a. Lengths for form.
    b. Sprint lengths for speed.
    c. Distance.

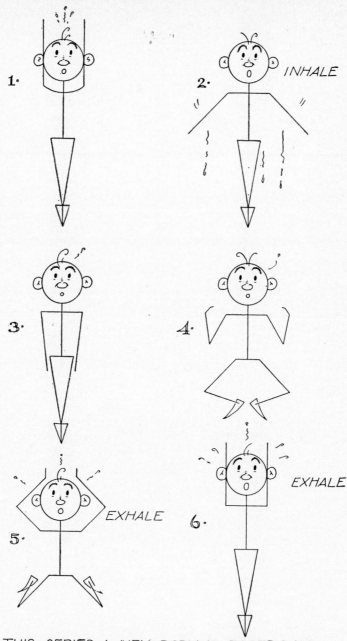

NOTE:- THIS SERIES WHEN BODY IS FACED DOWN, ILLUSTRATES UNDERWATER BREAST STROKE.

— INVERTED   BREAST   STROKE —

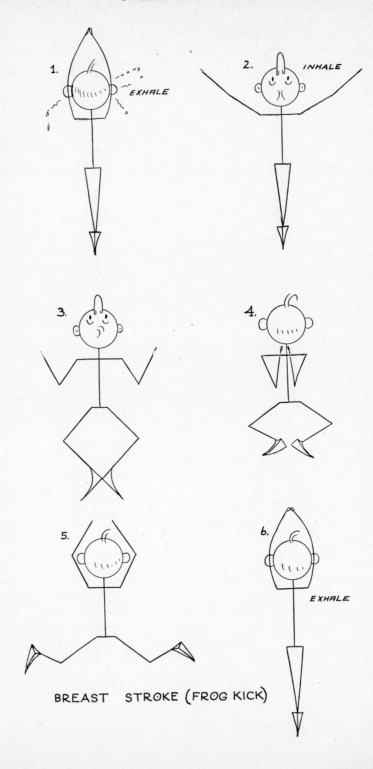

BREAST STROKE (FROG KICK)

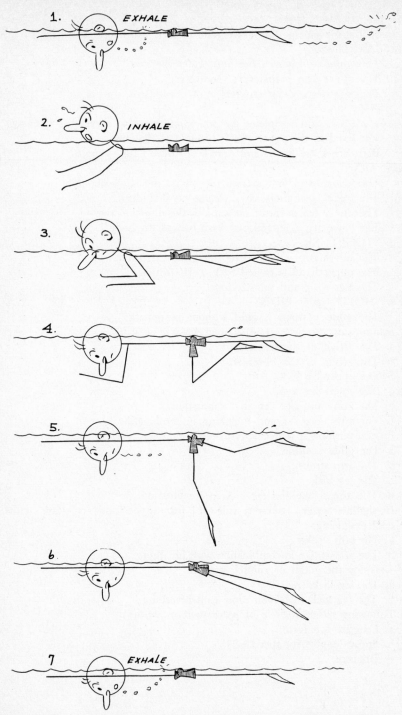

~BREAST STROKE WITH VERTICAL SCISSORS KICK~

Drills for the Side Stroke

37. Learn the movements that correspond to each word command:
    a. "AROUND."
       The lower arm begins the pull under the side.
       The upper arm prepares for recovery.
       The legs prepare for recovery.
    b. "UP."
       The lower arm completes the pull through and prepares for recovery.
       The hand of the upper arm is brought to the chest.
       Both knees are flexed and drawn up toward the stomach.
    c. "OUT."
       The lower hand moves from the hip to the lower shoulder.
       The upper arm circles away from the shoulder.
       The upper leg is thrust outward in the direction the body is facing.
       The lower leg is curved backward behind the body.
    d. "TOGETHER."
       The lower arm is pushed to full glide extension.
       The upper hand is pulled back to the thigh.
       The legs whip and squeeze together.
    e. "HOLD" or "GLIDE."
       The glide position is held without movement.
38. Standing on the deck or in shallow water, practice:
    a. The action of the upper arm.
    b. The action of the lower arm.
    c. The upper leg kick.
    d. The lower leg kick.
    e. The arms and one leg in combination.
    f. The arms, one leg and breathing in combination.
39. From a push-off, practice:
    a. The glide position.
    b. The arm stroke.
    c. The leg kick.
    d. The arm stroke and leg kick in combination.
40. In shallow water, assume a sideward leaning position and walk across the pool practicing:
    a. The arm stroke.
    b. The arm stroke in combination with breathing.
41. Grasping the gutter or gunnel, practice:
    a. The leg kick.
    b. The leg kick in combination with breathing.
42. Following either a circle or wave pattern, swim:
    a. Lengths for form.
    b. Sprint lengths for speed.
    c. Distance.

SIDE STROKE

Drills for the Crawl Stroke

43. While standing on the deck or in shallow water, practice:
    a. The arm stroke.
    b. The arm stroke and breathing.
44. From a push-off, practice.
    a. The prone glide with kick and arm stroke.
    b. The prone glide with kick, arm stroke and breathing.
45. Standing in shallow water, assume a forward leaning position and walk across the pool practicing:
    a. The arm stroke.
    b. The arm stroke in combination with breathing.
46. Grasping the gutter, in prone position, practice:
    a. The leg kick.
    b. The leg kick and breathing.
47. Following either a circle or wave pattern, swim:
    a. Lengths for form.
    b. Sprint lengths for speed.
    c. Distance.

Drills for the Trudgen Stroke

48. Grasping the gutter, with body in side down position, Practice:
    a. The scissor leg kick with underwater exhalation
49. Swim the side overarm stroke
50. Swim the side overarm stroke, but roll on to the stomach each time that the arm on the breathing side is recovered.
51. Swim the side overarm stroke but modify so that each arm, as it recovers, is brought forward out of water.
52. Following either a circle or wave pattern, swim:
    a. Lengths for form
    b. Sprint lengths for speed
    c. Distance.

Drills for the Inverted Crawl

53. Standing on the deck or in shallow water, practice the arm action.
54. Grasping the gutter, in back down position, practice the kick
55. From a push-off, in back down position, practice:
    a. The glide
    b. The arm action
    c. The glide and leg action
    d. The leg action in combination with sculling
    e. The leg kick and arm stroke in combination
56. Following either a circle or wave pattern, swim:
    a. Lengths for form
    b. Sprint lengths for speed
    c. Distance.

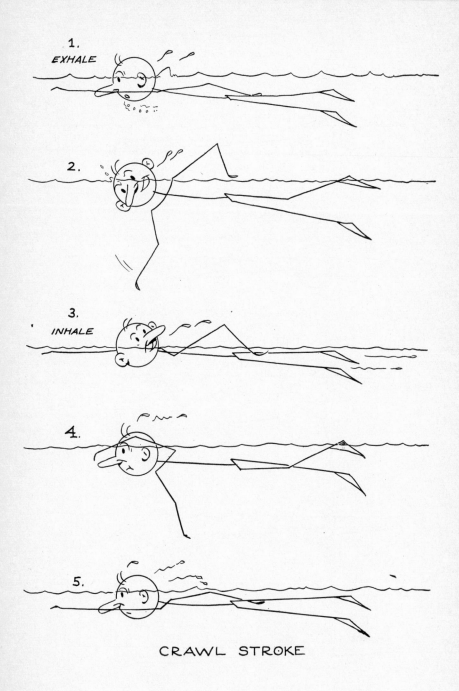

1. EXHALE

2.

3. INHALE

4.

5.

CRAWL STROKE

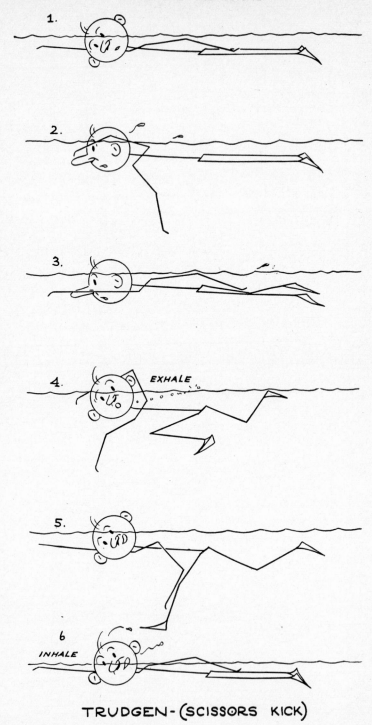

TRUDGEN-(SCISSORS KICK)

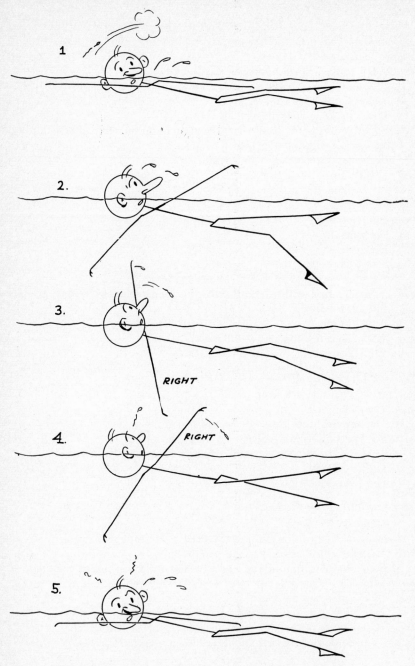

RACING BACK OR INVERTED CRAWL

Drills for Underwater Swimming

57. From a push-off, swim underwater and practice each of the four basic strokes.
58. From a push-off, swim underwater and practice the following stroke variations and combinations.
    a. Breast stroke with an horizontal scissor kick
    b. Breast stroke with a vertical scissor kick
    c. Breast stroke with a flutter kick
    d. Breast stroke with a trudgen kick
    e. Breast stroke, but with the hands continuing to pull through to the thighs.
    f. Side stroke with a flutter kick
    g. Elementary back stroke with a scissor kick
    h. Double arm pull with scissor kick, and with body in side stroke position
    i. Double arm pull with frog or scissor kick, and with the body in back stroke position
59. Swim underwater
    a. For form
    b. For speed
    c. For distance
    d. For short sprints away from point of jump entry.
    e. In combination with clothing skills, jumping, bobbing, strafing, retrieving and surface diving.
    f. With one arm only
    g. With hands tied together at the wrists
    h. With legs tied together at the ankles.

Drills for Elementary Diving

60. From the pool side, practice:
    a. The sitting dive.
    b. The kneeling dive
    c. The kneeling-standing dive.
    d. The dive from one leg, with opposite leg raised backward.
    e. The fall-in dive.
    f. The dive with spring.

Drills for Starts from the Deck

61. Standing on the deck:
    a. Swing arms to full extension overhead as if for a start
    b. Straighten the knees and spring into the air.
    c. Combine the spring of the legs with the upward swing of the arms.
62. Standing on the gunnel, take practice dives with emphasis upon:
    a. Clean entry into the water
    b. Maintaining streamlined position until the body stops gliding
    c. The addition of the kick when the glide speed is half spent.
    d. The addition of the arm stroke as the body surfaces.

Drills for Surface Diving

63. In deep water, practice surface diving:
    a. With tuck position on entry
    b. With pike position on entry
    c. With feet first entry
    d. While clothed, and swim underwater
    e. While wearing a deflated life jacket
    f. For a designated number of times, in quick succession
    g. And immediately make a 90 degree turn underwater
    h. To depth of at least two feet, remain submerged for 10 seconds, emerge and stay at the surface for 20 seconds. Repeat at least six times.
    i. With one arm bound to body
    j. With both hands tied together
    k. With both legs tied together.
    l. In pairs, two cadets extricate "insured" pilot from submerged replica of cockpit.

Drills for Bobbing

64. While standing in shallow water:
    a. Make at least five successive immersions. Exhale under water.
65. In deep water:
    a. Practice repeated submersions
    b. Combine bobbing with underwater swimming for a length of the pool
    c. Bob for a length of the pool by pushing-off against the bottom.
    d. Submerge to a depth of at least two feet for 10 seconds, emerge for five seconds, submerge again. Repeat at least 8 times.

Drills for Lines

Their use in and above water.

The correct methods of ascending and descending lines will be taught in gymnastics.

66. Ascend and descend a line suspended above the water:
    a. For form
    b. For speed against a stop watch
    c. For speed, competing group against group
    d. While wearing a life jacket

Drills for Cargo Nets

Their use in and above water

67. Ascend and descend a cargo net suspended above the water
    a. For form
    b. For speed against a stop watch
    c. For speed, competing group against group
    d. While wearing a life jacket
    e. That is hung against a ship's side.

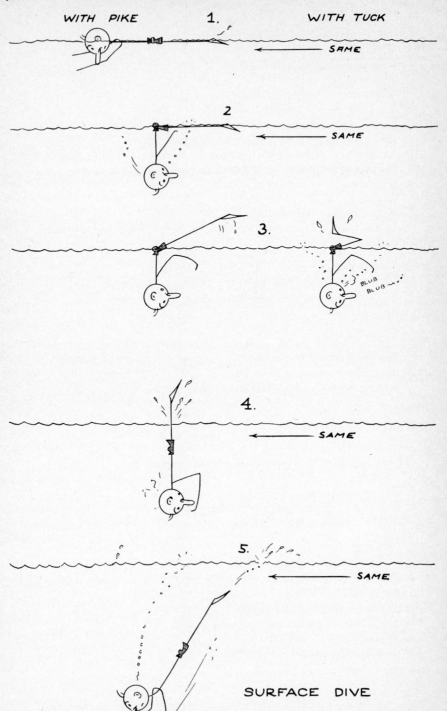

WITH PIKE   1.   WITH TUCK

← —————— SAME

2

← —————— SAME

3.

BLUB
BLUB

4.

← —————— SAME

5.

← —————— SAME

SURFACE DIVE

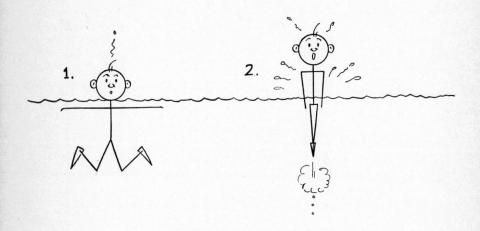

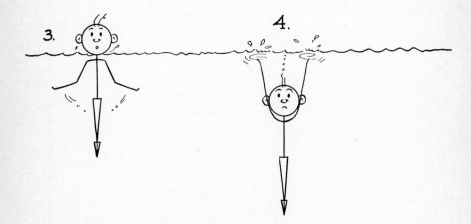

ADVANCED BOBBING—FEET FIRST-
SURFACE DIVE~•

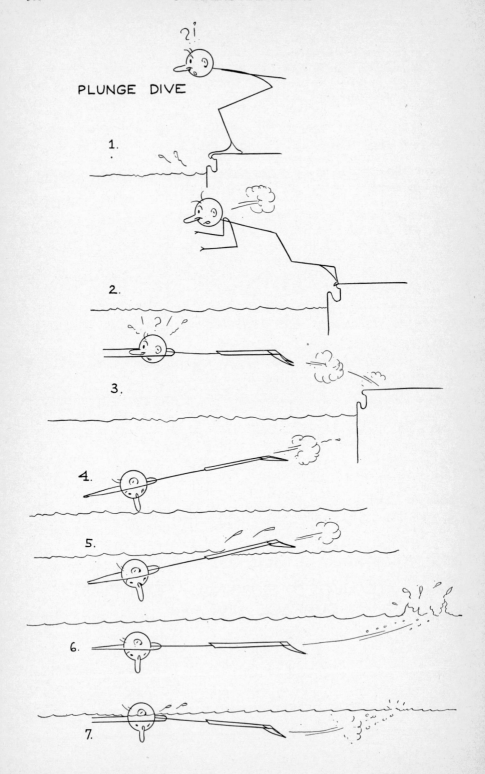

PLUNGE DIVE

1.

2.

3.

4.

5.

6.

7.

Drills for Jumping

68. From deck, 3 foot or 10 foot height, jump:
    a. In tuck position, hands extended sideward
    b. With legs in three-quarter frog or scissor position. Kick on entry.
    c. With legs straight and feet together. Hands against thighs
69. From a 10 foot height, jump:
    a. Feet together or crossed at ankles.
    b. Cover face, do not hold nose.
70. From a designated height, jump:
    a. While fully clothed and swim underwater
    b. While fully clothed and form a conga line or circle pattern
    c. For speed. As a group in least possible time.
    d. While wearing equipment.
71. Equipped with a life jacket, jump:
    a. With each hand grasping the jacket on top of the shoulder nearest to that hand
    b. With arms folded across the chest and grasping jacket
    c. With arms folded and hand of under arm covering face, heel of hand under chin
    d. Throw jacket into water, jump, retrieve it, put it on.
    e. After deflating jacket, then re-inflate orally.

Drill for Blindfold Swimming

72. Tie a towel or T-shirt over eyes. All cadets lower themselves into the pool by ladder or gunnel, and mill around in the water.

Drills for Debris

73. On an old wooden door or similar object:
    a. Ten to twenty men cling to it for support
    b. One cadet pulls another aboard
74. On a short piece of 4' x 4', tie shoes and jacket to it and support self without movement.

Drills for Wounds and Cramps

75. Swim a specified distance, both on the surface and underwater:
    a. With feet tied together at ankles
    b. With hands tied together at wrists
    c. With one arm and with both arms bound to the body.
    d. Sculling on the back with knees out of water

Technique for jumping from heights 20' or more

Hurry! Hurry!

Drills for Clothing

76. While fully clothed, swim a specified distance:
    a. For speed.
    b. Both on the surface and underwater
    c. While wearing a life jacket
    d. With sweeping breast stroke
77. While fully clothed, jump into the water, swim a specified distance, disrobe, inflate clothing and swim on it.
78. Inflate clothing and support self on it
    a. Shirt—by three methods.
    b. Pants—by four methods
    c. Make a life jacket of shirt
79. Transport a wounded man on inflated clothing

Drills for Equipment

80. Swim a specified distance:
    a. For speed, carrying a heavy stick or wooden rifle
    b. For distance, carrying a stick or wooden rifle
    c. While wearing a pack
    d. While fully clothed and equipped with emergency kit, packed parachute, life jacket.

Drills for Strafing

81. While in the center of the pool, sprint on signal for port and starboard bulkheads to escape an attacking plane traveling along the fore and aft line of the pool.
82. Submerge with surface dive, swim in circles underwater for 10 seconds, emerge, take a breath and repeat.
83. While aboard a rubber boat with from four to seven other cadets, capsize the boat on signal. Submerge for 10 seconds, emerge, right boat and climb in.

Drills for Frightening Sharks

84. Swim underwater with leather training knife and practice slashing.
85. While in a group, kick the feet to create splash.
86. While in a group assigned to a rubber boat, arrange a watch schedule whereby there is rotation of duty:
    a. Kicking
    b. Clinging to boat and resting
    c. Boarding boat and resting.

Drills for Abandoning Plane

87. List, in oral or written examination, the items of abandon plane equipment
88. Swim an obstacle course which simulates plane wreckage
89. Escape from a replica of a cockpit:
    a. In the manner prescribed for Intermediate check-out #1
    b. With one arm bound to body
    c. With hands tied together at the wrists
    d. With legs bound together at the ankles

e. While equipped with full winter flight gear

f. While the cockpit is turned upside down.

Drills for Abandoning Parachute

90. Extricate self from parachute in the manner prescribed for Intermediate check-out #3.

91. Attach a tow line to shrouds of a parachute without fabric, fix straps to self and attempt to effect an escape while being pulled at a rapid rate for the length of the pool.

Drills for Boat and Raft

92. In pool or ocean, demonstrate ability and knowledge:
    a. Boat inflation
    b. The use of equipment
    c. Correct rowing and manouvering techniques.
    d. Correct methods of entering and exit
    e. Procedure to avoid strafing
    f. Correct methods of righting the boat
    g. Correct methods for helping another aboard
    h. Correct methods for rigging a sail

93. In ocean, bring the boat in through surf by:
    a. The use of sea anchor
    b. Clinging to an attached line
    c. Clinging to the aft end of boat.

Drills for Rescue by Boat and Plane

94. Board a rescue plane while wearing life jacket.

95. While in groups of from five to 25, approach small rescue boat, stand by, move in according to prearranged order.

96. Maneuver a small rescue craft. Take charge of boarding and rescue procedures.

Drills for Surf, Tide and Currents

97. Come ashore in surf by:
    a. Swimming shoreward while in the trough, turning seaward to meet each wave.
    b. Swimming shoreward while in the trough, taking the first lift of the breaker and diving out of it.
    c. Body surfing

98. In stream, lake or ocean:
    a. Swim across the current.
    b. Swim diagonally into waves and away from shore.

Drills for Life Saving

99. Standing in shallow water, practice:
    a. Fireman's carry
    b. Saddleback carry

100. Standing on the deck or in shallow water, and in deep water, practice·
    a. Dive approach
    b. Jump approach
    c. Front surface approach
    d. Underwater approach
    e. Rear approach

f. Tired swimmer carry
g. Cross chest carry
h. Two man carry
i. Head carry
j. Hair carry
k. Clothing carry (3 methods)
l. Shallow water rescues (miscellaneous skills)
m. Retrieving shipmate from bottom
n. Supporting a shipmate
o. Release from front strangle (2 methods)
p. Release from back strangle
q. Release from double grip on one wrist,
r. Separating two people
s. Board and line tows.

DRILLS FOR WATER POLO AND NAVY BALL

Points to be Noted:

1. These games have a dual purpose:
   a. To provide mental and physical relaxation.
   b. To contribute to development of stamina, water ability and competitive spirit.
2. Drills should be accompanied by a knowledge of playing rules.
3. The following progression should be followed throughout the cadet training program and to instruct inexperienced officers and enlisted men.

Elementary Water Polo Drills:

1. Cadets line up in water, along bulkheads on both sides, facing center of pool, groups of eight, four on each side. Give each group a water polo ball (the hard, Olympic type ball). Start by learning to pick up the ball, taking the ball from underneath, and pass cross-pool.
2. Cadets swim short sprints with head well out of water.
3. Divide the cadets in teams of equal numbers. Repeat No. 2 as shuttle relay.
4. Cadets line up in shuttle relay formation, cross-pool or lengthwise. Dribble easily, ball in front of face and in pocket between arms. Swim well out of water, keep ball a little in front of head and shoulder, use the crawl or trudgen stroke.
5. Repeat No. 4 in obstacle course fashion. Require zig-zag and turn as well as straight ahead swimming.
6. Repeat No. 4 and No. 5 as shuttle relays for speed.
7. Dribble and pass relay. Place cadets in shuttle relay formation. Each cadet dribbles down the pool and passes to a teammate. The pass may be made any time after the dribbler is inside the penalty (4 yard) line.
8. Pass and score drill. For both Navy Ball and Water Polo goals. Shallow water. Divide each team in two equal lines. Men in (A) line pass to receiver in line (B) who is standing by goal. Receiver catches ball with one hand, scores, recovers ball and passes to next man in line (A). Passer then goes to end of line (B) and scorer goes to end of line (A). One group competes against another for greatest number of goals scored within time limit.
9. Repeat No. 8 in deep water.
10. Circle passing drill. (Deep water.) Form a number of circles, 8 men in each. Pass ball across circle the same as when passing cross-pool in No. 1. Try to

keep ball from hitting the water. Pass so that the receiver is required to reach up for the catch without the ball touching the water.

11. Repeat No. 10 with all men moving to the right. Use same stroke as in dribble, head high, eyes on the ball. Pass ball around and across circle. Every man alert, the next pass may be to him.

12. Repeat No. 11 with variations. Reverse direction to right or left on command. Speed up or slow down on command.

13. Repeat No. 10 and No. 11, with passes counted. Circles compete against each other for greatest number of passes made within time limit.

14. Play "It" or "Keepaway." Repeat No. 10 and No. 11 with one man in center of circle. Men in circle try to pass so center man cannot touch or catch ball. If center man touches ball, the cadet making the pass becomes "It."

15. From circle formation or moving down pool in column, swim with easy dribble, take two strokes and pass to cadet ahead. Pass the ball so that it lands ahead of receiver who continues swimming, dribbling two strokes before passing to man ahead of him. Until every man in the circle or column has handled the ball, speed up or slow down on command.

16. Repeat No. 15, requiring cadet to catch the ball as it is passed. When cadet is the next receiver, he must keep looking backward without changing speed or his position in circle.

17. Sprint drill. Line up teams as at the beginning of polo game. Sprint to get ball and pass back. Rotate men so each is in sprint position. Score one point for each successful sprint.

Advanced Water Polo Drills:

1. Develop the use of either hand. Right-handed men develop left-handed catch, life and pass. Progress from simple to complex (Drills 1-16, Elementary Water Polo.)

2. Guarding Drills. Divide each team into equal numbers and form two opposing columns. Cadet from Column A dribbles, cadet from Column B attempts to break it up.

3. Repeat No. 2 with two men against one guard, the dribbler may pass.

4. Repeat No. 3 with goal tenders in goal, to assist the guard. Team A tries to score.

5. Repeat No. 4 with all types of scoring shots. Rotate the men in positions.

6. Have two forwards attempt to score against two guards. Deception and "shifting" is important in this drill.

7. Repeat No. 6 with three forwards against two guards, and with three forwards against two guards and goalie.

8. Relay Race. Divide squad into two teams. Each man must dribble the length of pool, make pivot shot (repeat until score is made), dribble back to other goal, make backhand shot (repeat until score is made, and pass to next man on his team).

9. Repeat No. 8 but with two men at once from same team. Pass back and forth every two strokes. Either man may score.

10. Use offensive and defensive strategy drills, plays and formation for entire team.

11. Many drills used in basketball, soccer, and football are readily adaptable to water polo.

APPENDIX II

Lesson Plans

In preparing an instruction schedule, the swimming coach must bear in mind the age and experience of his students and the total amount of time available for lessons. An instructor at a community pool will have smaller and younger pupils, requiring a slower and different approach than for a college class. In a naval training program the instructor must be capable of making adjustments to provide for those men who are already expert swimmers. Men being trained in competitive swimming, and all students in advanced stages of proficiency, can be given increased instruction in distance swimming, relays and games of competitive skill. Always, the greater the students ability, the greater should be the endurance and time demands placed upon him.

A listing of the drills by number will be found in Appendix I. A detailed description of all drills may be found by checking the index and table of contents. Lesson plans are listed in order of increasing complexity; Lesson 1(A) is for children in the Non-Swimmer group. These lesson plans, which are primarily for civilian use, can be adopted for military use by stressing particular drills. Time allotment for each drill is based on a class period of 30 minutes. Military muster and dismissal procedures should take no more than a total of four minutes. Warm-up periods should be limited to five minutes. Nothing in these drills should be considered binding; successful coaching requires careful balance of time, capabilities, and facilities.

LESSON PLANS (A)

Length of the period in the water ....30 minutes
Number of lesson periods available 10
Age range of group .... 7–12 yrs.
Number in the class ....15 (Maximum)
Classification test passed: NON–SWIMMERS
Objectives of the course:

1. Face or prone float—regain feet
2. Breathing—10 consecutive times
3. Back float—regain feet.
4. Dog paddle—20 yds.
5. Scull—20 ft. (With use of feet)
6. Kneeling dive
7. Jump feet first in deep water—surface—swim to edge.
8. Reverse from dog paddle to position on back and vice versa.

Drill No.	New Drill	Time Allotment	*Short Description of drill*
			LESSON I(A)
1a	x	3	Face in water—5 seconds—repeat several times
1e	x	3	Face in water—walk as far as possible with arms extended
1c	x	2	Face in water—open eyes
1d	x	2	Face in water—exhale
46a	x	4	Flutter kick—grasp gutter—stress proper form
23a	x	4	Dog paddle—walk across pool—armstroke practice
3a	x	4	Prone glide to partner
3b	x	4	Prone glide—come to stand (regain feet)
3f	x	4	Prone glide—pushoff—flutter kick—repeat
			LESSON II(A)
		20	Review all of lesson #1
24a	x	7	Dog paddle (with or without aids)
1f	x	3	Successive inhalations and exhalations
			LESSON III(A)
		3	Successive inhalations and exhalations
		3	Prone glide—come to stand
		4	Flutter kick—hanging on gutter
		4	Flutter kick—with pushoff on prone glide
		10	Dog paddle—repeat—(with or without aids)
3c	x	4	Back glide with support
		2	Successive inhalations and exhalations (To be called Bobbing)
			LESSON IV(A)
		2	Bobbing
		3	Flutter kick—hanging on gutter
		3	Prone glide—regain feet—increase distance
		3	Prone glide—with flutter kick—increase distance
2a	x	2	Relax every muscle in body—slump in water
2b	x	2	Perform a tuck float (Jellyfish float)
		5	Dog paddle—increase distance (with or without aids)
		2	Back glide—with aid
3d	x	2	Back glide—regain feet without aid
		1	Bobbing
			LESSON V(A)
		2	Bobbing (increase number)
		2	Flutter kick—hanging on gutter
		2	Flutter Kick—from prone glide
		2	Perform tuck float

Drill No.	New Drill	Time Allotment	Short Description of drill
23b	x	2	Dog paddle arm action with underwater exhalation—walking
		6	Dog paddle—as much as possible without aids
		2	Back glide—with aid
		2	Back glide—regain feet without aid
29a	x	2	Back glide with flutter kick
3h	x	3	Swimming on back—turn to prone position without letting down
3i	x	2	Swimming in prone position—reverse above drill
		2	Bobbing

LESSON VI(A)

Test #2		2	First attempt for bobbing test
		2	Flutter kick—hanging on gutter
		2	Prone glide with flutter kick
		2	Dog paddle armstroke with underwater exhalation—walking
		4	Dog Paddle for distance—without aid
		2	Back glide—regain feet—without aid
		2	While swimming in prone position—reverse to position on back
		2	While swimming on back—reverse to prone position
		2	Back glide—with flutter kick
16	x	2	Sculling movements with support
17a	x	2	Back glide with sculling
17b	x	2	Back glide with sculling and flutter kick
60a	x	3	Sitting dive
		1	Bobbing

LESSON VII(A)

		2	Perform tuck float
		1	Bobbing
		2	Flutter kick—hanging on gutter
		2	Prone glide with flutter kick
		4	Dog paddle for distance
		3	Sitting dive
		3	Back glide—regain feet without aid
Test #8		4	Test for reversing positions in water
		3	Back glide with kick
		3	Sculling with flutter kick
68a	x	4	Jump from deck (tuck position) into 5-7 feet of water
		1	Bobbing

Drill No.	New Drill	Time Allotment	Short Description of drill

LESSON VIII(A)

Test #2		2	Bobbing test reviewed
Test #1		3	Prone glide—regain feet
		2	Prone glide—with flutter kick
Test #4		5	Dog paddle—20 yds.
43a	x	2	Crawl—arm stroke—standing
43b	x	2	Crawl—arm stroke and breathing combined—standing
		2	Sitting dive
60b	x	2	Kneeling dive
Test #3		4	Back float—regain feet
		2	Sculling with kick for distance
		2	Jump into deep water in tucked position
68c	x	2	Jump into deep water in position with legs straight

LESSON IX(A)

		1	Bobbing
		2	Prone glide with flutter kick
		5	Dog paddle—circular pattern in shallow water
44a	x	5	Crawl—flutter kick and armstroke—widths
44b	x	4	Crawl—flutter kick, armstroke and breathing—complete stroke
Test #6		4	Kneeling dive test
Test #5		4	Sculling 20 feet with aid of kick
Test #7		4	Jump into deep water—legs straight—surface—swim to edge
		1	Bobbing

LESSON X(A)

Retest #2		4	Bobbing
Retest #4		4	Bog paddle—20 yds.
Retest #5		4	Sculling with aid of kick
Retest #6		4	Kneeling dive
		14	Makeups and retests

LESSON PLANS (B)

Length of period in water . . . . 30 minutes
Number of lesson periods available 12
Age range of group . . . . any age
Number in the class . . . . 30 (Maximum)
Classification Test Passed:

> 1. Jump in deep water, surface, swim 20 yds. in prone position, roll to back-swim 20 ft. on back.

Drill No.	New Drill	Time Allotment	Short Description of drill

Objectives:

1. Breathing consecutively .... 20 times
2. Swim overarm .... 40 yds.
3. Swim elementary backstroke .... 60 yds.
4. Swim breaststroke .... 40 yds.
5. Swim sidestroke .... 60 yds.
6. Standing dive
7. Surface dive
8. Tread water vertically .... 1 minute
9. Remain afloat .... 5 minutes
10. Swim underwater .... 20 ft.

LESSON I(B)

Drill No.	New Drill	Time Allotment	Short Description of drill
1f	x	2	Bobbing (Successive inhalations and exhalations)
5	x	4	Horizontal float—partner or aid support
6	x	6	Back glide with arm and leg action of horizontal float
7	x	2	Above drill with water thrown in face
26b	x	3	Frog kick—standing—one leg then the other
29a, 34a	x	5	Frog kick—back and prone—hanging on gutter
28c-33c	x	3	Frog kick—prone and back—widths with pushoffs
60a, b	x	3	Sitting and kneeling dive
		2	Bobbing

LESSON II(B)

Drill No.	New Drill	Time Allotment	Short Description of drill
		2	Bobbing—shoulder depth
		3	Back glide with arm and leg action of horizontal float
		3	Frog kick—prone and back—hanging on gutter
		3	Frog kick—prone and back—widths with pushoff
26a	x	3	Elementary backstroke—armstroke—standing in shallow water
26c	x	2	Elementary backstroke—armstroke and one leg—shallow water
28b	x	3	Elementary backstroke—armstroke only—widths—pushoff
28e	x	4	Elementary backstroke—complete stroke with pushoff—widths
60c	x	3	Kneeling and standing dives
60d	x	2	Standing dive—one leg raised backwards

LESSON III(B)

Drill No.	New Drill	Time Allotment	Short Description of drill
		2	Bobbing
		3	Frog kick—hanging on gutter

Drill No.	New Drill	Time Allotment	Short Description of drill
		3	Frog kick—pushoff—widths
		3	E. Backstroke—arms and one leg—standing—in shallow water
		4	E. Backstroke—complete stroke—pushoff—widths
30a	x	6	E. Backstroke—complete stroke—widths—circular pattern
9	x	3	Jump in deep water—practice horizontal float—one minute
		4	Standing dive—one leg raised
		2	Bobbing

LESSON IV(B)

		2	Bobbing
		2	Frog kick—prone and back—hanging on gutter
		3	Frog kick—prone and back—pushoff—widths
32a	x	3	Breaststroke—armstroke—standing in shallow water
32c	x	2	Breaststroke—arms and one leg in combination—Standing
33d	x	4	Breaststroke—arms and legs with pushoff—complete—high breast
		5	E. Backstroke—widths—circular pattern
		3	Jump in deep—horizontal float—2 minutes
60e	x	3	Dive—fall in type
60f	x	3	Dive—spring type

LESSON V(B)

		2	Bobbing
		2	Frog kick-prone and back—hanging on gutter
		2	Breaststroke—arms only—standing
		3	Breaststroke—arms and one leg in combination—standing
		5	Breaststroke—arms and legs—pushoff—widths
		5	Breaststroke—complete stroke—widths in circular pattern
		5	E. Backstroke—widths—circular pattern
		2	Dive—with spring
		4	Jump in deep and practice horizontal float—3 minutes

LESSON VI(B)

		1	Bobbing
		2	Frog kick—prone and back—hanging on gutter
33e	x	3	Breaststroke—arms, legs and breathing—pushoff—widths

Drill No.	New Drill	Time Allotment	Short Description of drill
36a	x	6	Breaststroke—arms, legs and breathing—widths—circular pattern
		8	Breaststroke and E. Backstroke—alternate—circular pattern
58e	x	4	Underwater breaststroke—with full arm pull
		2	Dive—spring type
Test #1		4	Administer Test #1—rhythmical breathing—20 times

LESSON VII(B)

Drill No.	New Drill	Time Allotment	Short Description of drill
		1	Bobbing
41a	x	2	Sidestroke—Scissors kick—hanging on gutter
39c	x	2	Sidestroke—Scissors kick—pushoff—widths
38a, b, e	x	2	Sidestroke—Shallow water drills—standing
39a	x	2	Sidestroke—pushoff in glide position
39b	x	2	Sidestroke—pushoff—armstroke only
39d	x	3	Sidestroke—pushoff—arms and legs
		4	E. Back and breaststroke—alternate—widths—circular pattern
		2	Under water breaststroke—full arm pull
Test #6		3	Administer standing dive test
63a	x	3	Surface Dive—tuck position
		4	Jump in deep—3 minute horizontal float

LESSON VIII(B)

Drill No.	New Drill	Time Allotment	Short Description of drill
		1	Bobbing
		2	Sidestroke—scissors kick—hanging on gutter
		2	Sidestroke—scissors kick—hanging on gutter
		3	Sidestroke—arms and one leg in combination—pushoff—widths
		4	Sidestroke—arms and legs—pushoff—widths
42a	x	5	Sidestroke—complete stroke—widths—circular pattern
		3	E. Backstroke and Breast—alternate—circular pattern
59a	x	3	Underwater breaststroke swimming—for form
		2	Surface dive—tuck position
63b	x	2	Surface dive—pike position

LESSON IX(B)

Drill No.	New Drill	Time Allotment	Short Description of drill
		1	Bobbing
46a	x	3	Crawl—flutter kick—hanging on gutter
46b	x	1	Crawl—flutter kick—hanging on gutter—with breathing drill
45a	x	3	Crawl—armstroke—standing in shallow water

Drill No.	New Drill	Time Allotment	Short Description of drill
45b	x	2	Crawl—armstroke with breathing—standing in shallow water
44a	x	2	Crawl—armstroke and kick—pushoff—widths
44b	x	2	Complete stroke—pushoff—widths
		2	Sidestroke—scissors kick—hanging on gutter
		3	Sidestroke—complete stroke—widths—circular pattern
		4	Sidestroke and breaststroke—alternate—widths—circular pattern
Test #3		4	Administer test #3—60 yds.
Test #10		3	Administer test #10—swim underwater 20 ft.

LESSON X(B)

Drill No.	New Drill	Time Allotment	Short Description of drill
		1	Bobbing
		1	Crawl—flutter kick—hanging on gutter
		1	Crawl—flutter kick—hanging on gutter—with breathing
		2	Crawl—armstroke and kick—pushoff—widths
		2	Crawl—complete stroke—pushoff—widths
47a	x	4	Crawl—Complete stroke—widths—circular pattern
		4	Breast, Side, Back—alternate—widths—circular pattern
Test #4		4	Administer Test #4—40 yds. breaststroke
18a, b	x	3	Treading water—practice scissors kick and frog kick—hanging
Test #7		4	Administer test #7—surface dvie—either tuck or pike
Test #5		4	Administer test #5—60 yds—sidestroke

LESSON XI(B)

Drill No.	New Drill	Time Allotment	Short Description of drill
		1	Bobbing
		2	Crawl—kick and breathing—hanging on gutter
Test #2		6	Crawl—administer test #2—swim 40 yds.—crawl
		2	Treading water—practice kicks
19a, b	x	2	Treading water—hands alone—legs alone
Test #8		3	Treading water—administer test #8—tread water—1 minute
Test #9		5	Administer test #8—remain afloat—5 minutes
		9	Swim all four strokes—alternate—widths—circular pattern

LESSON XII(B)

Drill No.	New Drill	Time Allotment	Short Description of drill
		1	Bobbing
		10	Swim all four strokes—alternate—makeup for any of four

Drill No.	New Drill	Time Allotment	Short Description of drill
		15	Makeup and retesting
		4	Remain afloat 4 minutes

LESSON PLANS (C)

Length of period in water ....30 minutes
Number of lessons available 24
Number in class ....25 (Maximum)
Age of group ....any age

Classification Test Passed:

1. Remain afloat 3 minutes
2. Jump in deep-surface-swim 25 yds. in prone position-roll to back-swim 25 yds on back

Objectives:

1. Swim 200 yds. using the following strokes and in the order listed: Breast Sidestroke, Elementary Backstroke and Crawl. 50 yds. for each-no time limit.
2. Swim 50 ft. underwater starting from surface dive.
3. Perform surface dives in following manner-tuck and pike.
4. Tread water: 2 minute with or without hands.
5. Jump from 3 meter board fully clothed—swim 4 length of pool (25 yds.) using a different stroke each length—then disrobe.
6. Tired Swimmer's carry for 25 yds. with a turn at end.
7. Tow or carry other than above carry—25 yds.
8. Demonstrate Artificial Respiration.
9. Swim 1/4 mile wearing clothing.
10. Swim 1/2 mile using any stroke or combination of strokes.
11. Remain afloat 30 minutes.
12. Perform following dives from 1 meter board with proper approach:
   a) Running front dive
   b) Back Dive

LESSON I(C)

		5	Pool Regulations Explained
1f	x	2	Bobbing
3b	x	3	Face Float
pp-76	x	3	Jelly fish Float
3d	x	15	Back glide position
29a-34a	x	3	Frog Kick—prone and back position—hanging
3d	x	5	on gutter
28c-33c	x	5	Frog Kick—prone and back position—across pool
26a	x	3	E. Backststroke—armstroke—standing in shallow water
		1	Bobbing

Drill No.	New Drill	Time Allotment	Short Description of drill

LESSON II(C)

		2	Bobbing
		5	Frog kick—back and prone position—hanging on gutter
		5	Frog kick—back and prone position—across pool —widths
		3	Elementary Backstroke—arms only—standing in shallow water
26c	x	2	Elementary Backstroke—arms and one leg—in shallow water
28b	x	5	Elementary Backstroke—arms only—with pushoff —widths
28e	x	7	Elementary Backstroke—arms complete stroke— circular pattern
		1	Bobbing

LESSON III(C)

		2	Bobbing
		2	Frog kick—back and prone hanging on gutter
		3	E. Backstroke—Arms only—widths of pool
		5	E. Backstroke—Complete stroke—circular pattern
32a	x	4	Breaststroke—armstroke—standing in shallow water
32c	x	3	Breaststroke—Arms and one leg—in shallow water
33d	x	10	Breaststroke—complete high breaststroke—widths

LESSON IV(C)

		1	Bobbing
		5	Frog kicking—prone and back—widths of pool
		5	E. Backstroke—complete stroke—widths in circular pattern
		3	Breaststroke—arm movements—standing in shallow water
		3	Breaststroke—arms and one leg—in shallow water
		5	Breaststroke—Complete stroke—widths in circular pattern
		7	Breaststroke and E. Backstroke—alternate—circular widths
		1	Bobbing

LESSON V(C)

		1	Bobbing
		3	Frog kick—prone and back—widths of pool
		3	E. Backstroke—swimming widths in circular pattern

Drill No.	New Drill	Time Allotment	Short Description of drill
		3	Breaststroke—arms and one leg—standing in shallow water
		5	Breaststroke—Swimming widths in circular pattern
		10	Breaststroke and E. Back—alternate—circular pattern
68c	x	5	Jump into deep from 1 meter board—remain afloat —3 minutes

LESSON VI(C)

Drill No.	New Drill	Time Allotment	Short Description of drill
		1	Bobbing
		3	Frog kicking across pool
		3	E. Backstroke—widths of pool in circular pattern
		3	Breaststroke—widths of pool in circular pattern
		8	Breaststroke and E. Backstroke—alternate— lengths
41a	x	2	Side Stroke—scissors kick—hanging on gutter
39c	x	2	Side Stroke—scissors kick—pushoff—widths
38a, b, e	x	3	Side Stroke—shallow water drills
39d	x	5	Side Stroke—arms and legs—widths

LESSON VII(C)

Drill No.	New Drill	Time Allotment	Short Description of drill
		1	Bobbing
		2	Side Stroke—scissors kick—hanging on gutter
		3	Side Stroke—scissors kick—widths of pool
		2	Side Stroke—scissors and one arm across pool
		2	Side Stroke—scissors kick opposite arm—widths
42a	x	5	Side Stroke—complete stroke—widths—circular pattern
		2	E. Backstroke—widths
		2	Breaststroke—widths
		8	Breaststroke and E. Back—lengths in circular pattern
58e	x	3	Underwater swimming—regular breaststroke—full pull

LESSON VIII(C)

Drill No.	New Drill	Time Allotment	Short Description of drill
		2	Sidestroke—kick—widths of pool
		4	Sidestroke—complete stroke—widths in circular pattern
		2	E. Back—widths
		2	Breaststroke—widths
		10	Breaststroke and E. Back—lengths—circular pattern
59a	x	3	Underwater swimming for form
19d	x	3	Treading water—use 3 type kicks—scissors, frog, bicycling
		4	Jump in deep—remain afloat—3 minutes

Drill No.	New Drill	Time Allotment	Short Description of drill
			LESSON IX(C)
		2	Sidestroke—complete—widths—circular pattern
		2	E. Back—widths
		2	Breaststroke—widths
		10	Breaststroke, Side and E. Back—lengths—circular pattern
46a, b	x	4	Crawl—flutter kick—hanging on gutter
—	x	3	Crawl—flutter kick—pushoff—widths
43a, b	x	3	Crawl—armstroke and breathing—standing—shallow water
59c	x	3	Underwater swim for distance
		1	Bobbing—deep water
			LESSON X(C)
		2	Crawl—armstroke and breathing—standing in shallow water
		3	Crawl—kick—hanging on gutter
		3	Crawl—kick—pushoff—widths
44a	x	3	Crawl—pushoff—kick and stroke—widths
44b	x	2	Crawl—pushoff—complete stroke with breathing—widths
		10	Breast, Side, E. Back—lengths—circular pattern
60a-f	x	7	Diving—elementary
			LESSON XI(C)
		3	Crawl—prone and back—widths with pushoff
		2	Crawl—pushoff—kick and stroke—widths
		4	Crawl and E. Back—alternate—widths in circular pattern
		8	All four strokes—lengths—alternate—circular pattern
		5	Diving—elementary reviewed
19a, b, d, e	x	4	Treading water
59c	x	4	Underwater swimming for distance
			LESSON XII(C)
		10	Crawl and E. Back—lengths—circular pattern
		6	Breast and E. Back—lengths—circular pattern
		6	Side and E. Back—lengths—circular pattern
63a, b	x	4	Surface Diving
		4	Approach for board work
			LESSON XIII(C)
		4	Warmup—lengths—all four strokes
		8	Swim through Test #1

Drill No.	New Drill	Time Allotment	Short Description of drill
63a, b, c	x	4	Surface Diving—headfirst—tuck and pike—feet first also
		2	Treading water
		6	Diving Board—approach and bounce
		4	Underwater for distance
68c	x	2	Jump from 3 meter board

LESSON XIV(C)

		4	Breaststroke—swim 100 yds. continuously
		4	Side Stroke—swim 150 yds. continuously
		6	E. Backstroke—swim 200 yds. continuously
		5	Crawl—swim 100 yds continuously
pp	x	7	Diving Board—approach, takeoff and front dive
		4	Jump in from 3 meter board—remain afloat 3 minutes

LESSON XV(C)

pp	x	8	Artificial Respiration—introduction, demonstration, practice
		8	Jump from 3 meter board—tread 2 min.—disrobe
		8	Swim through Test #1
pp	x	4	Diving Board—review front dive—back dive
		3	Jump in deep—remain afloat 2 minutes

LESSON XVI(C)

		8	Artificial Respiration
Test #5		8	Jump from 3 meter board—swim 4 lengths—disrobe
		6	Diving Board—front and back dives
Test #2		5	Underwater swimming
		3	All 4 strokes—lengths—circular pattern

LESSON XVII(C)

Test #8		4	Artificial Respiration
100 f	x	6	Tired Swimmer's carry
Test #1		10	200 yds.—4 strokes—grade on form
53	x	2	Back Crawl—arm action
54	x	3	Back Crawl—kick—hanging on gutter
55b	x	2	Back Crawl—arm action—pushoff—width
55c	x	3	Back Crawl—leg action—pushoff—widths

LESSON XVIII(C)

		2	Back Crawl—kick—widths
55e	x	3	Back Crawl—complete stroke—widths

Drill No.	New Drill	Time Allotment	Short Description of drill
		6	Breaststroke—150 yds.
		6	E. Backstroke—200 yds.
		6	Sidestroke—200 yds.
		4	Crawl—100 yds.
		3	Tired swimmer's carry

LESSON XIX(C)

Drill No.	New Drill	Time Allotment	Short Description of drill
		5	Back Crawl—widths—circular pattern
PP	x	5	Butterfly stroke—armstroke—standing—shallow water
		2	Butterfly stroke—explanation of stroke, timing, etc
PP	x	3	Butterfly stroke—complete stroke—widths
Test #4		3	Treading water
Test #3		4	Surfacing diving
Test #12		6	Diving test —1 meter board—front and back dive
		2	Remain afloat

LESSON XX(C)

Drill No.	New Drill	Time Allotment	Short Description of drill
PP	x	4	Carry—other than x-chest, tired swimmer or hair
Test #6		4	Tired swimmer's carry
Test #9		22	Swim ¼ mile with clothing

LESSON XXI(C)

Drill No.	New Drill	Time Allotment	Short Description of drill
Test #10		—	Swim ½ mile
			Retest or makeups (Providing any time is left)

LESSON XXII(C)

Drill No.	New Drill	Time Allotment	Short Description of drill
Test #7		5	25 yd. tow or carry
		10	Swimming four strokes—alternating—lengths
		10	Retest and makeups
		5	Remain afloat

LESSON XXIII(C)

Drill No.	New Drill	Time Allotment	Short Description of drill
Test #11		30	Remain afloat entire 30 minutes

LESSON XXIV(C)

Drill No.	New Drill	Time Allotment	Short Description of drill
		10	Swim all four strokes
		20	Makeups and retests

APPENDIX III

Standards of Achievement and Testing

It is important that the program of swimming instruction for Naval Aviation Cadets should have continuity throughout all stages. As the cadet moves from one school or base to the next, he should face programs embracing skills progressively more difficult. Not only should the methods of organization and the nomenclature be of the same pattern, but also the syllabi. Every skill will be introduced at some point in this continuity and by means of review at successive bases will be developed and perfected.

A LIST OF THE PRINCIPAL STROKES AND SKILLS OF THE NAVAL AVIATION SWIMMING PROGRAM, WITH INDICATION OF THE STAGE AT WHICH EACH IS TO BE INTRODUCED.

"0"—Indicates the skill is to be reviewed in an advanced form.

STROKE OR SKILL	PREP	WTS	PRE-FLIGHT	PRIMARY	INTERM.	OPERAT'L	FLEET A.C.
Preliminary Skills							
Ducking	x	o					
Opening Eyes	x	o					
Regain Standing Position	x	o					
Prone Float	x	o					
Turtle Float	x	o					
Breathing	x	o	o	o	o	o	o
Holding Breath Submerged	x	o	o				
Leveling	x	o					
Changing Direction	x	o					
Push-Off and Glide	x	o					
Kick Glide	x	o					
Relaxation							
In Swimming Skills	x	o	o	o			
Carry-Over to Flying	x	o	o	o	o	o	o
Pool Rules, Standards							
5 Minute Float	x	o	o				
Sculling	x	o	o	o	o		
Finning	x	o	o				
Types of Kicks							
Frog	x	o	o	o	o	o	o
Vertical Scissors	x	o	o	o	o	o	o
Scissor	x	o	o	o	o	o	o
Trudgen	x	o	o	o	o	o	o
Flutter	x	o	o	o	o	o	o

STROKE OR SKILL	PREP	WTS	PRE-FLIGHT	PRIMARY	INTERM.	OPERAT'L	FLEET A.C.
Surface Diving							
Head First (tuck)	x	o	o	o	o	o	o
Head First (pike)	x	o	o	o	o	o	o
Feet First	x	o	o	o	o	o	o
Jumping Into Water							
From Pool Deck	x	o					
10 Feet			x	o	o	o	o
Clothed			x	o	o	o	o
With Equipment		x		x	o	o	o
From Ship Into Sea							x
Bobbing							
Simple	x	o	o	o			
In Imaginary Flame			x	o	o	o	
With Equipment				x	o	o	
Back Float	x	o					
Treading							
Arms and Legs	x	o					
For Time, Clothed			x	o	o		
Back Stroke							
Elementary	x	o	o	o	o	o	o
Inverted Breast			x	o			
Inverted Crawl			x	o	o		
Breast Stroke							
High (Rough Water Style)	x	o	o	o	o	o	o
Low (Exhale Head Under)	x	o	o	o	o	o	o
Side Stroke							
Orthodox	x	o	o	o	o	o	o
Side Overarm	x	o	o	o			
Overhand							
Trudgen	x	o	o	o	o	o	o
Crawl	x	o	o	o	o	o	o
Underwater Swimming							
20 ft. from Surface Dive	x	o	o	o	o	o	o
50 ft. from Surface Dive			x	o	o	o	o
Clothed, 25 Ft. from Surface Dive			x	o	o	o	o
Obstacle Course				x	o	o	o
Twisting and Changing Direction Getting Out of Plane					x	o	o
Competitive Games and Relays	x	o	o	o	o	o	o
Water Polo	x	o	o	o	o	o	o
Navy Ball	x	o	o	o	o	o	o
Racing Starts							
Swimming Clothed			x	o	o	o	o
Clothing Inflation			x	o	o	o	o

STROKE OR SKILL	PREP	WTS	PRE-FLIGHT	PRIMARY	INTERM.	OPERAT'L	FLEET A.C.
Lifesaving							
Rear Approach and Level			x	o	o	o	
Front Surface Approach			x	o	o	o	
Under Water Approach			x	o			
Surface Dive and Retrieve Person			x				
Cross Chest Carry			x	o	o		
Hair Carry			x	o			
Head Carry			x	o			
Tired Swimmer Carry	x	o	o	o			
Supporting Victim			x	o	o	o	o
Carrying Two Men				x	o		
Clothing Carries			x	o	o	o	o
Front Strangle				x			
Back Strangle				x			
Separating Two People				x			
Dive and Jump Approach			x				
Fireman and Saddleback				x			
Artificial Respiration			x	o			
Miscellaneous							
Board and Rope Tows				x	o		
Surf Rescues and Assistance						x	
Disrobing			x	o	o	o	
Use of Debris				x	o	o	
Swimming with Imaginary Cramps Wounds, or with Arms, Legs, Bound				x	o	o	
Swimming with Equipment; Firearms; Life Jacket				x	o	o	
Swimming in Cold Water—Where Possible					x	o	o
Use of Lines, Ropes and Cargo Nets							
Practice in Pool				x	o	o	o
From Ship Side or Tower				x	o	o	o
Abandoning Plane in Water (Ditching)							
Artificial Situation				x*	x	o	
Abandoning Parachute							
Artificial Situation				x*	x	o	
Rubber Boats Rafts							
Boarding				x	o	o	o
Helping Another Aboard				x	o	o	o
In Ocean Water						x	o
Boat Skills							
Boarding Rescue Craft					x	o	o
Method Judging Capacity					x	o	o
Emptying Water					x	o	o
Landing					x	o	o
Stay Away from Screws					x	o	o
How to Direct Rescue of Group					x	o	o

* Taught at Primary Base if Planes Are Flying over Water.

STROKE OR SKILL	PREP	WTS	PRE-FLIGHT	PRIMARY	INTERM.	OPERAT'L	FLEET A.C.
Surf Tide Rip Reefs—Where Possible					x	o	o
Avoid Props and Screws					x	o	o
Complete Abandon Ship and Ditching Routine					x	o	o
Sunburn, Sunstroke, Shock, Heatstroke (Review First Aid)					x		
Heaving Lines and Buoys						x	o
Handling Stretcher Cases						x	o
Shark, Barracuda, Physalia (Portuguese Man of War)						x	o
Concussion					x	o	o

MINIMUM REQUIREMENTS FOR EACH STAGE (IN TERMS OF SKILLS TO BE TAUGHT)

U. S. Navy Flight Preparatory School

MINIMUMS

Preliminary Skills
Relaxation
Rules, Standards, Hygiene
5 Minute Float
Sculling and Finning
Treading (simple)
Elementary Back Stroke
Breast Stroke (orthodox)
Rough Water Breast Stroke
Orthodox Side Stroke
Crawl
Long Time Swimming for Endurance
Long Distance

Types of Kicks
Surface Diving (head first)
Jumping (1 meter or from pool deck)
Bobbing (simple)
Back Float
Underwater (20 feet)

Competitive Games and Relays
Side Overarm Stroke
Trudgen

OPTIONAL

Starts and Turns (Sports Program)
Water Basketball
Miscellaneous Tows and Rescues
Chain, Hand, Foot Rescues
Backstroke Variations
  a—Inverted Trudgen
  b—Two Arm Overwater
  c—Alternate Arm Underwater

Arm Carries

Dog Paddle
Single Wrist Carry

Double Wrist Carry

War Training Service School

MINIMUMS

Present all of the skills included in Lessons 12-18 for Flight Preparatory and War Training Schools

Instruct in skills essential for the "B" test at Pre-Flight

Emphasize improvement in all strokes and skills presented at Flight Preparatory Schools

OPTIONAL

Present all of the skills included in Lessons 1-12 for Flight Preparatory Schools

U. S. Navy Pre-Flight Schools

MINIMUMS

Surface Dive, Advanced
Jumping 10 Feet, Clothed
Bobbing in Imaginary Flame

Underwater
20-50 Feet Clothed
Swimming, Clothed
Clothed Inflation
Lifesaving
Surface Approach
Underwater Approach
Cross Chest Carry
Hair Carry
Head Carry
Clothing Carries
Supporting a Shipmate in the Water
Lifesaving Dive and Jump Approach
Rear Approach and Level

Inverted Breast Stroke

Treading (advanced while clothed) for from 5-45 Minutes
Removing Clothing in Water

Endurance Swimming
Long Distance Swimming

Surface Dive and Retrieve Person

OPTIONAL

Optional skills not covered in Naval Aviation Preparatory Schools

Side Stroke with Double Kick with Flutter Kick
Trudgen with Double Kick

U. S. Navy Primary Flight Training Stations

MINIMUMS

Relaxation Carry-Over to Flying

High, Roughwater Breast Stroke

Jumping with Equipment
Bobbing with Equipment

Swimming with Jacket, Guns, Canteen, Flashlight and other Equipment
Swimming through and under Imaginary Fire

Swimming with Imaginary Cramps, Wounds, etc. Broken Leg, Arm. Arm or Legs Bound to Side

Long Time Swimming

Long Distance Swimming

Fireman and Saddleback Carries

Board and Rope Tows

Use of Debris for Support

Ascending and Descending Ropes and Cargo Nets, suspended above Pool.

Obstacle Course

Two-Man Carries

Front and Back Strangle Releases

Separating Two People

Simple Rubber Boat and Raft Skills

OPTIONAL
SPECIAL NOTE

Review Minimum Skills for Pre-Flight when some cadets obviously need further instruction

Thorough drills in artificial crash landings. (Suspend barrel or cockpit above pool and let it drop in the water with cadet in it.) This to be required if flying at this base is above water

Optional skills for Pre-Flight which were not presented at that stage

Thorough training in artificial parachute situation. Unbuckle chute, drop in water. This is to be required if flying at this base is above water

U. S. Navy Intermediate Flight Training Stations

MINIMUMS

Discuss Shark, Barracuda, Physalia

Underwater Swimming in Ocean

Surf Skills

  a—Rescues

  b—Landing in Waves—on Reefs, Rocky Shore, Precipitous Cliffs (wave back chop)

  c—Undertows. Rip Tides

  d—Currents and Run of Tides

  e—Kelp, Grass, etc.

Boat Drills; Boarding; Empty Water; Launching and Beaching

Long time Swimming

Long Distance Swimming

Swimming in Ocean

  With and Without Jacket

  With and Without Equipment

Thorough Training in Leaving Parachute while above water

Thorough Training in Abandoning Plane

OPTIONAL
SPECIAL NOTE

Sunburn, Sunstroke, Shock, Heat Stroke (Review First Aid)

Avoiding Props and Screws of Rescue Crafts, Large and Small, when Abandoning Ship

Organized Safety Plan

Recapitulate and Organize Skills Presented

Preparatory through Operational for Abandoning Ship and Ditching Plane

Directing Rescue by Small Craft

Optional Skills not Presented at Pre-Flight or Reserve Base

Ascending and Descending Ropes and Cargo Nets over Ships Sides

Utilizing, Inventing, Devising Water Canteens as Floats; Rubber Pads from Parachutes; Mattresses and Cushions from Planes; Powder Cans, etc., as Floats

Swimming through Imaginary Oil

Racing Starts (10 minutes only)
Swimming in Cold water (where possible)
Swimming in Current of Streams, with and without Equipment
Swimming in Swells, Choppy Seas

U. S. Navy Operational Flight Training Stations

MINIMUMS

Surf Rescue and Assistance
  a—Approach Methods
  b—Hazards
  c—Carries

A Complete Presentation of Information Relative to the Use and Control of Rubber Boats and Rafts in the Ocean:
  a—Precautions
  b—Capsizing and Righting
  c—Propelling

OPTIONAL

The Optional Skills not Presented at Preceding Stages of Training

Fleet Air Center

MINIMUMS

Every Officer and Man a Competent Swimmer
Maintenance of Skills and Conditions Acquired at Previous Training Schools and Bases
Jump from Ship to Sea

Complete Mastery of Abandon Ship Procedures
Swamp Tactics (If in that Area)

Ice Skills, Rescues, etc. (If in that Area)

OPTIONAL

Program of Reviews, Instruction or Competition or Recreational Swimming whenever Facilities Permit

Lifesaving, Abandon Ship, etc.
Organization and Review of Skills while at Sea

Olympic Swimming and Diving

Organization

Numerous pools have provided opportunities for the young and old to learn, to practice and to excel in swimming but it has remained for two agencies within the United States to sponsor and govern competition in these sports. These two agencies are the National Collegiate Athletic Association (NCAA) and the National Amateur Athletic Union (AAU). The National Collegiate Athletic Association has governed competition within our educational systems as far as legislation is concerned. The Amateur Athletic Union has governed and sponsored practically all competition outside of the schools and because this includes a number of divisions they will be listed below:

1. Men's Senior National AAU Meets (Indoor and Outdoor)
2. Women's Senior National AAU Meets (Indoor and Outdoor)
3. Men's Junior National AAU Competition (Indoor and Outdoor)
4. Women's Junior National AAU Competition (Indoor and Outdoor)
5. Junior Olympic Championship Competition (Boys and Girls)
6. Age Group Championships and Competition In Following Divisions: (Boys and Girls)
   a) 10 years and under
   b) 11 and 12 years of age
   c) 13 and 14 years of age
   d) 15 and 16 years of age

FINA

Federation Internationale De Natation Amateur better known as FINA is the international body that has governed world swimming and diving. This international group is composed of members elected from various countries of the world who meet to adopt legislation on swimming and diving, recognize applications for world records and finally set up the mechanism for the conduct of the Olympic Game competition in these sports.

Through this international competition the field of competitive swimming and diving has come to be recognized as one of the best and most universal in the sports world. The constant lowering of swimming records and the improved expertness of diving is a tribute to this fact. In the past few years many nations have exchanged ideas through State sponsored goodwill tours and as a result the training methods and skill techniques are in more or less general agreement all over the world. This has made for intense competition. No one nation has been able to dominate Olympics, Olympiad after Olympiad, and this condition has been very healthy for the sport.

History

The modern Olympic Games held in Athens, Greece, were restored in 1896 through the efforts of a Frenchman, Baron de Coubertin. These first modern Games had three swimming events for men:

1. 100 Meter Free Style
2. 500 Meter Free Style
3. 1200 Meter Free Style

No events for women were scheduled in the Olympics until the 1912 games. The only men's event from the 1896 Games still on the Olympic program is the 100 meter free style. The program has been altered many times; the 400 meter medley relay for both men and women was added in 1960.

1960 Program

Men	Women
1. 100 meter free style	1. 100 meter free style
2. 400 meter free style	2. 400 meter free style
3. 1500 meter free style	3. 100 meter backstroke
4. 100 meter backstroke	4. 100 meter butterfly
5. 200 meter breaststroke	5. 200 meter breaststroke
6. 200 meter butterfly	6. 3-meter diving
7. 3-meter diving	7. Platform diving
8. Platform diving	8. 400 meter (4 woman team) Relay
9. 800 meter (4 man team) Relay	(free style)
(free style)	9. 400 meter (4 woman team) Medley
10. 400 meter (4 man team) Medley	Relay
Relay	

Unquestionably if it were not for the great expense incurred in sending the Olympic teams to faraway countries the present program would be broader than it is at the present time. A slight retrenchment was made in the 1960 Olympic program when a limit of two entries to each individual event was placed on each countries' swimming and diving squad.

General Regulations

1. All swimming events are listed in meters.
2. The pool in which the competition is held must be 50 meters in length.
3. Qualification for finals based on times only (8 qualify for the finals).
4. Preliminaries and semi-finals are held in the 100 meter free style events.
5. Preliminaries are held in all other swimming events (except 100 meters).
6. Each nation is allowed two entries per event.
7. Each nation is allowed one relay team per relay event.
8. 3-Meter diving shall consist of Preliminaries, Semifinals and Finals.
   a) Preliminaries: Required from group I, III and V plus one optional
   b) Semifinals: Required from group II and IV plus two optionals
   c) Finals: Three remaining optional dives
9. Platform diving shall consist of Preliminaries, Semifinals and Finals.
   a) Preliminaries: 4 dives with *limit selected at option of diver
   b) Semifinals: 2 dives with *limit plus one dive without limit
   c) Finals: 3 dives without limit
10. Each country shall establish their own method of selection for team personnel.

---

* The total degree of difficulty for the 6 dives with limit cannot exceed 11

Olympic Record Holders

The following charts show the Olympic Record Holders in each event rather than the Olympic winners. It should be kept in mind that the Olympic records are not synonymous with world records although in a few cases this might be true.

	Men	
	100 Meter Free Style	
1896	Hajes (Hungary)	1:22.2
1904	De Halmay (Hungary)	1:02.8
1920	Kahanamoku (U.S.A.)	1:01.4
1924	Weissmuller (U.S.A.)	:59.0
1928	Weissmuller (U.S.A.)	:58.6
1932	Miyazaki (Japan)	:58.2
1936	Csik (Hungary)	:57.6
1948	Ris (U.S.A.)	:57.3
1956	Henricks (Australia)	:55.4
1960	Deavitt (Australia)	:55.2

	Women	
1912	Durack (Australia)	1:22.2
1920	Belibtrey (U.S.A.)	1:13.6
1924	Lackie (U.S.A.)	1:12.4
1928	Osipowicz (U.S.A.)	1:11.0
1932	Madison (U.S.A.)	1:06.8
1936	Mastenbroek (Netherl)	1:05.9
1956	Fraser (Australia)	1:02.0
1960	Fraser (Australia)	1:01.2

400 Meter Free Style — Men

1908	Taylor (Gr Br)	5:36.8
1912	Hodgson (Canada)	5:24.4
1924	Weissmuller (U.S.A.)	5:04.2
1928	Zorilla (Argentina)	5:01.6
1932	Crabbe (U.S.A.)	4:48.4
1936	Medica (U.S.A.)	4:44.5
1948	Smith (U.S.A.)	4:41.0
1952	Boiteux (France)	4:30.7
1956	Rose (Australia)	4:27.3
1960	Rose (Australia)	4:18.3

400 Meter Free Style — Women

1924	Noreilus (U.S.A.)	6:02.2
1928	Noreilus (U.S.A.)	5:42.8
1932	Madison (U.S.A.)	5:28.5
1936	Mastenbroek (Netherl)	5:26.4
1948	Curtis (U.S.A.)	5:17.8
1956	Crapp (Australia)	4:54.6
1960	Van Saltza (U.S.A.)	4:50.6

1500 Meter Free Style

1908	Taylor (Gr Br)	22:48.4
1912	Hodgson (Canada)	22:00.0
1924	Charlton (Australia)	20:06.6
1928	Borg (Sweden)	19:51.8
1932	Kitamura (Japan)	19:12.4
1952	Kone (U.S.A.)	18:30.0
1956	Rose (Australia)	17:58.9
1960	Konrads (Australia)	17:19.6

800 Meter Free Style Relay

1908	Great Britain	10:55.6
1912	Australia	10:11.6
1920	U.S.A.	10:04.4
1924	U.S.A.	9:53.4
1928	U.S.A.	9:36.2
1932	Japan	8:58.4
1936	Japan	8:51.5
1948	U.S.A.	8:46.0
1952	U.S.A.	8:31.1
1956	Australia	8:23.6
1960	U.S.A.	8:10.2

400 Meter Free Style Relay

1912	Great Britain	5:55.2
1920	U.S.A.	5:11.6
1924	U.S.A.	4:58.8
1928	U.S.A.	4:47.6

Men   Women

1932	U.S.A.	4:38.0
1936	Netherlands	4:36.0
1948	U.S.A.	4:29.2
1952	Hungary	4:24.4
1956	Australia	4:17.1
1960	U.S.A.	4:08.9

100 Meter Backstroke

1908	Bibenstein (Germany)	1:24.6	1924	Bauer (U.S.A.)	1:23.2
1912	Hebner (U.S.A.)	1:21.2	1928	Braun (Netherl)	1:22.0
1920	Kealoha (U.S.A.)	1:15.2	1932	Holm (U.S.A.)	1:19.4
1924	Kealoha (U.S.A.)	1:13.2	1936	Sneff (Netherl)	1:18.9
1928	Kojac (U.S.A.)	1:08.2	1948	Harup (Denmark)	1:14.4
1936	Kiefer (U.S.A.)	1:05.9	1952	Harrison (S. Africa)	1:14.3
1952	Oyakawa (U.S.A.)	1:05.4	1956	Grinham (Gr Br)	1:12.9
1956	Thiele (Australia)	1:02.2	1960	Burke (U.S.A.)	1:09.3
1960	Thiele (Australia)	1:01.9			

200 Meter Breaststroke

1908	Helman (Gr Br)	3:09.2	1924	Morton (Gr Br)	3:33.2
1912	Bathe (Germany)	3:01.8	1928	Schrader (Germany)	3:12.6
1924	Skelton (U.S.A.)	2:56.6	1932	Dennis (Australia)	3:06.3
1928	Tsuruta (Japan)	2:48.8	1936	Maehata (Japan)	3:03.6
1932	Tsuruta (Japan)	2:45.4	1956	Happe (Germany)	2:53.1
1936	Hamuro (Japan)	2:41.5	1960	Lonsbrough (Gr Br)	2:49.5
1956	Furukawa (Japan)	2:34.7			
1960	*Mulliken (U.S.A.)	2:37.4			

200 Meter Butterfly

1956	Verzyk (U.S.A.)	2:19.3
1960	Trey (U.S.A.)	2:12.8

100 Meter Butterfly

1956	Mann (U.S.A.)	1:11.0
1960	Schuler (U.S.A.)	1:09.5

400 Meter Medley Relay

1960	U.S.A.	4:05.4	1960	U.S.A.	4:41.1

Springboard Diving	Platform Diving	Springboard Diving	Platform Diving
'04 Sheldon (U.S.A.)	'08 Johasson (Sweden)	'20 Riggen (U.S.A.)	'12 Johasson (Sweden)
'08 Zuerner (Germany)	'12 Adlerz (Sweden)	'24 Becker (U.S.A.)	'20 Fryland (Denmark)
'12 Guenther (Germany)	'20 Pinksten (U.S.A.)	'28 Meany (U.S.A.)	
	'20 Wallman (Sweden)	'32 Coleman (U.S.A.)	'24 Smith (U.S.A.)
'20 Kuehn (U.S.A.)	'24 White (U.S.A.)	'36 Gestring (U.S.A.)	'28 Pinksten (U.S.A.)
'24 White (U.S.A.)	'24 Eve (Australia)	'48 Draves (U.S.A.)	'32 Poynten (U.S.A.)
'28 Desjardine (U.S.A.)	'28 Desjardine (U.S.A.)	'52 McCormick (U.S.A.)	'36 Peyton Hill (U.S.A.)
'32 Galitzen (U.S.A.)	'32 Smith (U.S.A.)	'56 McCormick (U.S.A.)	'48 Draves (U.S.A.)
'36 Degener (U.S.A.)	'36 Wayne (U.S.A.)		'52 McCormick (U.S.A.)

---

    * The 1960 Games were the first games in which the rules stipulated that the stroke must be swum on the surface.

    In the two Olympiads 1920 and 1924 there were both Plain High Diving and Fancy High Diving in Men's platform diving, hence the two winners were listed for those two Olympiads.

Springboard Diving	Platform Diving	Springboard Diving	Platform Diving
'48 Harlan (U.S.A.)	'48 Lee (U.S.A.)	'60 Kramer (Germany)	'56 McCormick (U.S.A.)
'52 Browning (U.S.A.)	'52 Lee (U.S.A.)		'60 Kramer (Germany)
'56 Clotworthty (U.S.A.)	'56 Capilla (Mexico)		
'60 Tobian (U.S.A.)	'60 Webster (U.S.A.)		

Summaries of the Record Charts

An analysis of these swimming record holders reveals that the United States, Australia and Japan have dominated men's division while the women's division has been led by the United States, Australia, Netherlands and Great Britain. Ten countries have had Olympic Record holders among the men while nine countries have held this honor among the women.

The second observation that is quite obvious shows the United States holds a decided superiority in both men's and women's 3-meter diving and platform diving. In the 3-meter springboard diving neither the men nor the women had lost a title since the 1920 Games until a German girl won the '60 gold medal. The platform diving has been about the same with only one loss apiece for the men and women of the United States in the past eight Olympiads.

A third conclusion points out the dominance of the United States in the relay events. In the 1960 Games the U.S. teams not only won the four relay events and set new records but they won them handily over their nearest rivals. This relay power does give some insight into the depth of swimming power in the United States.

Australia appears to have the edge in free style events especially in the longer distances. Japan has been outstanding here too.

Australia leads in backstroking too at the present time although the United States held a monopoly for many Olympiads. It is very close between these two countries with the Aussies winning the top spot and the United States following with very close over all competition.

The breaststroke finds the two leading powers much weaker than they appear in other strokes. Japan has held the lead here although this superiority was evident when the stroke was swum underwater as well as on the surface. The rules governing this stroke have been changed often and it was difficult to draw any conclusions as to the relative strength of the various nations.

In the short history of the butterfly stroke the United States has dominated the world. This stroke is a product of U.S. swimming and we did have a start on other nations.

In Conclusion

It is very evident to anyone with a basic knowledge of sports that desire alone cannot lower marks. It might be well to point out the reasons for these record smashing performances.

1. There has been a re-evaluation of the amount of work that the body can stand and profit by through over-work. At one time a mile per day was considered a good workout but now topflight swimmers may swim as much as 5-6 miles per day when in training.

2. Training methods have been improved. Interval swimming is one of the new training procedures that has proven very helpful.
3. Recognition of the fact that it takes strength to swim fast just as it takes strength to perform well in other physical feats. The muscles that are to be used in swimming must be developed in this body building program.
4. Development of new and better stroke techniques. Actually this has been the least important of the four points listed.

Index